THE PATHFINDER PROJECT

EXPLORING THE POWER OF ONE

TEACHER'S MANUAL

Robert J. Marzano

Diane E. Paynter

Jane K. Doty

Pathfinder Education, Inc.

ISBN 0-9743142-0-X

Holly LeMaster, Editor

Judy Counley, Desktop Publisher

Shae Isaacs, Writer

Leticia Steffen, Writer

Pathfinder Education, Inc.
P. O. Box 531
Conifer, CO 80433
www.PathfinderUSA.com

THE PATHFINDER PROJECT
TABLE OF CONTENTS

This book is dedicated

To Todd. Your courage and dedication have inspired me and countless others.

Robert J. Marzano

To my mother Mildred, whose life is an inspiration to me. Thanks for always believing in me.

Diane E. Paynter

To my parents, Sue and Dave, who inspired and motivated me and opened the world to the endless possibilities life has to offer.

Jane K. Doty

CHAPTER 1
WHAT IS THE PATHFINDER PROJECT?

I have spent my life stringing and unstringing my instrument while the song I came to sing remains unsung. Tagore (1861-1941)

Most people have something in life they dream of accomplishing. Interestingly, some people realize their dreams, while others seem to spend their days "stringing and unstringing their instruments." Why do some people realize their dreams and others do not? Why is it that some, maybe most people, never even try to accomplish their dreams? Is it that those who accomplish their goals believe that they will succeed if they try hard enough? Is it the belief that they have the skills and resources necessary to accomplish their dreams? Is it because there is someone along the way who inspires them or encourages them to take the first step?

The Pathfinder Project is a program designed to help students identify goals that are intensely important to them, and give them the skills necessary to accomplish their goals and to function successfully in life. Since students learn these skills in the context of something that is enormously important to them, they come to realize that *if* they are deeply committed and willing to act on their dreams, they *can* accomplish great things.

One question commonly asked about the Pathfinder Project is, "How was it named?" Why is it called Pathfinder? To answer this question, let's consider what a pathfinder is. According to the dictionary, a pathfinder is "a person who makes a path, way, or route through a previously unexplored or un-traveled wilderness." When pursuing a deeply held desire to accomplish something, we forge new insights. We discover new paths into who we are as human beings, the

nature of the world around us and its meaning to us. Students who engage in the activities provided in this program are truly pathfinders in terms of their own lives; hence the name, the Pathfinder Project.

The subtitle to the Pathfinder Project is "Exploring the Power of One." As students learn about the great accomplishments other ordinary people have made and discover their own potential for greatness, they confront one of the most profound awarenesses an individual can have: one committed human being can effect extraordinary change, for better or for worse.

The Principles on Which the Pathfinder Project Is Founded

The Pathfinder Project is founded on four general principles:

1. Everyone has deeply-held desires to accomplish something that is highly meaningful to them and deeply personal.

2. When engaged in the pursuit of these accomplishments, individuals bring to bear energy and abilities that are otherwise difficult, if not impossible, to access.

3. When engaged in the pursuit of these accomplishments, individuals frequently learn a great deal about themselves.

4. Commonly, these deeply-held desires are awakened by an inspirational event.

Although there is a strong theory and research base for these principles (see Seligman, 1991; Harter, 1999; Bandura, 1997; Csikszentmihalyi, 1990; Covington, 1992), all four also have an intuitive ring of truth to them because most of us have experienced the principles operating in our own lives.

We have all been inspired by the actions of others. It might have been through a movie we saw, a story we read or heard, or an incident we actually observed. This inspirational event, the specifics of which might not have even been related to the details of our lives, reminded us of something we wanted to accomplish. The inspirational event might also have given us the courage to try something we have always wanted to do but were hesitant to begin.

Standing on this moment of inspiration, we began to move into action, maybe for the first time in our lives. We set goals and started working toward them. As we worked on our goals, we discovered a level of energy we may never have had before. We even discovered skills and abilities we didn't know we had. We approached problems differently. We approached decisions differently. We became aware of aspects of our personality that were new to us.

Perhaps most importantly, while working on our goals, we experienced a level of satisfaction and fulfillment we had never previously achieved.

As common and widely understood as this dynamic is, it is not systematically used in K-12 education as a basic structure for students to develop skills and abilities that would otherwise lay dormant, or to engage them in the pursuit of goals that provide deep personal satisfaction. **The purpose of the Pathfinder Project is to bring this power and potential to K–12 education.**

The Structure of the Pathfinder Project

The Pathfinder Project consists of:

- A set of inspirational stories and quotes
- A framework for a personal project
- Activities for learning essential life skills

These elements are depicted in more detail in Figure 1.1.

Figure 1.1 Structure of the Pathfinder Project

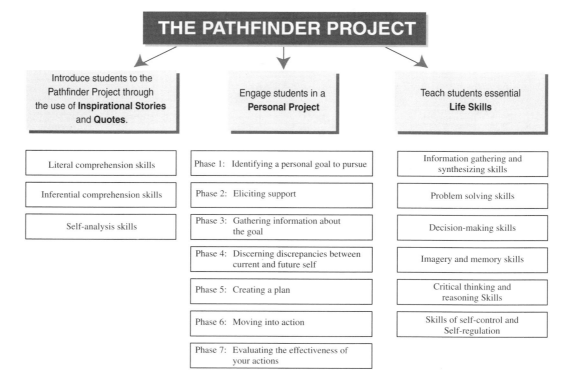

I. Inspirational Stories and Quotes

Stories are a staple of the Pathfinder Project, as they provide the guidance and inspiration for students to set and accomplish personal goals. A set of stories about different individuals who have accomplished unusual, and in some cases extraordinary, things are provided in Chapter 8 of this Manual. These stories are about real people, some of whom have come from backgrounds similar or even identical to the students who will read their stories.

One of the purposes of presenting inspirational stories to students is to help them realize that people who have accomplished extraordinary things in their lives have followed similar patterns of behavior. Students are presented with this pattern in the context of the first story they read. As students read additional stories, they are asked to identify how the people in these stories followed that same general pattern—a pattern that becomes the framework for students to follow as they set and pursue their own personal goals.

The inspirational stories also provide a convenient venue for teaching and reinforcing comprehension skills, which are taught, modeled, and reinforced. After reading a story, students are asked basic literal comprehension questions that help them better understand the basic message of the story and practice the comprehension skills that can be used when they are reading other information. As most teachers know, these are the very skills required to do well on the reading portion of many state and standardized tests.

In addition to questions that address important literal comprehension skills, questions are asked that require students to make inferences about issues not specifically addressed in the stories. When answering these inferential comprehension questions, students are asked to explain and justify the assumptions that lead to their conclusions.

Self-analysis questions are the third type. Here, students are asked to place themselves in the same position experienced by the person in the story, and to describe and explain how they might have behaved.

In addition to the inspirational stories, the Pathfinder Project also provides a series of inspirational quotes that can be used to motivate students. These are found in Chapter 9. There are more than 900 quotations that can be used on a daily basis to help remind students of the importance of pursuing their passions and the necessary actions they must take to do so.

II. The Personal Project

The centerpiece of the Pathfinder Project is the personal project. Here students identify and gather information about something they might want to do in the future. The critical feature of the personal project is that students are intensely interested or, ideally, passionate about pursuing and achieving a particular goal. The purpose of the personal project is to help students:

- Identify a personally relevant goal they would like to achieve.
- Learn a process they might follow to achieve such a goal.
- Develop the knowledge and skills necessary to help them achieve this goal and function successfully in life.

The personal project is divided into seven phases that parallel the general pattern underlying the inspirational stories. Each phase is facilitated by specific classroom activities guided by the teacher, as described in detail in Chapter 3 of this Manual and briefly summarized below:

Phase One: Identifying a Personal Goal to Pursue

This phase of the project provides students with opportunities to think about their future outside the constraints of limiting belief patterns. From this perspective, students identify a future goal that they would like to pursue.

Phase Two: Eliciting Support

In this phase, students explore the importance of establishing support; how heroes, role models, and mentors can be used as support; and the importance of eliciting appropriate support. Although students begin to elicit support for their project during this phase, they continue to examine the nature of support throughout the entire project.

Phase Three: Gathering Information About the Goal

Once students have begun to establish a circle of support, they gather information on the topic they have selected. They also construct a description of themselves in the future at a time when they have accomplished their goal. This "future possible self" description serves as a concrete target and inspiration for each student.

Phase Four: Discerning Discrepancies Between Current and Future Self

Armed with the description of their "future possible selves," students identify the differences or "discrepancies" between where they are now and where they want to be. This phase of the project provides a concrete list of tasks and milestones that must be addressed if students are to realize their goals.

Phase Five: Creating a Plan

Based on their look into the future through the description of their "future possible selves" and their discrepancy analysis, students create a detailed plan. This involves planning backwards. As the name implies, this is accomplished by selecting a date in the future by which the goal will be accomplished, and then planning the events that must occur for them to reach the goal within that timeframe. Stated differently, they make a timeline of future activities and events working backwards from their look into the future.

Phase Six: Moving into Action

Up to this point in their projects, students have been gathering a great deal of information and speculating about actions they will take in the future. Now, it is time for them to put their thoughts and words into action. While students at the middle and high school levels might not be able to take major steps toward their goals, they can still take at least small steps in this phase of the project.

Phase Seven: Evaluating the Effectiveness of Your Actions

The final phase of the personal project requires students to examine the effectiveness of their efforts relative to the personal project. This includes examining the progress they have made toward their goals, reviewing the lessons learned, and evaluating their level of proficiency in selected skills.

III. Activities for Learning Essential Skills

As students are engaged in reading the inspirational stories, they are taught literal comprehension skills, inferential comprehension skills, and self-analysis skills. As they work on their personal projects other skills can be taught and reinforced, including:

1. Information-gathering and synthesizing skills
2. Problem-solving skills
3. Decision-making skills
4. Imagery and memory skills
5. Critical thinking and reasoning skills
6. Skills of self-control and self-regulation

These skill areas are described in depth in Chapter 4 of this Manual. Virtually all of these skills are important to success in school as well as success in life.

The first skill area—information-gathering and synthesizing skills—can be directly addressed as students gather information about various aspects of their projects. That is, as they collect information about the goal they have selected, they are taught about various information sources, ways to gather information, how to take notes and record information, and how to synthesize that information.

The other five areas are addressed via the use of specific instructional activities that the teacher intersperses throughout the program. These instructional activities can be organized in a variety of ways and used to change the pace and focus of instruction.

Students are given a general problem-solving strategy that can be applied to real life challenges. When they understand the method, they are asked to apply it to problems in their lives. Additionally, throughout the Pathfinder Project, students are presented with engaging academic problems and a process for solving them. These academic problems are used as "sponge activities"—activities that "soak up" dead time when students are finding it difficult to concentrate.

Decision-making skills are approached in a manner similar to real life problem-solving skills. Students are presented with a generic strategy and then provided practice with real life decisions.

The imagery and memory skills presented to students have a variety of applications. Imagery, in and of itself, can be used to help students clarify their goals, think through the implications of their actions, and test out possible courses of action. The memory skills (which are based on imagery techniques) can be used by students to improve their ability to remember important information in both academic and non-academic situations. Additionally, developing expertise in

memory strategies gives students a keen awareness of the power of the human mind.

The critical thinking and reasoning skills presented to students give them tools for analyzing the logic of their own conclusions and those of others. They also provide a grounding in the many types of informal fallacies they hear and read. In this day and age of geometrically-expanding access to information from the Internet, television, and other media, critical thinking and reasoning skills might very well be the foundation skills of a democratic society.

The final skill area addressed in the Pathfinder Project involves self-control and self-regulation skills. They are presented to students under the title of "The Inner Game of Success." Here students are taught that their thinking and the manner in which they control their thinking has a great deal to do with their success in life as well as their experience of life. The self-control and self-regulation skills include: the importance of inner dialogue, the nature and importance of optimistic thinking, and the importance of self-management.

How the Pathfinder Project Might be Used

The Pathfinder Project can be used in a variety of settings that include:

- A unit or course that lasts a few weeks
- A unit or course that lasts a quarter or a semester
- A language arts course that focuses on writing
- An after school program
- A home study course that parents and children might engage in together

Each of these venues is described in more detail in Chapter 6.

Materials

The materials used in the Pathfinder Project include:

1. This Teacher's Manual, which describes how to use the program and provides all necessary instructional materials.
2. A Student Notebook, which contains all the materials and activities students will use throughout their personal projects.

The Student Notebook is described in Chapter 7 of this Manual.

How This Manual is Organized

This Manual includes ten more chapters. Chapter 2 describes how the inspirational stories and quotes might be used, and explains how to teach and reinforce comprehension skills when using the stories. Chapter 3 describes the personal project in depth. Chapter 4 describes the essential life skills that can be developed throughout the Pathfinder Project. Chapter 5 describes how evaluation and grading of students might be addressed within the context of the Pathfinder Project. Chapter 6 describes various ways the Pathfinder Project can be used. Chapter 7 describes the Student Notebook. Chapter 8 contains the inspirational stories, along with their associated comprehension questions. Chapter 9 contains more than 900 inspirational quotations, and a discussion about how they might be used. Chapter 10 contains reproducible exercises and activities for a variety of aspects of the Pathfinder Project. Chapter 11 contains blackline masters for various aspects of the Pathfinder Project. In short, this Manual is a comprehensive resource for the implementation of the Pathfinder Project.

CHAPTER 2
USING INSPIRATIONAL STORIES AND QUOTES

Albert Einstein (1879-1955), a mathematical physicist of German birth, profoundly influenced the world. In fact, a great deal of modern scientific theory is rooted in Einstein's work. He is probably best known for his enunciation of a theory of relativity, which states: if a body emits a certain amount of energy, the mass of that body must decrease by a proportionate amount. That relationship is expressed in the famous equation $E = mc^2$. It is hard to imagine that this man, who had such an impact on the field of science, was once asked to leave school because he was considered a nuisance by his teachers.

We wonder what made Einstein great. Was it simply the power of his mind, or were there people or experiences that inspired him—that helped him accomplish goals that were beyond the dreams he had for himself? He gives some clues in his personal writings. He tells of a time when he was 12 years old, reading a booklet on Euclidean plane geometry. He says, "Here were assertions, as for example the intersection of the three altitudes of a triangle in one point, which—though by no means evident—could nevertheless be proved with such certainty that any doubt appeared to be out of the question. This lucidity and certainty made an indescribable impression on me." (Schlipp, 1951, p. 9) In short, one source of motivation for Einstein was the pristine beauty of Euclidean geometry, which invoked a sense of wonder and excitement within him.

Einstein goes on to explain that it was the people in his life and his interactions with those people that helped him eventually become clear about his life path. One influential individual in Einstein's life was his uncle, an engineer, who provided a sounding board for Einstein's early thoughts about physics. Another influential individual was a medical student who ate dinner with him once a week and gave Einstein the courage to try new ideas, even though failure might be inevitable. In fact, Einstein once noted, "Anyone who has never made a mistake has never tried anything new." (Schlipp, 1951, p. 10)

We see two complementary forces working in Einstein's life: inspiration and support. It is true that each of us may not impact the world with the same magnitude as Einstein; however, that does not diminish the fact that *everyone* can accomplish extraordinary things if they are inspired and have the support to turn inspiration into action. The Pathfinder Project is designed to provide both the inspiration and the initial stages of support for students, and this chapter addresses how the inspirational stories and quotes can be used to that end.

Chapter 8 contains stories of ordinary people who have accomplished a personal goal and, as a result, influenced the lives of others and increased their joy in life and their capacity to accomplish even greater things. These events may not have made the papers or the nightly news. Nonetheless, they profoundly affected the individuals who accomplished them and, in many cases, profoundly affected and even inspired those people with whom the individuals had contact.

Inspirational Stories

Besides being a source of inspiration to students, the stories presented in Chapter 8 have a two-fold purpose.

1. They illustrate a general pattern of action that students can follow as they pursue their own personal goals.

2. They are the basis for teaching and practicing comprehension skills.

Providing a General Pattern for Students to Follow

Like most people, students typically like to hear inspirational stories and often wish that they could be like the people in those stories. Sometimes these stories spur students on to action. All too often, however, students are impressed by a story, but assume that their personal circumstances, their access to resources, or their ability to overcome obstacles vary so greatly from the situation in the story that they see no correlation between the story and their own lives. Thus, many inspirational stories lose their power to influence the lives of the students who read them.

In the Pathfinder Project, the stories are a means to help students step outside of the specifics of a given situation and comprehend a general pattern of behavior followed by successful people across a wide array of circumstances. When students understand this general pattern, they can move beyond the specifics of a particular story and see how to use the behavior in their own lives.

In the Pathfinder Project, the general pattern of action followed by the people in the stories presented in Chapter 8 includes the following elements:

1. An individual is inspired to make a decision about pursuing a personal goal.

2. The individual receives guidance, support, and encouragement for pursuing this goal.

3. The individual identifies the knowledge, skills, and resources necessary to obtain this goal.

4. The individual must overcome obstacles and barriers to meeting the goal.

5. Planning, determination, and hard work make it possible for the individual to meet and overcome obstacles and barriers.

6. The individual reaches or even exceeds his or her goal.

To help students recognize and understand this general pattern, you might begin with Todd's story (the first one in Chapter 8). Todd's personal goal was to become a jet fighter pilot. Begin by reading the story with students. You might have them read the story silently, you might read the story aloud, or both. Then, ask students to identify what Todd did to accomplish his goal,

Figure 2.1 Blackline Master B

Todd's Story	General Pattern
1. After watching the movie *Top Gun*, Todd decided that he wanted to be a jet fighter pilot.	1. An individual is inspired to make a decision about pursuing a personal goal.
2. Todd's parents encouraged Todd to pursue his goal.	2. The individual receives guidance, support and encouragement for pursuing this goal.
3. Todd researched what he would have to do to become a fighter pilot.	3. The individual identifies the knowledge, skills, and resources necessary to obtain this goal.
4. Todd found out that he lacked the necessary academic knowledge and skills to become a fighter pilot.	4. The individual must overcome obstacles and barriers to meeting the goal.
5. Todd took courses, studied hard, and purchased a program to improve his vision. Because he did these things, when he applied to Navy flight school, he was accepted. Flight school challenged Todd but he worked even harder to finish in the top 20% of his class, the requirement needed to fly jets.	5. Planning, determination, and hard work make it possible for the individual to overcome the obstacles.
6. Todd was accepted as a Top Gun pilot and has a career in the United States Navy.	6. The individual reaches or even exceeds his or her goal.

Teacher's Manual

listing their comments on the board. Next, present students with the general behavior pattern and point out how the specifics of Todd's story fits that pattern (see Figure 2.1 on page 8). Blackline Master B, found in Chapter 11 of this Manual, can be used for this purpose.

Next, ask students to consider another story they have heard (or one you provide for them) that demonstrates the various elements of the general pattern. As they relate the specifics of the new story, they should record their responses using Blackline Master C (found in Chapter 11 of this Manual and depicted in Figure 2.2 below).

As students read the other inspirational stories, periodically ask them to show how the new story fits the general pattern, again using Blackline Master C. By discussing the details of the various stories as they relate to the general pattern, students come to better understand how they might use the general pattern as a means to pursue their own goals.

Teaching and Practicing Comprehension Skills

The stories in Chapter 8 can also be used to enhance students' comprehension skills. There are three sets of questions at the end of each story in Chapter 8. In the context of the Pathfinder Project, these inquiries move students from conversations about specific details in each story (literal comprehension questions), to making inferences about information not specifically stated in the story (inferential comprehension questions), and finally, to an analysis of how the information in the story might be applied to their own lives (self-analysis questions). Below we consider how you might address each category of question.

The first set of questions following each story is *literal* in nature. These are typically *who, what, when, and where* questions, the answers to which can be identified within the text of the story. These literal questions help students develop the skills important to doing well on the reading portion of many state and standardized tests.

Figure 2.2 Blackline Master C

General Pattern	New Story or Example
1. An individual is inspired to make a decision about pursuing a personal goal.	
2. The individual receives guidance, support and encouragement for pursuing this goal.	
3. The individual identifies the knowledge, skills, and resources necessary to obtain this goal.	
4. The individual must overcome obstacles and barriers to meeting the goal.	
5. Planning, determination, and hard work make it possible for the individual to overcome the obstacles.	
6. The individual reaches or even exceeds his or her goal.	

Some literal comprehension questions around Todd's story might be:

- What are the major events that led Todd to become a fighter pilot?
- What did Todd do to make sure that his eyesight was adequate to be a pilot?
- What is the process involved in landing a plane on an aircraft carrier?

The second set of questions following each story is *inferential* in nature. To answer this type of question, a student must think well beyond information explicitly provided in the text, reasoning from the basic beliefs he or she has about people and the nature of the world. When answering inferential questions, students should be asked to explain the assumptions that lead to their conclusions. Additionally, they should be asked to explain how they came to these basic assumptions. This kind of interaction helps sharpen students' inductive and deductive reasoning abilities.

In Todd's story, the following inferential comprehension questions might be asked:

- What do you think might have been one of Todd's lowest moments or most discouraging moments?
- From Todd's perspective, what do you think was his greatest triumph?

The third type of question involves *self-analysis.* These are questions that place the students in the same position experienced by the person in the story. Typically, questions in this category ask the students to think about what they would have done in a specific situation, how they would have handled a specific situation, or how they would have reacted to a specific situation. To answer these questions, students must reason from basic beliefs and assumptions they have about themselves.

Relative to Todd's story, students might be asked the following self-analysis question:

- Imagine that you are Todd. You know that you have to get into and graduate from a good college to even be considered for the Navy's flight school. But, at age 17, you don't have the necessary grades to get into college or the money to pay for college. What are some ways you might consider solving these problems?

To help students answer the literal and inferential questions, it is useful to provide them with the following strategy:

Step 1 *Have students determine if they know the answer to the question without going back to consult the text. This might be the case if they remember the answer from the passage, or it might be a question that they could answer without having read the story at all.*

Step 2 *If they can't remember or don't know the answer, students should go back to the point in the text where the answer is most likely to be found. This is probably the most crucial aspect of this step because students must consider the question, the type of information that would answer the question, and where that type of information might be found in the text. This requires a fairly good sense of the general structure of the story. Consequently, before looking for the information, it is useful for students to do a quick mental review of the basic sequence of events presented in the text (what happened first, what happened next, and so on).*

Step 3 *If students don't find the information relatively quickly, they should go to the beginning of the text and quickly scan each part of the story sequentially.*

Step 4 *If the answer to a question is not explicitly stated in the text, students must infer the answer. This requires students to find clues in the text to help answer the question. With this information, students make an educated guess as to the answer.*

Present these steps to students using Blackline Master D from Chapter 11. The process is stated in "student friendly" language, and reads as follows:

Step 1 *Do you know the answer?*

Step 2 *If you don't, go to where it might be in the story.*

Step 3 *If you still can't find it, scan the whole story.*

Step 4 *If you still can't find it, look for clues to the answer and make your best guess.*

It is highly advisable to model each step for students as you explain the type of thinking discussed above. The best way to do this is to *think aloud* as you go through the various steps in your own mind.

Unlike literal and inferential comprehension questions, self-analysis questions do not lend themselves to a specific strategy. They require students to examine how they would react to a situation. Even though you can't provide "steps" for answering these questions, you can make students aware that the way they answer these questions reveals something about themselves. Consequently, as students answer these self-analysis questions, you might also ask them to address questions such as:

"How sure are you that you would have acted or reacted this way?"

"What is it about you that would have driven you to act or react that way?"

"What does your answer tell you about yourself?"

Inspirational Quotations

Have you ever heard a quotation that stuck with you, caused you to take a more focused look at your life, or even changed your life? This is not an uncommon experience. Quotations can alter the actions of individuals, societies and even entire countries. Consider some of the quotations that have influenced the actions of many people in the United States:

"I have a dream."

-Martin Luther King, Jr.

"Ask not what your country can do for you. Ask what you can do for your country."

-John F. Kennedy

In Chapter 9 of this Manual, you will find a variety of inspirational quotes organized by topic. Most of these quotes are from well-known individuals who have achieved some degree of greatness. These quotes can inspire students as they reflect and work on their personal goals and counteract negative self-talk.

It is quite common for students to engage in negative self-talk, particularly when they are attempting to do something beyond their expectations for themselves. The goals students select in conjunction with the Pathfinder Project often push them beyond their comfort zones and can produce a great deal of negative self-talk, especially when things are not going smoothly. Inspirational quotes are a great antidote to this form of self-sabotage.

The Student Notebook contains a section dedicated to quotations that are personally meaningful to each student. Some ways the quotations might be used to inspire students and counteract their negative self-talk are:

- Place quotes around the classroom for students to read.

- Each day, introduce students to a different quote and ask them to discuss what they think the quote means in general and what it means relative to their lives.

- Ask students to identify negative self-talk they may be experiencing and identify quotes that might help them overcome it. When they find quotes that are particularly meaningful to them, they can memorize them and repeat them when they need an emotional lift.

- Ask students to interview people they know to determine if they were motivated to accomplish a goal through an inspirational quote.

- Ask students to create their own quotes, and discuss the degree to which other members of the class relate to or are motivated by them.

- Have students record the quotes that inspire them in their Notebooks, and periodically review their favorite ones.

CHAPTER 3
THE PERSONAL PROJECT

As described in Chapter 1, the personal project is the centerpiece of the Pathfinder Project. While not required, it is highly recommended that you, the teacher, engage in a personal project along with your students. Specifically, we suggest that you do the activities with the students regarding something you would like to accomplish in your life—something you are passionate about. This will produce benefits to you personally, and will also put you in a better position to answer students' questions and provide examples related to their personal projects.

The personal project is organized into seven phases which parallel the general pattern of the inspirational stories (see Figure 3.1). In each of the seven phases, students engage in teacher-led activities that help them construct and complete their personal projects. As you will see in Chapter 4, the essential life skills (problem-solving skills, decision-making skills, information-gathering and synthesizing skills, and so on) can be interspersed throughout the phases of the personal project.

Each participating student should have a Student Notebook, which outlines the activities and phases of the personal project and contains the inspirational stories (it is described in more depth in Chapter 7). It is also useful for you, the teacher, to have your own copy of the Student Notebook for reference.

Figure 3.1 Personal Project Phases

General Story Pattern	Seven Phases in Personal Project	Activities
1. An individual is inspired to make a decision about pursuing a personal goal.	*Phase One* Identifying a Personal Goal to Pursue	• Overcoming Fear of Failure • Breaking Patterns of the Past • Identifying a Future Accomplishment or Goal
2. The individual receives guidance, support and encouragement for pursuing this goal.	*Phase Two* Eliciting Support	• Identifying a Circle of Support • Learning from Heroes, Role Models, and Mentors • Constructing the Winner's Profile • Understanding the Nature of Support
3. The individual identifies the knowledge, skills, and resources necessary to obtain this goal.	*Phase Three* Gathering Information About the Goal	• Identifying Your Future Possible Self • Articulating Necessary Experiences, Accomplishments, and Schooling
4. The individual must overcome obstacles and barriers to meeting the goal.	*Phase Four* Discerning Discrepancies Between Current and Future Self	• Completing a Discrepancy Analysis
5. Planning, determination, and hard work make it possible for the individual to overcome obstacles.	*Phase Five* Creating a Plan	• Planning Backwards • Making Declarations
6. The individual reaches or even succeeds his or her goal.	*Phase Six* Moving into Action	• Taking Small Steps
	Phase Seven Evaluating the Effectiveness of Your Actions	• Re-Evaluating Plans • Creating Aphorisms • Evaluating Success

Phase One: Identifying a Personal Goal to Pursue

Students begin their personal projects by identifying a personal goal. Three focused activities are useful to this end, each of which is facilitated by a Student Activity Sheet from the Student Notebook.

Activity: Overcoming Fear of Failure

One of the first activities students are asked to undertake is to respond to the query, "What would you do if you knew you wouldn't fail?" (See Student Activity Sheet 1 in the Student Notebook.) The basic purpose of this activity is to provide a platform for students to think about the future outside the constraints of limiting beliefs about themselves, the opportunities that are available to them, the nature of the world around them, and so on. Both research and theory tell us that students, at a very early age, start limiting their dreams because they assume some dreams are not attainable.

Before asking students to engage in this activity, have a discussion with them about the consequences of *not* following dreams. You might relate some examples from your own life, or examples you have heard.

After students have responded to the prompt, "What would you do if you knew you wouldn't fail?" have a discussion with them about the limiting nature of our beliefs and how the possibility of failure often stops us from beginning things that we might like to do.

Activity: Breaking Patterns of the Past

Breaking from the past is another critical aspect of the personal project (see Student Activity Sheet 2). For some students, responding to the question, "What would you do if you knew you wouldn't fail?" will cause them to consider possibilities that go well beyond what they have ever admitted to others, and maybe even to themselves. These possibilities might cause a complete break from their current reality and belief sets.

The mere idea that it is possible to break from past patterns is revolutionary for some students. Consequently, it is advisable to have a discussion with them about this phenomenon. Specifically, you might emphasize that breaking from our patterns is frequently necessary to accomplish our deeply-held goals and desires. Additionally, breaking from our patterns of the past is often the most difficult part of the journey to success because our patterns have frequently become habituated.

Link this activity to the first one, in which students identified what they would do if they knew they wouldn't fail. Have them select one of the things they identified during that activity, and then list the behaviors they currently engage in which must be changed or stopped to accomplish the goal. The more specific they are about their responses to this activity, the better. If students address this activity thoughtfully and specifically, they will begin to identify the current actions and behaviors that produce negative consequences in their lives.

Activity: Identifying a Future Accomplishment or Goal

The next activity in the personal project is for students to identify a specific future accomplishment or goal they would like to work toward. There should be no constraints on the accomplishments they select (unless they are immoral or illegal). They can be careers that students would like to pursue (e.g., becoming a doctor or a baseball player), projects that are beneficial to others (e.g., inventing a car that doesn't pollute the environment), or problems that students would like to solve for themselves or for others (e.g., developing a cure for an illness).

Again, the more specific, the better. Student Activity Sheet 3 asks the following questions:

- What do you want to accomplish?
- Where and how will you be living?
- What are some things you will be doing?
- What will you look like?
- What type of people will you be working with?
- How will you feel about yourself?

As students answer these questions, encourage them to imagine the answers they are generating.

Phase Two: Eliciting Support

In this phase, students address the nature of support and the importance of support in accomplishing their goals. They are asked to identify heroes, role models, and mentors as sources of encouragement, positive reinforcement, and advice. They also consider the general characteristics of these successful people.

Throughout this phase, students come to understand that some types of support are more beneficial than others. Although they begin to elicit support in this phase of their personal project, they continue to identify and use various sources of support throughout the entire project. Four activities constitute this phase.

Activity: Identifying a Circle of Support

To some students, the concept of a circle of support will be new. Consequently, you might have to spend time discussing the importance of support, particularly when trying to accomplish something that is personally challenging. This is best accomplished by presenting examples of how people rely on and use support. The inspirational quotes in Chapter 9 should be useful to this end, and you might also provide students with examples from your own life or from the inspirational stories.

The objective of this step is for students to identify those people who currently provide support in their lives, as well as other people who could provide the support they need (Student Activity Sheet 4 explicitly addresses these issues). Another question for students to address is, "How do you get people to support you?" Ask them to identify a time when they became excited about what someone else was doing and wanted to help them—a time when they were moved to support someone else. For example, some students might have helped somebody build something or solve a particular problem, or they might even have become involved in some type of drive or political campaign. By identifying what it was about those experiences that inspired them to get involved, they can start to see how support is elicited.

Some of the important aspects of eliciting support include:

- People will become excited about your project when they see that you are excited.
- People will become excited about your project when they see the value in it.
- People will become excited about your project when they see that you are truly committed to it.

Activity: Learning from Heroes, Role Models, and Mentors

This activity begins by asking students to identify heroes, role models, and mentors. Although these categories of people share certain common characteristics, you might point out some important differences. *Heroes* are people who have actually accomplished the goals we are striving for, but with whom we have no contact. In fact, they might not even be living at the present time. A *role model* is someone who has accomplished the goal we aspire to and whom we might be able to contact. Finally, a *mentor* is someone who has accomplished what we are striving for, or who can be a source of support for us even though he or she has not accomplished our specific goal. Mentors are people we have access to and who are willing to be actively involved in our lives. It is ideal for each student to find a mentor for their goal, although it might be difficult. Student Activity Sheet 5 is designed to help students identify potential heroes, role models, and mentors.

Spend some time discussing the importance of these people in our lives—even heroes with whom we have no contact. They are important because they provide us with a concrete example that our goals can actually be reached. To a great extent, they provide us with a constant source of inspiration—someone who has actually accomplished our dreams or who reminds us about our aspirations.

It is not enough for students to simply identify a hero, role model, or mentor. They should also gather detailed information about their lives, including:

- Where and when they were born
- Where they are now
- Their major accomplishments
- The major obstacles they overcame
- The support they had along the way
- Why the student selected them
- What can be learned from them

Activity Sheet 6 provides guidelines about the kinds of information to gather about their heroes, role models, and mentors.

For this activity, you may have to spend time introducing students to various information sources in the library or on the Internet. Since some students will identify people they actually have access to, you might also present interviewing techniques. Additionally, all

students can be provided with some strategies for gathering information. Related skills and techniques are covered in the section of Chapter 4 entitled "Information-Gathering and Synthesizing Skills."

Activity: Constructing the Winner's Profile

The Winner's Profile is a logical extension of students gathering information about their heroes, role models, and mentors. In this activity, students compare the characteristics of their heroes, role models, and mentors. While the process of gathering information about their heroes, role models, and mentors is fairly factual in nature, the process of creating the Winner's Profile is highly inductive. For a characteristic to be listed on the Winners' Profile, it does not have to be possessed by each individual the students have researched; however, it should be a characteristic of at least a majority of the individuals.

The Winner's Profile can be done as a whole class activity, in small groups, or both. That is, students might break into small groups to create Winner's Profiles, and then come together as a whole class to construct a composite Profile. It is useful to keep this Profile displayed prominently in the classroom so you can add to it and alter it as students learn more about their projects, about themselves, and about others who have accomplished great things in their lives.

Figure 3.2 on page 17 is provided for students in Student Activity Sheet 7.

Activity: Understanding the Nature of Support

It is important for students to understand that support might look quite different from occasion to occasion, and is not always positive. Student Activity Sheet 8 asks students to identify times when they received support, and to analyze the nature of that support. Some of the major distinctions they should understand relative to support are:

- People who support us do not always tell us what we want to hear.

- People who support us will do so only if they see us trying.

- People are not supporting us if they do things for us that we really should be doing for ourselves.

- It is common and very useful to get support from more than one person.

- Different types of people provide different types of support, all of which can be helpful.

- When people provide support in the form of advice, we are always free to *not* follow that advice.

To help students recognize and understand these aspects of support, you might provide personal examples from your own life. For each point, have students identify examples from the lives of their heroes, role models, and mentors and/or from the inspirational stories. Encourage them to record the information they gather and their reactions in their Student Notebooks.

Phase Three: Gathering Information About the Goal

Once students have addressed the issue of support, they begin to gather information about their goal. This involves answering questions such as:

- How long does it take to accomplish my goal?

- What types of experiences are required or useful to have?

- What type of schooling is required?

- What physical skills are required?

- What mental skills are required?

Throughout the personal project, this information becomes critical, as it is the basis for creating an action plan. Students can use a number of resources to gather information regarding the goal they have selected, including the Internet. You might provide class time for students to gather information over the Internet about their goals. They can also use more traditional sources such as books, journals, and newspapers found in the library. A third source is the people students have identified as their heroes, role models, and mentors: some of these individuals might be accessible for the students to interview, making them "primary sources" of information.

Figure 3.2 Student Activity Sheet 7

Successful People	Trait 1	Trait 2	Trait 3	Trait 4
Person 1				
Person 2				
Person 3				
Person 4				

This third phase of the project is a perfect opportunity to teach and reinforce important information-gathering and synthesizing skills (found in the section of Chapter 4 entitled "Information-Gathering and Synthesizing Skills"). If you want students to write a formal report during the project, this is the appropriate point to do so. Traditional writing and research skills can be taught and reinforced within the context of the written report such as: mechanics, word choice, cohesion, and bibliographic format.

Students engage in two major activities during this phase.

Activity: Identifying Your Future Possible Self

Identifying their future possible self is one of the more creative activities students engage in as part of the personal project. Here students construct a description of themselves in the future—at a time when they have accomplished their goal. They initiated this activity when they first identified the topic of their personal projects and answered the questions about how old they were, where they were living, and so on (see Student Activity Sheet 3). Now, it is time to formalize the exercise.

Prior to engaging in this activity, it is useful to have a conversation about the importance of creating a future image of oneself, particularly when you are trying to accomplish something extremely difficult. You might facilitate this discussion by simply asking students, "Why is it important to have an image about ourselves in the future?" It might help to let them know that researchers have determined that successful people are able to generate detailed images of themselves in the future. That is how the term *future possible self* was coined. Note that this description employs the word "possible" because these images are just that—possibilities. Even though these images only represent possibilities, without actively cultivating them, our chances of accomplishing something great in our lives are severely hindered.

Student Activity Sheet 9 introduces the concept of a future possible self to students and provides questions like the following to stimulate their thinking:

- How old will I be when I accomplish my goal?
- Where will I live?
- What will an average day be like?
- How will I feel about myself?
- What will I look like?
- Who will my friends be?

Finally, students should construct a written description of themselves in the future. Their descriptions can be short or long, depending on how much you want to emphasize writing skills throughout the Pathfinder Project.

Activity: Articulating Necessary Experiences, Accomplishments, and Schooling

The future possible self-description articulates a detailed vision of what life might be like when the student achieves the goal, and the next major activity helps them actually begin the journey toward the goal. Within this activity, students identify the experiences, accomplishments, and schooling necessary to realize the vision they have created. Specifically, *necessary experiences* refer to background experiences that are important to a specific goal. For example, if a student has identified a future possible self of being a doctor, then it might be useful for her to have experiences such as volunteering in a hospital, and actually observing a surgery. *Necessary accomplishments* involve milestones and skills. For example, a high school student seeking to become a doctor will have to take the SAT and obtain a certain score. She will also have to develop certain study skills. Finally, *necessary schooling* is just that—the types and levels of schooling a student must complete to reach her goal. In this example, the student seeking to become a doctor must have a high school degree and a college degree, typically with a major in science.

Student Activity Sheets 10 and 11 provide questions that help students identify their necessary experiences, accomplishments, and schooling. Students should have adequate class time to gather the information necessary to answer the questions in these worksheets.

Phase Four: Discerning Discrepancies Between Current and Future Self

With their future possible self-descriptions completed, students are asked to engage in a "discrepancy analysis." The purpose of the discrepancy analysis is for students to see the difference or "discrepancy" between where they are now and where they want to be. It is not meant to discourage them, but rather to provide a reality base for their dreams and aspirations. Here students are asked to:

1. Identify the experiences, accomplishments, and schooling that are required to realize their future possible self.

2. Identify their current status relative to each of these elements.

3. Identify what they need to do if they haven't obtained a given skill or accomplishment.

The discrepancy analysis will prepare students to more realistically create and execute a plan to achieve their goals.

Activity: Completing a Discrepancy Analysis

The discrepancy analysis can be quite an eye-opener for students. As its name implies, while doing the discrepancy analysis, students contrast where they are now with where they will be once their future possible self is realized.

Figure 3.3 depicts Student Activity Sheet 12.

Students should first fill out the column entitled, "What experiences, accomplishments, and schooling will I need to become my future possible self?" This information comes directly from the previous activities in Student Activity Sheets 10 and 11.

The second column requires students to list their current status relative to each of the items listed in the first column. For many of the items, nothing concrete will have been done. For example, a middle school student who has listed,

Figure 3.3 Student Activity Sheet 12

What experiences, accomplishments, and schooling will I need to become my future possible self?	What is my current status in this area?	What can I do now?	What will I have to do in the future?
1.			
2.			
3.			
4.			

"Take the SATs and receive a score of at least 1200" in column one will have nothing concrete to put in the second column. It is useful to explain to students that this is quite natural when someone identifies a goal that is long term in nature. However, if students are currently doing anything relative to a given item, even if it is quite indirect, they should record it. The middle school student in the example has a few years until she will take the SATs; however, if she is currently talking to older students about test strategies, she should record that activity in column two.

The third and fourth columns are where students start to identify specific steps they must take—some right now, some far off in the future. For example, the student who listed the SAT might record that, right now, she will buy a book on the SAT to get a feel for what it will be like to take the test. She might also record that, starting at the end of her sophomore year in high school, she will take at least one practice examination per month.

Phase Five: Creating a Plan

This phase of the project asks students to create a plan for achieving their personal goals, and then make a commitment to carry out the plan. This does not assume that students will be able to achieve their goals in the period of time designated for the personal project, but rather that they identify a time in the future when their goal will be accomplished. From that point of time in the future, students plan the specific steps they will take to accomplish their goals. There are two activities within this phase.

Activity: Planning Backwards

With the discrepancy analysis completed, students plan backwards. In this activity, students begin at the point in time at which their future possible self-description is realized, and then identify what must be done before that in a rough timeline. For example, if a student has written a future possible self-description that is situated 25 years in the future, the student begins at that point in time and develops a rough timeline indicating the significant events that must occur between that future date and today. Figure 3.4 depicts Student Activity Sheet 13 which you can use to facilitate this process.

Explain that the entry in the top row simply reads, "My future possible self-description becomes a reality." Because they created this description in some detail during Phase Three of the project, they don't have to restate it here. The entry in the bottom row of the form is the current date. The major task for students in this activity is to fill out the rows with specific activities, accomplishments, and dates. This should be fairly straightforward since students have already identified specific activities they must undertake in the discrepancy analysis. Emphasize that, as they begin to plan backwards, students may have

Figure 3.4 Student Activity Sheet 13

Date	My future possible self-description becomes a reality
Date	Event
Date	Event
Date	Event
Date	Event
Today	

to adjust their future possible self-descriptions, particularly *when* they might reach their goals.

Activity: Making Declarations

One of the most dramatic activities students engage in during the personal project is the construction of personal declarations. This process will probably seem a bit unusual to most of the students. A declaration is a statement of what will be. It is not offered as a prediction, but rather as a promise. The reason we make declarations about projects we are involved in is to place ourselves in a position where others have expectations about our actions. In a sense, making a declaration to other people is like asking them to hold us accountable for what we say we are going to do. It is a technique to make ourselves accountable for what we have said we are going to do. The following prompt (provided in Student Activity Sheet 14) is a suggested format for student declarations:

About my project, you can count on me to_____.

Encourage students to take the time to carefully craft these statements. If they are willing, you might also have students read their declarations to the class.

Phase Six: Moving into Action

Once students have completed a plan for achieving their goals, they should identify actions they can take immediately. This phase of the project will help students realize that accomplishing a challenging goal involves doing small things consistently, over a long period of time. There is one major activity in this phase of the project.

Activity: Taking Small Steps

In this activity, students are asked to identify a small step. This should be something they can begin working on immediately. Up until this point in the project, students have been working at a conceptual, "what if?" level. In contrast, their small step is something they can begin working on right away.

The small step might even be something indirect. For example, if a student has identified becoming a professional athlete as her future possible self, her small step might be to begin weight training. Or, the small step might be something more directly related to a specific accomplishment. For example, a student might actually sign up to take the SAT test. Emphasize that people who successfully accomplish what they desire to do in life typically work on their projects every day, even if it is only for a few moments per day.

In short, the important aspect of this part of the personal project is that students begin doing something immediately to realize their future possible selves. Students should record their small steps on Student Activity Sheet 15 of their Notebooks, as shown below in Figure 3.5.

Figure 3.5 Student Activity Sheet 15

Date:
Date by which I will accomplish my small step:
A description of what I will accomplish by that date:
What I will need to do to accomplish my small step?

A copy of this form should be given to you, the teacher, along with a self-addressed stamped envelope. (Blackline Master M in Chapter 11 contains a copy of the form.) Keep these forms for a set period of time (perhaps a month), and then mail them back to students so they can evaluate how far they have progressed with their small step. It is very powerful if you take the time to include a handwritten note from you to each student providing some encouraging words about them and their projects.

Phase Seven: Evaluating the Effectiveness of Your Actions

The final phase of the personal project requires students to evaluate their progress. Both the student and you, the teacher, can be involved in this process. This phase also gives students the opportunity to create their own quotes that, hopefully, will continue to be a source of inspiration to them and to others who know them. The creation of these quotes or "aphorisms" is the culminating activity for the project.

It may be that, for some classes, you must assign a grade for the personal project. This phase of the project will facilitate grade construction. There are three activities in this phase.

Activity: Re-evaluating Plans

The purpose of this activity is to make students aware that the plans we make frequently, and often necessarily, change once we actually begin to work on them. This is not only natural but advisable. What seems like a good idea when we begin a project often does not work out the way we anticipated. Consequently, we must periodically re-evaluate our plans, adding new steps, changing old steps, or even deleting some. To help provide this awareness, have students answer the following questions about the small step they have taken by completing Student Activity Sheet 16.

- What has happened that you did not expect?
- What has happened that you did expect?
- What changes have you made, or do you still need to make, in your thinking about your project?

Before answering these questions, the students must have spent some time working on their small steps. The culminating action for this activity should be that students make any necessary changes to the plans they have made for accomplishing their goals.

Activity: Creating Aphorisms

Creating an aphorism is one of the last activities in the personal project. In simple terms, an aphorism is a "short saying embodying a truth or astute observation." Throughout the personal project, students have been presented with quotations about such things as inspiration, dedication, and the power of support. Most of

Figure 3.6 Student Activity Sheet 18

Some things I did well on my project are:
Some of the things I did not do well are:
Some things I would do differently are:
Something I learned about myself is:

these were aphorisms. At this point, students are asked to create their own aphorisms to present to the rest of the class. Perhaps the best way to provide students with a sense of what is expected of their aphorisms is to go back over some of the quotations you previously presented. Students can analyze the ones they like particularly well, making a list of the critical features of a powerful aphorism. Student Activity Sheet 17 provides a framework for students to create their own aphorisms.

Activity: Evaluating Success

During this last phase of their projects, students are asked to determine how effective they have been, not only in making progress on their goal, but also in developing important academic and life skills throughout the project. If you wish, this can be done at a general level by using Student Activity Sheet 18, as depicted in Figure 3.6 on page 22 of this Manual.

At a more formal and detailed level, you can have students evaluate themselves on the following skills:

- Literal and inferential comprehension
- Information-gathering and synthesizing
- Problem-solving
- Decision-making
- Imagery and memory
- Critical thinking and reasoning
- Self-control and self-regulation

Chapter 5 provides rubrics for both you and the student to evaluate these skills. It also provides you with a scheme for assigning student grades for their performance, if you so desire.

CHAPTER 4
TEACHING AND REINFORCING ESSENTIAL SKILLS

This chapter provides detailed information regarding the following "essential skills" and how they can be integrated into the personal project:

- Problem-solving skills
- Decision-making skills
- Information-gathering and synthesizing skills
- Imagery and memory skills
- Critical thinking and reasoning skills
- Self-control and self-regulation skills

In Chapter 1, we referred to these as essential skills because they generalize so well to many life situations. It is important to realize that you do not have to teach and reinforce *all of* these skills (although we recommend that you do). Rather, you can tailor the personal project to the needs of your students and your particular goals for students by emphasizing certain skills. This feature makes the Pathfinder Project very flexible: you emphasize what you wish.

Problem-Solving Skills

Introduction to the Skills

We are presented with problems nearly every day—both problems that can be solved easily and immediately, and problems that require a great deal of time and effort. By definition, a problem is a situation in which you have a clearly defined goal with obstacles standing in your way. For example, assume you have the goal of getting medical treatment for a sick pet. Perhaps you don't have enough money to pay for the treatment, or the veterinary clinic is closed when your pet becomes ill. Solving this problem, or any other problem, involves overcoming the obstacles that prevent you from reaching your goal.

In this section we provide both a simplified and an expanded version of the problem-solving process. You can present either approach to students, depending on how deeply you wish to go into the topic of problem solving. Additionally, we present a strategy to help students engage in solving content-related, academic problems.

Problem Solving: Simplified Version

Even though students have already solved many problems in life, it is important to give them a specific strategy or set of steps. You might do this by first describing a problem you recently faced, identifying both the goal and the obstacles. List all the options that were available to you, identify the option you selected, and explain why this was (or why *it wasn't*) the best option in the situation.

Next, have students describe specific problems they have faced. Help them identify the obstacles involved, the options they considered, and the reasoning they used to decide what to do.

You might also present students with a clear example of a problem-solving situation using an example that is currently in the news or one of the inspirational stories from Chapter 8. Here's a good example:

Paul Martin had always enjoyed participating in athletics. But at the age of 25, he was in a car accident that resulted in the amputation of his lower left leg. After the accident, Paul did not know if he would be able to participate in athletics again, and he established that as a personal goal. A prosthetics designer told Paul he could run a marathon with the right prosthetic leg. After testing several different prosthetic legs, Paul found the one that worked well for him. Paul's persistence paid off. He finished the New

York Marathon, the Iron Man Triathlon, and many other difficult and prestigious competitions.

After reading a story or providing other examples, ask students to identify the goal, the obstacle, the possible solutions, and the final solution. In Paul Martin's story, these elements are:

- **Goal:**
  Paul wanted to participate in athletic competition.

- **Obstacle:**
  Paul had only one leg, and his athletic activities required both.

- **Options:**
  Paul could have:

  ➢ *explored athletic competitions open to one-legged athletes;*

  ➢ *tried to find alternatives to athletic competition;.*

  ➢ *found ways to compensate for his lost leg (e.g., artificial limbs, etc.); or*

  ➢ *given up on athletic competition altogether.*

- **Solution:**
  Paul was fitted with a prosthetic leg that enabled him to compete as if he had two legs.

Next, write out the steps to the problem-solving process (simplified version) and present them to students. (Blackline Master F in Chapter 11 can be used for this purpose.)

Step 1 *State the intended goal.*

Step 2 *List the obstacles to the goal.*

Step 3 *Create a list of options for overcoming the obstacles.*

Step 4 *Determine which option is best and try it out.*

Step 5 *If your first option doesn't work, try another option.*

Once students have a basic understanding of the problem-solving process, have them analyze the problems they encounter while working on their projects or outside of school. As they do so, they should record their insights and reactions in the Personal Reflections section of their Notebooks.

Problem Solving: Expanded Version

You might wish to present a more detailed approach to problem solving than the "simplified version" described above. The expanded problem solving process involves the following steps:

Step 1 *Determine whether you really have a problem. Is the goal truly important to you, or is it something you can ignore?*

Step 2 *If you determine that you really do have a problem, take a moment to affirm the following beliefs:*

- *There are probably a number of ways to solve the problem, and I will surely find one of them.*

- *Help is probably available if I look for it.*

- *I am perfectly capable of solving this problem.*

Step 3 *Start talking to yourself about the problem. Verbalize the thoughts you are having.*

Step 4 *Start looking for the obstacles in your way—what's missing? Identify possible solutions for replacing what is missing or overcoming the obstacle.*

Step 5 *For each of the possible solutions you have identified, determine how likely it is to succeed. Consider the resources each solution requires and how accessible they are to you. Here is where you might have to look for help.*

Step 6 *Try out the solution you believe has the greatest chance of success and fits your comfort level for risk.*

Step 7 *If your solution doesn't work, clear your mind, go back to another solution you have identified, and try it out.*

Step 8 *If no solution can be found that works, "revalue" what you are trying to accomplish. Look for a more basic goal that can be accomplished.*

This process is much more detailed than the simplified version, and introduces a number of fairly sophisticated and powerful concepts. Each step should be presented, discussed, and exemplified with students. (You can use Blackline Master G in Chapter 11 to facilitate this process.) Examples can be provided from your own life, from the stories students are readinxfrom stories in the news.

Step 1 introduces the concept of determining whether you really have a problem when an obstacle is met. In some situations, the goal we are striving for is really not that important to us and it might be just as easy to temporarily ignore it. For example, if your goal is to go to a movie tonight but you don't have enough money, you are involved in a problem situation—at least on the surface. You have a goal and there is an obstacle in the way; but going to a movie is probably not critically important. Consequently, involving yourself in a detailed and stressful process of trying to overcome the obstacle (i.e., the lack of money) simply might not be worth it. This first step teaches students that not all problems are worth the energy and time it takes to solve them. In life, there are some times when it is better to accept the reality of our current situation and use our energies on more important issues.

Step 2 addresses the negative self-talk that commonly occurs whenever we are faced with particularly difficult problems. Although this is quite natural, negative self-talk has a profoundly deleterious affect on our ability to solve problems. If we are thinking about all the reasons why we can't solve a problem, we will have little

mental energy left to actually solve the problem. This natural tendency can be overcome, however, by replacing negative self-talk with positive self-talk. Step 2 is designed to do just that. Students are encouraged to affirm the beliefs that:

- There are a number of ways to solve the problem, and they will surely discover at least one of them.
- Help is available if they look for it.
- They are perfectly capable of solving the problem.

Step 3 encourages students to begin verbalizing the problem; in essence, to start talking to themselves about the problem. The act of verbalizing our thoughts helps us see the problem more clearly.

Step 4 prompts students to begin looking for the obstacle in their way, recalling that, by definition, a problem is a situation in which there is an obstacle in the way of a goal. They also start to look for ways to overcome the obstacle, the various possible solutions to the problem.

Step 5 asks students to consider the resources required for each solution they have identified and the accessibility of those resources—both important factors. The solutions that seem the most straightforward might require resources that are very difficult to obtain.

Step 6 prompts students to select the solution they believe has the greatest chance of success. It also introduces the concept of risk. Some possible solutions might have a high probability for success but carry a fair amount of risk. In fact, some solutions might be so risky that they are not worth trying. The risk factor for each possible solution should be examined to determine if it fits within our tolerance. Attempting a solution that is beyond our tolerance level for risk causes tension and ultimately distracts us.

Step 7 directs students to try other solutions if their initial selection doesn't work.

Step 8 introduces the concept of "revaluing." This is a strategy good problem solvers use when no solution can be found: they identify another goal that *can* be reached. For example, assume your goal is to get to work in the morning but your car won't start. After repeated attempts to solve the problem have failed and you simply have to accept the fact that you cannot get to work that day, you engage in revaluing by identifying a related goal that you can accomplish that day. For example, staying home might allow you to get some work done that you cannot do at the office because of frequent interruptions from phone calls or from colleagues. Revaluing turns unsolved problems into opportunities.

In Chapter 10, exercises are provided for a number of steps in the expanded version of the problem-solving process. These exercises can be used to help students understand and practice the steps. Again, once students understand the process, they should use it as they are engaged in their projects. They can also apply the process to problems that occur outside of school. As they do so, ask students to record their insights and reactions in the Personal Reflections section of their Notebooks.

Solving Academic Problems

In addition to the problems students have to solve in their day-to-day lives, they frequently face content-related problems in school. We refer to these as academic problems. In Chapter 10 you will find exercises for four categories of academic problems:

- Problems of unusual thinking
- Quantitative problems
- Spatial problems
- Analogy reasoning problems

These exercises are challenging as well as highly engaging. They are designed to be used as "sponge activities" to soak up the unproductive time that can occur during any class.

Consider frequently mixing the types of problems you present to students. That is, one day you might give students quantitative problems, the next time you have them solve spatial problems, and so on. The advantage to this approach is that it provides students with a great deal of variety and holds their interest.

Another approach would be to exhaust the exercises for a given problem type before moving on to another category of academic problems. The advantage to this approach is that students will have a firm grasp of a given problem type once they have exhausted all the related exercises and examples.

Although designed to be fun, these are the kind of problems that students will encounter on cognitive ability tests. Additionally, exercises can teach students important lessons about themselves and the way they approach problems. The recommended process for solving academic problems is:

Step 1 *Read over or look over the entire problem and get a sense of what you are being asked to do.*

Step 2 *Listen to your self-talk. If your self-talk is negative, replace it with statements like:*

- *"These problems might by tricky, but once I know how to do them, they are easy."*

- *"I can figure this out if I work at it and give myself time."*

- *"It's okay if I have to ask for help and there is plenty of help available to me."*

- *"Putting energy into these problems will pay off for me later."*

Step 3 *State the problem in your own words.*

Step 4 *Try representing the problem in some way by drawing a picture of it or making a model of it.*

Step 5 *Try out different ways to solve the problem. If one solution doesn't work, move on to another.*

Step 6 *When you have come up with an answer, ask yourself, "Does this answer make sense?"*

Step 7 *When you've completed the problem or problems, answer the questions:*

- *What did I do that worked well?*
- *What did I do that did not work well?*
- *What have I learned about myself as a problem solver?*

Step 1 encourages students to obtain a sense of the whole problem and consider it deeply before they try to solve it. Too often, students rush to find a solution before they have a good grasp of the problem.

Step 2 asks students to examine their self-talk and replace negative self-talk with positive affirmations. As is the case with everyday problems, academic problems commonly stimulate negative self-talk, inhibiting our ability to think well.

Step 3 tells students to restate the problem in their own words, helping them examine the problem in some detail. Oftentimes, students don't truly understand a problem until they have tried to restate it.

Step 4 asks students to represent the problem in some pictorial way, or to even make a physical model of the problem. This helps them see the problem more clearly.

Step 5 encourages students to think of and try out multiple solutions. This step is designed to keep their thinking open and flexible.

Step 6 is executed after a solution is identified. It encourages them to examine the reasonableness of the solution and constitutes a rough check on their answer.

Finally, **Step 7** encourages students to consider some questions about the effectiveness of their thinking and their approach to problem solving.

Blackline Master E in Chapter 11 can be used to facilitate this process. Each of these steps should be explained and exemplified to students by presenting one of the academic problems from Chapter 10 and using the steps of the process to solve it. The problems entitled "Problems of Unusual Thinking" are probably the best examples to start with. As you solve the sample problem, "think aloud," allowing students to observe your thinking during each step.

Decision-Making Skills

Introduction to the Skills

Although we make decisions every day, not every decision requires serious analysis. We probably don't have to spend a lot of time weighing our options about what kind of sandwich to have for lunch, but we should put a lot of time and serious thought into what kind of career to pursue or where to go to college. Big decisions such as these require careful and organized thinking.

As with problem solving, the Pathfinder Project provides both a simplified and an expanded approach to decision making. You can present either to students, depending on how deeply you wish to focus on the process.

Decision Making: Simplified Version

Introduce the topic of decision making by differentiating between trivial decisions and important decisions we face in our lives. As an example, present decisions from your own life, some of which were trivial and did not require the use of a process, and others that were important and required careful thought and analysis.

Next, have students identify decisions they have made or are currently making in their own lives and ask them to distinguish between those that require the use of a process and those that do not.

Then, present students with a clear example of a decision-making situation. You might wish to use an example from one of the inspirational stories in Chapter 8, like Dave Liniger's:

> *Dave Liniger was in the military, and he was unhappy with the direction his life was going. He knew he wanted a better life. He started reading books and considering various options. He knew that he wanted to make a good deal of money and he also wanted an exciting lifestyle. He decided to pursue a career in real estate. He began taking real estate courses and studied to get his real estate license. Dave worked as a real estate agent until he began his own company.*

After reading the story or listening to another example you provide, have students identify the decision being made, the alternatives being considered, the criteria used to select an alternative, and the alternative that best met the defined criteria. These elements in the Dave Liniger story are:

- **Decision**
  Dave's decision dealt with the career path he should follow.

- **Alternatives**
  Dave may have considered putting more time into his military career, or he may have also considered options depicted in the books he read.

- **Criteria**
  One condition for Dave was that he wanted to make more money. He also wanted to do something enjoyable and fulfilling .

- **Alternative selected**
  Dave decided to get into real estate because he saw this option as the one that allowed him to make more money. It was also something Dave enjoyed and felt fulfilled doing.

Next, write out the steps to the decision-making process (simplified version) and display them somewhere in the classroom (Blackline Master H in Chapter 11 lists these steps; it can be duplicated and presented to students).

Step 1 *Clearly state the decision you are faced with.*

Step 2 *State the options or alternatives available to you.*

Step 3 *Consider the criteria or attributes a good decision will meet.*

Step 4 *Identify the alternative that best meets the defined attributes.*

Once students have a basic understanding of the decision-making process, have them analyze the decisions they encounter while working on their projects and outside of school. As they do so, have them record their insights and reactions in the Personal Reflections section of their Notebooks.

Decision Making: Expanded Version

You may wish to present a more detailed approach to decision making. The steps to the expanded version of decision making are:

Step 1 *Identify the alternatives you are considering.*

Step 2 *Identify the attributes or criteria that your ideal decision will meet.*

Step 3 *For each attribute, assign an importance score (very important =3, moderately important =2, not terribly important =1).*

Step 4 *For each alternative, assign a score indicating the extent to which it* *possesses each attribute (possesses the attribute to a great extent = 3, possesses the attribute moderately = 2, possesses the attribute to a small degree = 1, doesn't possess the attribute at all = 0).*

Step 5 *Multiply the importance score for each attribute by the score depicting the extent to which each alternative possesses the attribute.*

Step 6 *For each alternative, add up the product scores. The alternative with the highest total score is the most logical choice.*

Step 7 *Based on your reaction to the selected alternative, determine if you want to change the importance scores for attributes, or even add or delete attributes.*

Step 8 *If you have changed something, go back and re-compute the scores.*

This process is much more detailed than the simplified version, and introduces a number of fairly sophisticated and powerful concepts. Each step should be presented, discussed and exemplified with students (you may use Blackline Master I in Chapter 11 for this purpose). Examples can be provided from your own life, from the stories students are reading, and from stories in the news.

Steps 1 and 2 are similar to the steps in the simplified version—students identify the alternatives they are considering and the attributes or criteria they will use to choose from among the alternatives.

Step 3 introduces a numerical way of evaluating the importance of the attributes. To use this numeric-coding scheme, it is useful to have students construct a decision-making matrix as depicted in Figures 4.1 – 4.3 (pages 31–32).

To illustrate, assume that a student is using the expanded decision-making process to determine which summer job to take. The alternatives available to the student might be: *Lifeguard, Store Clerk and Retirement Home Aide.* These options are placed in the columns of the decision-making matrix. The attributes the student has identified as being important are: *Work Outside, Meet Other Young People,* and *Help Others.* These are placed in the rows of the decision-making matrix. Next, a numeric importance score is assigned to each attribute as depicted in Figure 4.1 below.

Figure 4.1 Decision-Making Matrix A

Attributes	ALTERNATIVES		
	Lifeguard	Store Clerk	Retirement Home Aide
Work outside (1)			
Meet other young people (2)			
Help others (3)			

Here, the student has assigned an importance score of 1 to *Work Outside*, an importance score of 2 to *Meet Other Young People*, and an importance score of 3 to *Help Others*.

Step 4 directs students to assign a score, on a scale of 0 to 3, indicating the extent to which each alternative possesses each attribute. This is depicted in Figure 4.2.

Figure 4.2 Decision-Making Matrix B

Attributes	ALTERNATIVES		
	Lifeguard	Store Clerk	Retirement Home Aide
Work outside (1)	3	0	0
Meet other young people (2)	3	3	1
Help others (3)	3	1	3

In this example, the student has assigned a score of 3 to the *Lifeguard* alternative, indicating that being a lifeguard fulfills the attribute of working outside to a great extent. The scores of 0 for *Store Clerk* and *Retirement Home Aide* indicate that these alternatives do not fulfill the attribute of working outside at all.

In **Steps 5 and 6**, the students multiply the importance score for each attribute by the score indicating the extent to which each alternative possesses the attribute, and then add up those products for each alternative as depicted in Figure 4.3.

Figure 4.3 Decision-Making Matrix C

Attributes	ALTERNATIVES		
	Lifeguard	Store Clerk	Retirement Home Aide
Work outside (1)	1 x 3 = 3	1 x 0 = 0	1 x 0 = 0
Meet other young people (2)	2 x 3 = 6	2 x 3 = 6	2 x 1 = 2
Help others (3)	3 x 3 = 9	3 x 1 = 3	3 x 3 = 9
TOTALS	**18**	**9**	**11**

In the example above, the alternative with the highest total score is *Lifeguard*. At face value, this is the most logical selection.

Step 7 introduces an aspect of the decision-making process not addressed in the simplified version. We sometimes discover that we have assigned importance scores to alternatives incorrectly. This happens when our original thinking does not truly reflect what we value. Consequently, we might want to change the importance scores we have assigned to attributes, or even add or delete attributes.

Step 8 directs students to re-compute the products and the total scores for alternatives if they have changed anything as a result of Step 7. In effect, *the best decisions are the ones for which we keep repeating Steps 7 and 8 until we reach a decision that truly reflects our values.*

Chapter 10 includes exercises for some of the decision-making steps that can be used to help students understand and practice the skills. Once students understand the decision-making process, they should use it while they work on their projects as well as outside of school. Ask students to record their insights and reactions in the Personal Reflections section of their Notebooks.

Information-Gathering and Synthesizing Skills

Introduction to the Skills

In this information-rich society there are endless sources of information. However, this does not mean that students know how to effectively gather or synthesize the information from them.

As a part of their personal projects, students are asked to compile a great deal of information. For example, they gather content about their heroes, role models, and mentors. They also gather information about the specific goal they want to accomplish, and data to help them construct their future possible self-descriptions. These activities provide opportunities for students to learn about and practice a variety of information-gathering and synthesizing skills.

Information Sources and Synthesizing Skills

Start by introducing students to various types of information sources that are available to them. These might include:

- The Internet
- Newspapers
- Books and journals
- Direct contact with people

Next, identify specific attributes of each source that will aid students in using them. Some examples are:

Internet

- Teach students how to use search engines like "Google" and "Yahoo."
- Show students how to organize and store information electronically in files on the computer.

Newspapers

- Teach students about the different kinds of newspapers, and the type of information they contain.
- Teach students how to access newspaper articles on-line or using microfiche at the library.

Books and Journals

- Have students visit with the school librarian to determine the types of journals available.
- Introduce students to various types of indexes and reference books that might be useful to their projects.

Direct Contact with People

- Introduce students to various interviewing techniques.
- Provide students with questioning strategies for gathering information.

Regardless of the sources of information used by students, they will have to take and organize notes for the information to be truly useful to them in their projects. In the context of the personal project, taking notes on index cards is highly useful because it allows students to easily sort and organize information. Some useful note-taking strategies you might teach students include:

- Don't try to take notes "verbatim."
- Capture only what seems important to their projects.
- Don't worry about spelling or handwriting, but write legibly enough to read what was written.
- Occasionally write summaries of the information in their notes.

For notes to be useful, students need to synthesize the information into categories. To this end, a useful thing to teach students is a simple sorting strategy. Have them lay out all their notes and organize them into piles of related information (this is one of the reasons why taking notes on index cards is advisable). Next, write a brief description for each of the piles on a single sheet of paper or a single note card. Piles can also be coded with a Roman numeral or letter, and each note card coded along with the pile it belongs to.

Imagery and Memory Skills

Introduction to the Skills

Human thinking occurs in two primary forms: as words and as images. It is sometimes easier to observe our thinking in words because it manifests as inner speech or inner dialogue. That is, we talk to ourselves. We will consider inner dialogue and memory techniques later in this chapter; for now, we will focus on imagery.

The ability to think in images is one of the most useful and flexible mental abilities we possess. Scientists David Lewis and James Greene (1982)

describe the power of imagery, or "wordless thinking" as they call it, in their book *Thinking Better: A Revolutionary New Program to Achieve Real Mental Performance*. One of the most powerful wordless thinking examples they provide comes originally from Albert Einstein. In Chapter 1, we considered what inspired and motivated Einstein. Now let's examine a technique Einstein used to aid him in his thinking: a technique he referred to as "thought experiments." Lewis and Greene describe Einstein's thought experiments as follows:

Einstein developed this technique of wordless thought to such high levels of perfection that his favored method of investigation was to perform these experiments in the mind.

"When I examined myself and my methods of thought," he once wrote, "I came to the conclusion that the gift of fantasy has meant more than my talent for absorbing positive knowledge."

He started using this approach at the age of sixteen when considering the physical properties of light, ideas which would later form the basis of his two theories of relativity. In an attempt to visualize how light might appear, if no longer "blurred" by its tremendous velocity, Einstein imagined himself traveling in a space vehicle alongside the speeding beam. In his mind he constructed a vivid image of how the light would then appear, an image which led to his monumental discovery of photons...

In the early 1900s Einstein performed a thought experiment that was to shake the world of physics to its foundations. He had begun to realize that Newton's theory of gravitation, until then the unchallenged dogma, was seriously flawed. To explore the concept he pictured himself as the passenger in an elevator hurtling through the farthest reaches of space at a speed faster than light. He then visualized a slot opening on one side of the elevator cage so that a beam of light was projected onto the opposite wall. This enabled him to realize that if the elevator were moving with sufficient velocity, it would travel a finite distance in the time required for the beam to pass across the cage so that an observer in the cage would see the light beam as curved. (Lewis and Greene, pp. 244-245)

Exploring the Power of Imagery

To give students a sense of the power of their wordless thinking, present them with this example about Albert Einstein or some other story that demonstrates the potential power of imagery. For example, there are many illustrations of the use of imagery in the world of sports. Then, engage them in a few brief activities that provide practice in constructing mental images (some sample activities are listed below).

As you go through these activities with students you will notice that they emphasize taste, touch, smell, sound, kinesthetic sensations, and emotions as much as mental pictures. This is because all of these senses go into the formation of a mental image. To illustrate, assume that you are remembering a picnic that you went to last summer. If you concentrate on your recollection of that picnic you will notice that you have the ability not only to see what was happening, but you also can smell the food cooking, hear the sound of laughter, taste the hamburgers, feel the warm breeze on your face, and re-experience the contentment you felt. Images, then, are not just mental pictures: they include all of our sensations.

Mental Imagery Activities

1. Have students think back to when they first opened their eyes that morning. Ask them to recall the mental pictures, physical sensations, and emotions they experienced.

2. Have students imagine that they have won a gold medal (or some other award). Ask them to create and describe a mental picture of the event, along with the physical sensations and emotions they experienced.

3. Have students practice generating mental pictures using the directions below:
   - Imagine a blue ball.
   - Change your mental image of that ball by making the ball more intense in color.
   - Imagine the ball to be much closer to you than it was before.
   - Imagine the ball to be much farther away.
   - Rotate the ball to the left.
   - Rotate the ball to the right.
   - Move the ball back to its original position.

4. Have students practice generating mental sensations of "taste" using the directions below:
   - Imagine the taste of peanut butter.
   - Change the taste to milk chocolate.
   - Change the taste to lemon.
   - Change the taste to orange juice.

5. Have students practice generating mental sensations of "touch" using the directions below:
   - Imagine what it feels like to touch a silk scarf.
   - Change that to touching a piece of sandpaper.
   - Change that to petting a rabbit.
   - Change that to touching an ice cube.

6. Have students practice generating mental sensations of "smell" using the directions below:
   - Imagine what a cup of coffee smells like.
   - Change that smell to a cup of hot chocolate.
   - Change that smell to a skunk.
   - Change that smell to a flower.

7. Have students practice generating mental sensations of "sound" using the directions below:

- Imagine what a high note on a flute sounds like.
- Change that to the same sound on an organ.
- Change that to the sound a washing machine makes when it goes through the rinse cycle.
- Change that to the sounds toast makes when it pops out of the toaster.

8. Have students practice generating mental "kinesthetic" sensations using the directions below:

- Imagine what it feels like to be running around on a racetrack at full speed.
- Change that to how it feels to be trotting around the track.
- Change that to how it feels to be picking up something very heavy.
- Change that to how it feels to be falling through the air.

9. Have students practice generating mental "emotions" using the directions below:

- Imagine what it feels like to be on stage in front of 1,000 people.
- Change that to how it feels to be in the audience.
- Change that to how it feels to be lost in a big city.
- Change that to how it feels to walk in on your surprise birthday party.

Once students have a sense of the components of well-formed mental images and some practice in generating them, give them strategies for using mental images to aid in their recall of information. These strategies give students tools they can use to remember academic content, coupled with *a tremendous sense of the power of their minds*. It literally enables them to perform acts of memory that appear impossible to the untrained observer.

A number of imagery-based memory strategies follow. They are all grounded in the simple concept of generating images that include a mental picture, smells, tastes, sounds, kinesthetic sensations and even emotions. They also include the technique of talking to yourself as you form the image.

Remember that self-talk is one of the two forms of thought. In general, then, memory technique employs the general strategy of creating a mental image and talking to yourself about whatever it is you want to remember. To illustrate, assume you want to remember information about George Washington. Specifically, you want to remember that he was the first president of the United States, and that he kept his army together at Valley Forge during a particularly difficult winter. You would create a rich mental picture of George Washington on his horse in a valley during the winter. You would let yourself feel the cold wind stinging your face and making your hands and feet numb. You would smell the campfires and taste the falling snow melting on your tongue. You would hear the crunching of the horse's footsteps as it walks through the crispy snow. You would then expand the image to include soldiers huddled in tents with disgruntled looks on their faces and having discussions about the fact that they should probably surrender to the British forces. All the while you were creating these images, you would repeat the important information you want to remember in the form of inner speech: "George Washington was the first president of the United States. He kept the forces together at Valley Forge … and so on."

This is the basic strategy employed in most memory techniques. Below we consider six such techniques:

- *Using symbols and substitutes*
- *The link strategy*
- *The rhyming peg word method*
- *The number/keyword method*
- *The number picture method*
- *The familiar place method*

Present these methods to students by explaining and exemplifying them. Then, have students practice using the methods by giving them lists of things to remember. As you present these techniques, encourage students to use them to remember subject-matter information presented in their various classes.

Using Symbols and Substitutes

It is easy to create images for some types of information and difficult to do so with others. Creating images for factual information about Abraham Lincoln is fairly easy because you can picture him (with his tall top hat and long beard), the log cabin where he grew up, the theatre in which he was assassinated, and so on. But it may be more difficult to create images of abstract information, like the basic elements of water: two hydrogen atoms and one oxygen atom. However, if you use symbols and substitutes, it becomes relatively easy to create images for even abstract concepts.

A symbol is something that suggests the information you are trying to remember. For example, an oxygen tank might symbolize oxygen to you. A substitute is a word that is easy to picture and sounds like the information you want to remember. For hydrogen, you might think of the word "hydrant."

The symbol for oxygen and the substitute for hydrogen can now by used to create an image for the information that water is made of two parts hydrogen and one part oxygen. You would simply create an image of two hydrants placed atop an oxygen tank.

The Link Strategy

The link strategy is commonly used with symbols and substitutes linked together in a chain of events or narrative story. To illustrate, a student may wish to remember the 13 original colonies: Georgia, New Jersey, Delaware, New York, North Carolina, South Carolina, Virginia, New Hampshire, Pennsylvania, Connecticut, Rhode Island, Maryland, and Massachusetts. Since it is difficult to mentally picture the actual states, the student could use symbols and substitutes.

A football jersey could represent New Jersey, and the Empire State Building could be a symbol for New York. The name George sounds like Georgia, and the words Christmas carol provide good reminders for the two Carolinas. Dinnerware could be a symbol for Delaware and so on. The students would link these mental images for each of the 13 original colonies into one story. For example, the students might picture George Washington (Georgia) wearing a football jersey (New Jersey). Then the students would imagine George holding dinnerware (sounds like Delaware) as he stands on the top of the Empire State Building (New York) and sings Christmas carols (North and South Carolina). With his left hand George is using the dinnerware to cut into a Virginia ham (Virginia and New Hampshire). In his right hand, George is holding a pen (Pennsylvania) and connecting dots (Connecticut) on a puzzle. These dots join to form a picture of a road (Rhode Island) and Marilyn Monroe (Maryland) is riding on this road on her way to mass (Massachusetts).

The Rhyming Pegword Method

The rhyming pegword method is a simple system that can be used to remember information organized in a list format. The method utilizes a set of easily remembered words because they rhyme with the numbers 1 through 10:

1 is a bun

2 is a shoe

3 is a tree

4 is a door

5 is a hive

6 is a stack of sticks

7 is heaven

8 is a gate

9 is a line

10 is a hen

While the "pegwords" bun, shoe, tree, and so on are easy to remember, they are also concrete and easy to picture. If a student wanted to connect information to pegword #1 (the bun), she would form a mental image of the bun interacting with that information. For example, assume the student wanted to remember the following information about the Incas of Peru:

- They had complex irrigation systems.
- They were skilled surgeons and dentists.
- They cultivated their crops and developed new kinds of vegetables and fruits.

To remember this, the student might picture a hot dog bun with a faucet tapped into it (representing irrigation), a doctor might be sitting on the bun examining the faucet (surgeons and dentists) while fruits and vegetables pour out of the faucet (modern agriculture).

Similar images can be used to connect information to each of the other "pegwords." (Blackline Master J in Chapter 11 can be used to help students learn the rhyming pegword method.)

The Number/Keyword Method

The number/keyword method may first appear complex, but it is actually quite simple and effective. In this system, each digit from 0 through 9 is assigned a unique sound (always the sound of a consonant). So 0 is s (if you turn the z in zero around it looks like an s), 1 is t (t has one vertical bar), 2 is n (n has two vertical bars), 3 is m (m has three vertical bars), 4 is r (four ends in r), 5 is L (L is the Roman numeral for 50), 6 is j (turn the letter j around and it resembles 6), 7 is k (turn the letter k around and it resembles 7), 8 is f (when f is written in script, it looks like an 8), 9 is p (turn the letter p around and it looks like 9).

Using this system you can create "keywords" for as many slots as necessary. For example, if you need a word for slot 21, the letters "n" and "t," the word "net" would work. If you need a word for slot 41, "rt," the word "rut" would work. Below are keywords for 20 slots:

1 = t = golf tee	11 = t + t = tot
2 = n = necktie	12 = t + n = tin
3 = m = maypole	13 = t + m = time
4 = r = roof	14 = t + r = tire
5 = l = lips	15 = t + l = tile
6 = j = jar	16 = t + j = tire jack
7 = k = kitten	17 = t + k = tack
8 = f = football	18 = t + f = turf
9 = p = pole	19 = t + p = tape
10 = t + s = toes	20 = n + s = news

With keywords identified, the system works the same way as the rhyming pegword method. For example, to link the keyword for slot #1 (golf tee) to the fact that the Incas of Peru had a complex irrigation system, the students would create an image involving the irrigation system and the golf tee.

The Number/Picture Method

The number/picture system is used to remember number combinations like the multiplication tables. It is similar to the rhyming pegword system in that it allows students to associate information with digits. But the operating principle with this system is that each of the digits 0-9 resembles objects that are easy to imagine. For example, 0 looks like a big egg, 1 looks like a tall man, 2 looks like a swan, 3 looks like a bird, 4 looks like a flamingo with one leg bent, 5 looks like a snake, 6 looks like mouse, 7 looks like a cane, 8 looks like a snowman, and 9 looks like the head of an elephant. These associations are depicted below:

0 = big egg

1 = tall man

2 = swan

3 = bird

4 = flamingo with one leg bent

5 = snake

6 = mouse

7 = cane

8 = snowman

9 = head of elephant

If a student wishes to remember that 7 x 8=56, then he would create an image with the symbols for 8 (snowman), 7 (cane), 5 (a snake) and 6 (a mouse). That image might be organized in the form of a story: A snowman (8) goes for a walk with his cane (7) and sees a snake (5) chasing a mouse (6).

The Familiar Place Method

Familiar place frameworks are some of the easiest memory techniques to use. To create a familiar place framework, the student imagines a place that is very familiar to him, like his bedroom. Then he mentally goes around the room identifying familiar objects in the order in which they appear in the room. He might see a door first, then a dresser, then a mirror, then a bed, then a lamp, then a window. The objects in this framework (the objects in the room) become slots in which information can be stored. For example, if the student wishes to remember information about the Inca's complex irrigation system, he forms a mental image of that information, and the door of his bedroom, and so on.

Another example of a familiar place method is a "familiar route" you commonly travel (e.g., the drive from home to school). You can identify familiar places along the route (e.g., the fast food restaurant, the shopping mall, the gas station, the park, etc.) and use these as slots to store information. (Blackline Master K in Chapter 11 can be used to help students devise familiar place frameworks.)

Critical Thinking and Reasoning Skills

Introduction to the Skills

Critical thinking skills are those skills we use to analyze our own thinking and the thinking of others. One might make the case that, in a free society where information flows with little or no monitoring, the ability to critically analyze information is essential to the effective functioning of that society. In the Pathfinder Project, two aspects of critical thinking are stressed: analyzing errors and analyzing deductive conclusions.

Analyzing Errors

The ability to analyze errors is useful in our everyday lives, where we are bombarded with information attempting to persuade us. Advertisements try to convince us to buy certain products. Politicians try to convince us to vote for them based on their platforms. Occasionally, we might be convinced to do things or to act in ways that we regret when we stop to think more carefully.

When we are influenced by information or arguments containing errors, the consequences are frequently insignificant (e.g., we may buy one kind of dish soap instead of another). However, being persuaded by faulty arguments can influence the quality of our life or even impact the outcome of life-and-death situations. The rigor with which we must analyze information for errors depends on the extent to which the information can affect us. When the stakes are high, more attention to an argument is required. Recognizing high-stake situations and increasing our level of attention and depth of analysis will decrease the possibility of doing things we later regret.

To help students understand why the process of analyzing errors is important, discuss the different types of information that confronts the average U.S. citizen on a daily basis. List these on the board, and then explore how important it might or might not be to analyze the errors in the various sources and situations you have listed. Guide students to understand that analyzing errors in the remarks of a political candidate might be more important than analyzing errors in a commercial about running shoes.

Next, present examples of messages that contain obvious, as well as subtle, errors. Advertisements make perfect examples. You might also include examples from editorials, speeches, and articles in print and electronic media. You can tape record or purchase transcripts of radio and television talk shows to illustrate the errors that people make when they are discussing issues, or provide examples from everyday situations that students can relate to (e.g., a school friend who states, "Everybody is doing…").

Once students have a sense of the nature and importance of analyzing errors, provide the following step-by-step process:

Step 1 *Determine whether the information presented to you is intended to influence your thinking or your actions.*

Step 2 *If the information is intended to influence you, identify things that seem wrong—statements that are unusual or go against what you know to be true.*

Step 3 *Look for errors in the thinking that underlies the statements you have identified.*

Step 4 *If you find errors, ask for clarification.*

At first, you will have to demonstrate this process to students in a "think aloud" fashion. You might start by providing information from a commercial or a political ad. To exemplify the first step, say: "Wait. This information is trying to convince me to…Something is funny here. This isn't like what I have heard before," and so on. As you talk through the process, emphasize the steps by referring to Blackline Master L1 in Chapter 11.

Once they have a sense of the steps in the process of analyzing errors, familiarize students with the four types of common errors in thinking below. To help them become more proficient in recognizing these types of errors, use the exercises in Chapter 10 entitled "Errors in Thinking." You can also use Blackline Master L2 from Chapter 11 to familiarize students with these types of errors.

Common Types of Errors in Thinking

Four common categories of errors in thinking are: faulty logic, attacks, weak references, and misinformation.

Faulty logic can occur in seven different ways:

1. *Contradiction*—presenting conflicting information. If a politician runs on a platform supporting term limits, then votes against an amendment that would set term limits, that politician has committed the error of contradiction.

2. *Accident*—failing to recognize that an argument is based on an exception to a rule. For example, if a student concludes that the principal always goes to dinner at a fancy restaurant on Fridays because she sees him at one on a given Friday which just happens to be his birthday, that student has committed the error of accident.

3. *False cause*—confusing a temporal (time) order of events with causality, or oversimplifying the reasons behind some event or occurrence. For example, if a person concludes that the war in Vietnam ended because of the anti-war protests, he is guilty of ascribing a false cause. The anti-war protests might have had something to do with the cessation of the war, but there were also many other interacting causes.

4. *Begging the question*—making a claim and then arguing for the claim by using statements that are simply the equivalent of the original claim. For example, if a person says that product x is the best detergent on the market and then backs up this statement by simply saying that it is superior to other detergents, he is begging the question.

5. *Evading the issue*—changing the topic to avoid addressing the issue. For example, a person is evading the issue if he begins talking about the evils of the news media when he is asked by a reporter about his alleged involvement in fraudulent banking procedures.

6. *Arguing from ignorance*—arguing that a claim is justified simply because its opposite has not been proven true. For example, if a person argues that there is no life on other planets because there has been no proof of such existence, he is arguing from ignorance.

7. *Composition/division*—asserting something about a whole that is really only true of its parts is *composition*; on the flip side, *division* is asserting about all of the parts something that is generally, but not always, true of the whole. For example, if a person asserts that Republicans are corrupt because one Republican is found to be corrupt, she is committing the error of composition. If a person states that a particular Democrat supports big government simply because Democrats are generally known for supporting government programs, he is committing the error of division.

Attacks can occur in three ways:

1. *Poisoning the well*—being so completely committed to a position that you explain away absolutely everything that is offered in opposition to your position. This type of attack represents a person's unwillingness to consider anything that may contradict his/her opinion. For example, if a political candidate has only negative things to say about his opponent, she is poisoning the well.

2. *Arguing against the person*—rejecting a claim using derogatory facts (real or alleged) about the person who is making the claim. If a person argues against another person's position on taxation by making reference to his poor moral character, she is arguing against the person.

3. *Appealing to force*—using threats to establish the validity of a claim. If your landlord threatens to evict you because you disagree with her on an upcoming election issue, she is appealing to force.

Weak reference occurs in five ways:

1. *Sources that reflect biases*—consistently accepting information that supports what we already believe to be true, or consistently rejecting information that goes against what we believe to be true. For example, a person is guilty of bias if he believes that a person has committed a crime and will not even consider DNA evidence indicating that the individual is innocent.

2. *Sources that lack credibility*—using a source that is not reputable for a given topic. Determining credibility can be subjective but there are some characteristics that most people agree damage credibility, such as when a source is known to be biased or has little knowledge of the topic. A person is guilty of using a source that lacks credibility when he backs up his belief that the government has a conspiracy to ruin the atmosphere by citing a tabloid journal known for sensational stories that are fabricated.

3. *Appealing to authority*—invoking authority as the last word on an issue. If a person says, "Socialism is evil" and supports this claim by saying that the governor said so, she is appealing to authority.

4. *Appealing to the people*—attempting to justify a claim based on its popularity. For example, if a girl tells her parents she should have a pierced belly button because everyone else has one, she is appealing to the people.

5. *Appealing to emotion*—using a "sob story" as proof for a claim. For example, if someone uses the story of a tragic accident in her life as a means to convince people to agree with her opinion on war, she is appealing to emotion.

Misinformation occurs in two different ways:

1. *Confusing the facts*—using information that seems to be factual but that has been changed in such a way that it is no longer accurate. For example, a person is confusing the facts if he backs up his claim by describing an event but leaves out important facts or mixes up the temporal order of the events.

2. *Misapplying a concept or generalization*—misunderstanding or wrongly applying a concept or generalization to support a claim. For example, if someone argues that a talk-show host should be arrested for libel after making a critical remark, the person has misapplied the concept of libel.

Developing an awareness of these four types of errors takes time and energy. It is best to address one category of errors at a time using the exercises in Chapter 10. When students have completed an exercise, they should be asked to find or generate their own examples of the specific types of errors within a given category.

When students have a good sense of the four categories of errors and the process for analyzing errors, have them use the process on information they gather as a part of their personal projects.

Analyzing Deductive Conclusions

We reason deductively when we draw conclusions from specific premises. For example, you are thinking deductively when you conclude that your automobile, which you have just picked up from a repair shop, has been checked for oil because that shop always checks the oil in the cars that it repairs. Your reasoning might be stated in the following way: My car just came from the repair shop; the repair shop always checks the oil in cars; therefore, the oil in my car has been checked.

Deductive conclusions can be expressed as categorical syllogisms. Categorical syllogisms have a specific format, as follows:

a. All new commercial airplanes have radar on board to detect wind sheer.

b. This is a new commercial airplane.

c. Therefore, it has radar to detect wind sheer.

Statements a and b are the premises in the syllogism. Statement c is the conclusion. Syllogisms have two premises and a conclusion.

In the example of deductive reasoning about your car, the embedded categorical syllogism might be stated as follows:

a. The repair shop where I take my car always checks the oil.

b. My car has just come from the repair shop.

c. Therefore, my car has been checked for oil.

While it is true that you don't always hear syllogism stated formally in oral language or see them in written language, many statements of conclusion contain hidden syllogisms. For example, if you are sitting in an airplane next to someone and the plane experiences turbulence, the person next to you might say, "Don't worry, this plane is new. It has radar to detect wind sheer." In fact, this statement is based on the first syllogism above; however, the syllogism is implicit as opposed to explicit.

The ability to identify and evaluate implicit syllogisms in what we read or hear is one of the most powerful critical thinking skills we can develop. Fostering this in students requires some initial instruction in the nature of categorical syllogisms, as well as a strategy for solving them.

One of the best ways to teach students how to identify and evaluate syllogisms is to introduce them to Euler diagrams, which use circles to represent membership in a set. Specifically, with Euler diagrams, each of the three elements in a categorical syllogism is represented by a circle. Circles are inside, outside, or overlapping one another based on the relationships expressed in the premises of the categorical syllogism. Consider the following syllogism:

• All mammals breathe air.

• All porpoises are mammals.

• Therefore, porpoises breathe air.

The three elements in this syllogism are:

• A = mammals

• B = breathe air

• C = porpoises

If we represent each of these elements by a circle, the first premise can be represented in the following way:

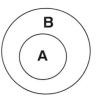

The second premise states that the circle for porpoises, C, should be placed inside the circle for mammals. Therefore, the entire categorical syllogism can be represented as follows:

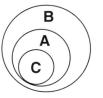

When the circles representing the premises in a categorical syllogism match up this way, we know it is valid to conclude that all porpoises breathe air (all C are B) based on the premises that all mammals breathe air (all A are B) and all porpoises are mammals (all C are A).

The Euler diagram can also show that a conclusion based on premises is *not* valid. To illustrate, consider the following two premises:

- All A are B
- All C are B
- Therefore _____

Based on the two premises, you might be tempted to conclude that A and C have some type of relationship. However, Euler diagrams show us that we really aren't sure. To illustrate, let's diagram the first premise.

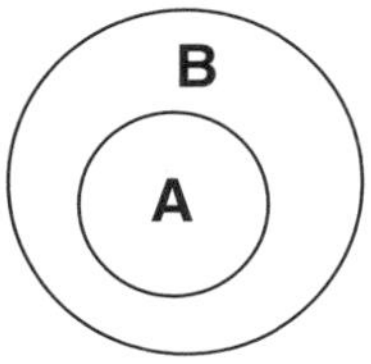

Now let's add the second premise. It states that the C circle is inside the B circle (just as the first premise states that the A circle is inside the B circle). However, we aren't sure where inside the circle it goes. In fact, it could be in any of the positions depicted below:

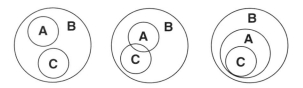

Consequently, there is no valid conclusion that can be made about the relationship between A and C based on the first two premises.

To help students obtain a sense of how to use the Euler diagram to test the validity of categorical syllogisms, give them practice problems like the ones in Figures 4.4 and 4.5 below:

Figure 4.4 Syllogisms Matrix A

SECOND PREMISE	FIRST PREMISE			
	All A are B	Some A are B	No A are B	Some A are not B
All B are C	All A are C	Some A are C Some C are A	Some C are not A	
Some B are C			Some C are not A	
No B are C	No A are C No C are A	Some A are not C		
Some B are not C				
All C are B			No A are C No C are A	Some A are not C
Some C are B			Some C are not A	
No C are B	No C are A No A are C	Some A are not C		
Some C are not B	Some C are not A			

Figure 4.5 Syllogisms Matrix B

SECOND PREMISE	FIRST PREMISE			
	All A are B	Some A are B	No B are A	Some B are not A
All B are C	Some A are C Some C are A	Some A are C Some C are A	Some C are not A	Some C are not A
Some B are C	Some A are C Some C are A		Some C are not A	
No B are C	Some A are not C	Some A are not C		
Some B are not C	Some A are not C			
All C are B	All C are A		No C are A No A are C	
Some C are B	Some C are A Some A are C		Some C are not A	
No C are B	Some A are not C	Some A are not C		
Some C are not B				

Are these valid conclusions?

All A are B.

All C are B.

Therefore, C are A.

All C are B.

No B are A.

Therefore, no C are A.

Worksheets 1 and 2 in the section of Chapter 10 entitled "Analyzing Deductive Conclusions" present syllogisms with this format. While the answers to each problem are provided, Figures 4.4 and 4.5 summarize the valid conclusions that can be drawn for different types and arrangements of premises.

Once students have a general understanding of how to validate categorical syllogisms that are stated in symbolic form using letters, have them validate syllogisms that are stated in sentence form. To do this, present students with exercises like the following:

Is this a valid syllogism?

1. All people from Colorado vote Republican in elections.
2. Bill is from Colorado.
3. Therefore, Bill will vote Republican in the next election.

Worksheets 3 and 4 in the section of Chapter 10 entitled "Analyzing Deductive Conclusions" contain exercises like this.

When syllogisms are stated in sentence form, you can address the most important aspect of syllogistic reasoning: the truth versus the validity of a syllogism. A syllogism is *valid* if the conclusion logically follows from the premises. The example above is valid. However, for a syllogism to be *true*, it must be valid **and** the premises from which the conclusion is drawn must be true. Let's apply this criterion to the syllogism about people from Colorado voting

Republican. Given the premise that "all people from Colorado vote Republican in elections" and the premise that "Bill is from Colorado," it is valid to conclude that "Bill will vote Republican in the next election." However, the premise that "all people from Colorado vote Republican" is not true. Therefore, the conclusion in this syllogism is *valid* but *untrue*.

This is a very important distinction, since much of our faulty reasoning results from valid conclusions based on untrue premises. In fact, one might say that the heart of prejudicial thinking is valid reasoning from untrue premises. Worksheet 5 in Chapter 10 provides students with practice in determining the truth of conclusions.

The final step in developing the ability to analyze deductive conclusions is to have students **standardize** statements they read or hear. Standardization is the term for translating a statement into a syllogistic form with two premises and a conclusion. This idea might be presented as "finding the hidden syllogisms" in statements. To illustrate, consider the sentence, "He is going to vote Republican in the next election because he is from Colorado." To standardize this statement, you would state it in the following way:

a. All people from Colorado vote Republican.
b. He is from Colorado.
c. Therefore, he will vote Republican in the next election.

As we have seen, this is a valid syllogism but it is untrue. Worksheet 6 in Chapter 10 requires students to standardize statements. Be sure students use Euler diagrams to complete these exercises.

Once students have some skill at syllogistic reasoning, they can look for hidden syllogisms in the media and in what they read. They might bring these to class and discuss their validity and truth. More importantly, they can look for and evaluate hidden syllogisms in their own thinking about themselves and about their projects.

Self-Control and Self-Regulation Skills: Teaching the "Inner Game of Success"

Introduction to the Skills

The knowledge and skills described in this section are referred to collectively as self-control and self-regulation skills. However, with students you might refer to them as the "Inner Game of Success" because they deal with our inner thoughts and emotions and our ability to control them. The skill of controlling our inner thoughts and emotions is usually not observable in terms of explicit behaviors. Rather, it occurs inside our mind; hence, the title "Inner Game of Success." There are three basic aspects of self-control and self-regulation or the "Inner Game of Success": controlling inner dialogue, the power of effort, and power thinking.

Controlling Inner Dialogue

The concept of inner dialogue, or inner speech, was introduced in the discussion of imagery and memory strategies. Here we consider it in more depth.

Although it goes on almost all of the time, we are rarely aware of our inner speech—the manifestation of the thoughts and beliefs we carry into each new situation. For example, whenever we encounter something new or challenging, our inner dialogue frequently articulates our beliefs about the situation: how confident we are, how committed we are, whether we have a negative or a positive attitude, and so on.

One of the first activities to help students become aware of the nature and function of inner dialogue is to have them analyze their self-talk relative to their future possible self-descriptions.

To this end, the following questions are very useful:

- What are some things I say to myself about my future possible self that make me feel like working harder?

- What are some things I say to myself about my future possible self that make me want to quit?

- How can I change my negative inner dialogue?

You can present these questions to students using Blackline Master N in Chapter 11. This activity will provide a general awareness for students that their inner dialogue can either motivate them to work harder or make them want to give up.

Next, have a conversation with students about the nature and function of inner dialogue, emphasizing the fact that it can be controlled. Finally, have students analyze their inner dialogue for a set period of time (e.g., a day). On the negative side, they might find particular areas of weakness in their self-talk. For example, they might become aware of a number of thoughts about their lack of ability, lack of resources, and so on. On the positive side, they might find that their self-talk is motivational in nature and involves statements about doing something good for others or accomplishing something no one else has done.

The Power of Effort

The belief that effort can overcome almost any obstacle is one of the most powerful thinking tools you can cultivate in students. Begin by relating a story that illustrates the power of effort—a story demonstrating how someone overcame great difficulty simply by persevering in his efforts, trying no matter how bleak the situation appeared. You can use one of the stories in Chapter 8, a story you have heard about, or a story from your own life.

Next, have students identify a time or times when they persisted at something and succeeded. Also have them identify a time when they gave up on something they wanted because they thought they didn't have the necessary resources. For each situation, ask them to identify what they say to themselves, the physical sensations they have, the mental pictures they have, and their emotions. (Blackline Master O in Chapter 11 walks students through these questions.)

These questions help students identify a profile of the things they commonly say to themselves, the bodily sensations they have, and the mental pictures they have when they try hard even in the face of adversity. It will probably be necessary to have some discussion with students about the relationship between inner dialogue, physical sensations, and mental pictures. Recall from the discussion on imagery and memory strategies that imagery involves mental pictures along with associated smells, tastes, sounds, kinesthetic sensations, and emotions.

Power Thinking

The culmination of the discussions about inner dialogue and the power of effort is the strategy of power thinking. As referred to here, power thinking is a systematic way of thinking that elicits effortful behavior. It involves students consciously engaging in a type of thinking that will help them optimize any situation.

Start by giving students the steps to the power thinking process. (Blackline Master P in Chapter 11 lists these steps.)

Step 1 *Before you engage in a new activity—one that is challenging to you—stop for a moment and remind yourself that effort is the key to success. Little effort will probably bring little success.*

Step 2 *If you don't feel strongly motivated to work hard on this new task:*
- *Change your inner dialogue to statements that make you want to work hard.*
- *Change your physical sensations to those that make you want to work hard.*
- *Change your mental pictures to those that make you want to work hard.*
- *Change your emotions to those that make you want to work hard.*

Step 3 *Next, set a specific goal for what you want to accomplish or have happen.*

Step 4 *As you are engaged in the activity:*
- *Keep reminding yourself about your goal.*
- *Keep monitoring your inner dialogue.*
- *Keep monitoring your physical sensations.*
- *Keep monitoring your mental pictures.*
- *Keep monitoring your emotions.*

Step 5 *When you have completed the activity, ask yourself if you accomplished what you set out to do. If your answer is yes, acknowledge your success. If not, ask yourself what you did that worked well, what you did that did not work well, and what you would do differently. Even if you have accomplished your goal, it is useful to ask these questions. Once you have answered them, put the incident behind you and move on to your next challenge.*

There are a number of aspects of the power thinking process you might want to go over with students. **Step 1** directs students to stop before engaging in a new activity (particularly one that is challenging) and think before they act. To a great extent, this first step is about creating a mental set that is conducive to success. Such a mental set involves inner dialogue, physical sensations, mental images, and emotions that are conducive to learning. This step also reminds students of the importance of effort.

You might liken this first step to the checklist an airplane pilot goes through before taking off. No matter how long a pilot has flown or how routine the flight, the pilot still goes through a checklist to ensure that he and the plane are ready to fly. So, too, should we go through a checklist before engaging in difficult tasks to ensure that we are ready to take on something challenging.

Next, address the importance of setting an explicit goal (even for fairly short tasks) and then monitoring progress toward that goal **(Steps 2 and 3).** Setting a goal helps us identify what is important to attend to and what is not. Those things that are directly related to the goal should receive the lion's share of our attention.

Step 5 is the self-evaluation component of powerful thinking; the component that helps us learn from our actions. One of the critical aspects of this step is, once we have analyzed what we did and did not do well, we put the experience in the past. Even if we failed miserably, we have learned something. After Step 5 has been completed, there is little need to continually go over our actions, particularly if we have failed. Learning involves failure, and it does us no good to dwell on failures once we have identified what we would do differently in the future.

After reviewing the steps of the power thinking process with students, relate a personal story about how specific aspects of the process have helped you in life. Then invite students to identify situations in their own lives where certain aspects of the power thinking process were beneficial to them.

Ask students to systematically employ the power thinking process, particularly when they are faced with challenging situations. Have them record their reactions to the power thinking process in the Personal Reflections section of their Notebooks as they work through their projects.

CHAPTER 5
EVALUATING STUDENTS

As you implement the Pathfinder Project, you will want to provide students with feedback on their performance. You might even wish to, or be required to, assign grades to students. Eight aspects of the Pathfinder Project can be evaluated and used as the basis for grading if you so choose.

They are:

1. Overall progress in the personal project
2. Literal and inferential comprehension skills
3. Information-gathering and synthesizing skills
4. Problem-solving skills
5. Decision-making skills
6. Imagery and memory skills
7. Critical thinking and reasoning skills
8. Self-control and self-regulation skills.

The personal project and the literal and inferential comprehension skills are intended to be standard fare in all implementations of the Pathfinder Project. You may or may not choose to focus on the other areas in your implementation. We recommend that you evaluate students on any aspect of the program that you implement, and we strongly recommend the use of rubrics as a primary evaluation tool.

A *rubric* is a description of varying levels of understanding or performance. You will notice that rubrics are provided for you (the teacher) and for students in each of the eight areas that might be evaluated. You should discuss with students the rubric for each area you wish to evaluate, going over the various levels of understanding or performance.

We recommend that these rubrics be used throughout the personal project on a weekly basis so that multiple scores are collected over time for each assessed area. You evaluate students using the teacher rubrics; students evaluate themselves using the student rubrics.

As students complete Phase Seven of the personal project, the final activity asks them to assign an overall score for their progress in the evaluated areas. Using the student rubrics, they should consider their weekly scores as well as their growth over time. Their final score for each area should represent their level of knowledge or performance at the *end* of the Pathfinder Project. You should do the same for each student in each evaluated area.

Students should then be given the opportunity to discuss any discrepancies between the final scores you have computed and their final scores for each area. Ideally, each final score should be one that you and the student agree is an accurate representation of their status at the end of the project.

If you wish to, or are required to, compute an overall grade for the Pathfinder Project, then you can simply combine the final scores for each student on the areas evaluated into some type of average.

For example, assume that you have evaluated the following areas:

- Overall progress on the personal project
- Literal and inferential comprehension skills
- Information-gathering skills
- Problem-solving skills
- Critical thinking and reasoning skills

Also assume that a particular student received the scores (on a scale of 1.0 – 4.0) depicted in Figure 5.1 at the end of the Project on those areas.

Figure 5.1 Scoring Illustration

Area Evaluated	Student's Final Score
Overall progress on the personal project	3.0
Literal and inferential comprehension skills	2.5
Information-gathering skills	3.0
Problem-solving skills	3.0
Critical thinking and reasoning skills	2.5
AVERAGE	**2.8**

If you wish to weight some areas more than others (e.g., have the personal project account for 50 percent of the grade), then you would simply construct a weighted average for the areas evaluated. Convert the average or the weighted average of a student's final scores to a letter grade using the scale depicted in Figure 5.2 (or another scale that you devise):

Figure 5.2 Grading Scale Illustration

Range for Final Average	Letter Grade
4.00 – 3.65	A
3.64 – 3.26	A –
3.25 – 3.09	B+
3.08 – 2.92	B –
2.91 – 2.76	B
2.75 – 2.50	C+
2.49 – 2.25	C
2.24 – 2.00	C –
1.99 – 1.84	D+
1.83 – 1.67	D
1.66 – 1.50	D –
1.49 – .000	F

Using the scale depicted in Figure 5.2, the student with a final average score of 2.8 would receive a letter grade of B-.

Scoring Rubrics

In this section, two rubrics have been provided for each of the eight possible evaluation topics. The first rubric is written for the classroom teacher; the second rubric is written for students. (Blackline Masters are provided in Chapter 11 for each of these rubrics.) As described above, these should be reviewed on a weekly basis. The scale for each rubric runs from 1 to 4. It is important to note that "half scores" can be used; i.e., if you believe that a student's score in a given area is between rubric scores of 3 and 4, then you should assign a score of 3.5.

Figure 5.3 Blackline Master Q

The Personal Project

Teacher Rubric	Student Rubric
4. The student has a clear and detailed vision of the outcome of his or her project and the steps that must be taken to realize that vision. Additionally, the student is taking concrete steps toward the vision.	4. I know what I want to accomplish in my personal project, and I know what I must do to get there. Additionally, I am doing things right now to help me accomplish my goal.
3. The student has a clear and detailed vision of the outcome of his or her project and the steps that must be taken to realize that vision.	3. I know what I want to accomplish in my personal project, and I know what I must do to get there.
2. The student has a vision of the outcome of his or her project but it is not clear and/or the student is not clear about the steps that must be taken to realize that vision.	2. I know what I want to accomplish in my personal project, but I haven't thought through what I need to do to accomplish my goal.
1. The student has no vision of the outcome of his or her project.	1. I don't really know what I want to accomplish in my personal project.

Figure 5.4 Blackline Master R

Literal and Inferential Comprehension Skills

Teacher Rubric	Student Rubric
4. The student provides complete and accurate answers to literal and inferential comprehension questions. Additionally, the student understands the strategies he or she uses to answer these questions.	4. After reading a story, I can answer questions about information that is obvious in the text as well as information that is not obvious but can be figured out. Additionally, I can describe the strategies I use to answer these types of questions.
3. The student provides complete and accurate answers to literal and inferential comprehension questions.	3. After reading a story, I can answer questions about information that is obvious in the text as well as information that is not obvious but can be figured out.
2. The student provides answers to literal and inferential questions. However, these answers commonly have inaccuracies.	2. After reading a story, I make an attempt to answer questions about information that is obvious in the text as well as information that is not obvious but can be figured out. However, I tend to get confused and I'm not very certain about my answers.
1. The student cannot answer literal or inferential comprehension questions.	1. When questions are asked about a story, I don't really try to answer them in any systematic way.

Figure 5.5 Blackline Master S

Information-Gathering and Synthesizing Skills

Teacher Rubric	Student Rubric
4. The student can accurately gather information from a variety of sources and can identify the key elements of the information he or she has gathered. Additionally, the student can organize the key points into conceptual categories that are useful to the completion of his or her project.	4. I know of and can use a variety of sources to gather information about a topic. As I gather information, I can identify the information that is most important to my topic. Additionally, when I have gathered the information, I can organize it into categories that makes it useful to me.
3. The student can accurately gather information from a variety of sources and can identify the key elements of the information he or she has gathered.	3. I know of and can use a variety of sources to gather information about a topic. As I gather information, I can identify theinformation that is most important to my topic.
2. The student can gather information from a variety of sources but is not very accurate when doing so, and/or the student has difficulty identifying the key elements of the information he or she has gathered.	2. I know of and can use some sources to gather information about a topic, but I have a hard time identifying which information is important.
1. The student cannot gather information from a variety of sources.	1. I don't really know many sources from which to gather information about a topic.

Figure 5.6 Blackline Master T

Problem-Solving Skills

Teacher Rubric	Student Rubric
4. The student clearly identifies obstacles to the goal and ways of overcoming the obstacle, and carries out the most effective ways of overcoming the obstacle. Additionally, the student understands the process he or she is using to solve the problem.	4. When I face a problem, I can identify the obstacle in my way. I can identify possible solutions and try out the one that has the best chance of working. Finally, I can describe the strategies I am using to solve the problem.
3. The student clearly identifies the obstacles to the goal and ways of overcoming the obstacle, and carries out the most effective ways of overcoming the obstacle.	3. When I face a problem, I can identify the obstacle in my way. I can identify possible solutions and try out the one that has the best chance of working.
2. The student provides a rough attempt to solve the problem but does not clearly identify the obstacle to the goal or does not clearly identify ways of overcoming the obstacle.	2. When I face a problem, I have a difficult time identifying the obstacle in my way, or I have a difficult time identifying ways of overcoming the obstacle.
1. The student makes no systematic attempt to solve the problem.	1. When I face a problem, I really don't have a systematic way of solving it.

Figure 5.7 Blackline Master U

Decision-Making Skills

Teacher Rubric	Student Rubric
4. The student clearly identifies the alternatives and the criteria used to select among them. The student selects the alternative that best meets the criteria. Additionally, the student understands the process he or she is using to make the decision.	4. When I face a decision, I can identify the alternatives that are available and an approach to select the best alternative. Additionally, I can describe the strategies I am using to make the decision.
3. The student clearly identifies the alternatives and the criteria used to select among them. The student selects the alternative that best meets the criteria.	3. When I face a decision, I can identify the alternatives that are available and an approach to select the best alternative.
2. The student provides a rough attempt to make the decision but does not clearly identify the alternatives or the criteria used to select among them.	2. When I face a decision, I have difficulty identifying the alternatives available to me or an approach to select the best alternative.
1. The student makes no systematic attempt to make the decision.	1. When I face a decision, I really don't have a systematic way of making it.

Figure 5.8 Blackline Master V

Imagery and Memory Skills

Teacher Rubric	Student Rubric
4. The student uses imagery and memory strategies to better understand and recall information. Additionally, the student understands why these strategies work.	4. I can use imagery and memory strategies to help me understand and remember information. I can explain how and why these strategies work.
3. The student uses imagery and memory strategies to better understand and recall information.	3. I can use imagery and memory strategies to help me understand and remember information.
2. The student makes a rough attempt to use imagery and memory strategies but does so in a way that diminishes the effectiveness of these strategies.	2. I try to use imagery and memory strategies, but I have trouble making them work well for me.
1. The student makes no systematic attempt to use imagery and memory strategies.	1. I don't really try to use imagery and memory strategies.

Figure 5.9 Blackline Master W

Critical Thinking and Reasoning Skills

Teacher Rubric	Student Rubric
4. The student can analyze his or her thinking and that of others in terms of its logic and the extent to which it contains errors. Additionally, the student understands the process used to do so.	4. I can analyze my own thinking and other people's thinking in terms of how logical it is and whether it contains errors. Additionally, I can explain the strategies I am using to do so.
3. The student can analyze his or her thinking and that of others in terms of its logic and the extent to which it contains errors.	3. I can analyze my own thinking and that of other people in terms of how logical it is and whether it contains errors.
2. The student attempts to analyze his or her thinking and that of others in terms of its logic and the extent to which it contains errors. However, the student exhibits misconceptions or misunderstandings in doing so.	2. I try to analyze my own thinking and that of other people in terms of how logical it is and whether it contains errors. However, I get confused about how to do this.
1. The student makes no systematic attempt to analyze his or her thinking, or that of others, in terms of its logic or the extent to which it contains errors.	1. I really don't try to analyze my own thinking or that of other people in terms of how logical it is or whether it contains errors.

Figure 5.10 Blackline Master X

Self-Control and Self-Regulation Skills

Teacher Rubric	Student Rubric
4. The student has an understanding of the influence of his or her internal thoughts, as manifested by inner dialogue and mental images, on his or her ability to accomplish things and has identified strategies for controlling those thoughts. Additionally, the student actively uses those strategies to enhance his or her ability to accomplish things.	4. I am aware of the things I say to myself, the thoughts I have, and how they affect me. I can control them.
3. The student has an understanding of the influence of his or her internal thoughts, as manifested by inner dialogue and mental images, on his or her ability to accomplish things and has identified strategies for controlling those thoughts.	3. I am aware of the things I say to myself, the thoughts I have, and how they affect me. I have strategies for controlling them, but I don't always use these strategies.
2. The student has an awareness of the influence of his or her internal thoughts, as manifested by inner dialogue and mental images, on his or her ability to accomplish things but has no strategies for controlling those thoughts.	2. I am aware of the things I say to myself and the thoughts I have, but I have no way of controlling them.
1. The student is not aware of the influence of his or her internal thoughts, as manifested by inner dialogue and mental images, on his or her ability to accomplish things.	1. I am not aware of the things I say to myself and the thoughts I have.

CHAPTER 6
DESIGNING A COURSE OF STUDY

*T*he first five chapters of this Manual identify and describe the component parts of the Pathfinder Project. This chapter provides you with a description of the various ways it can be implemented and adapted. These options include: 1) a nine-week course, 2) a three- to four-week course, 3) a semester-long course, 4) a language arts course, 5) an after school program, and 6) a home study course with parents. As you read the descriptions of these venues, note that the sequence and pacing of activities are recommendations only; that is, you should feel free to make alterations as you see fit.

A Nine-Week Course Offered Daily

Even if you are not planning to use the Pathfinder Project in the context of a nine-week course, it is helpful to read this description thoroughly as it is the most detailed reference point for the other venue descriptions.

Figure 6.1 depicts the learning objectives and the corresponding sections from this Manual for each lesson in a nine-week course offered daily.

Figure 6.1 Nine-week Lesson Plan

Week	Lesson #	Learning Objectives	Chapter of Teacher's Manual	Activities/ Skills
1	Lesson 1	• Help students understand the purpose and component parts of the Pathfinder Project. • Help students understand the role of inspirational stories and quotes within the context of the personal project. • Introduce students to a comprehension strategy.	Chapter 1 Chapter 2	• Introduction to the Pathfinder Project • Inspirational Stories • Inspirational Quotes • Comprehension Skills
	Lesson 2	• Introduce students to the comprehension strategy. • Introduce students to the academic problems that will be used throughout the program and their role in the program.	Chapter 2 Chapter 4	• Inspirational Stories • Comprehension Skills • Solving Academic Problems
	Lesson 3	• Introduce students to the phases of the personal project so they can begin setting a personal goal. • Introduce students to the notion of taking on something big in their lives – overcoming fear of failure.	Chapter 3 Phase One	• Overcoming Fear of Failure
	Lesson 4	• Help students understand that if they are going to do something big, they must break from the past. • Provide students additional experience in solving academic problems.	Chapter 3 Phase One	• Breaking Patterns of the Past • Solving Academic Problems
	Lesson 5	• Help students identify a specific future accomplishment that taps into their dreams and strong desires.	Chapter 3 Phase One	• Inspirational Quotes • Identifying a Future Accomplishment or Goal

Week	Lesson #	Learning Objectives	Chapter of Teacher's Manual	Activities/ Skills
2	Lesson 6	• Provide students additional experience in developing comprehension skills. • Introduce students to the concept of identifying a circle of support.	Chapter 2 Chapter 3 Phase Two	• Inspirational Quotes • Inspirational Stories • Comprehension Skills • Identifying a Circle of Support
	Lesson 7	• Introduce the concept of heroes, role models, and mentors. • Provide students additional experience in solving academic problems.	Chapter 3 Phase Two Chapter 4	• Inspirational Quotes • Learning from Heroes, Role Models, and Mentors • Inspirational Stories • Solving Academic Problems
	Lesson 8	• Have students begin collecting information about their heroes, role models, and mentors. • Provide students support for gathering and synthesizing information.	Chapter 3 Phase Two Chapter 4	• Learning from Heroes, Role Models, and Mentors • Information-Gathering and Synthesizing Skills
	Lesson 9	• Introduce students to the general problem-solving process. • Provide students additional time to collect and gather information about their heroes, role models, and mentors.	Chapter 3 Phase Two Chapter 4	• Inspirational Quotes • Problem-Solving Skills • Learning from Heroes, Role Models, and Mentors • Information-Gathering and Synthesizing Skills
	Lesson 10	• Provide students additional time to collect and organize information about their heroes, role models, and mentors. • Provide further information and practice in the general problem-solving process.	Chapter 3 Phase Two Chapter 4	• Problem-Solving Skills • Learning from Heroes, Role Models, and Mentors • Information-Gathering and Synthesizing Skills

Week	Lesson	Learning Objectives	Chapter of Teacher's Manual	Activities/ Skills
3	Lesson 11	• Provide students with the opportunity to present what they have learned about their heroes, role models, and mentors. • Introduce the concept of the "Winner's Profile."	Chapter 3 Phase Two	• Inspirational Quotes • Learning from Heroes, Role Models, and Mentors • Information-Gathering and Synthesizing Skills • Constructing the Winner's Profile
	Lesson 12	• Help students understand that not all support is equal, that some types of support are more useful than others, and that they should select support that will be most useful to them.	Chapter 3 Phase Two	• Understanding the Nature of Support
	Lesson 13	• Provide students additional experience in developing comprehension skills. • Introduce students to the concept of creating "future possible self."	Chapter 2 Chapter 3 Phase Three	• Inspirational Quotes • Inspirational Stories • Comprehension Skills • Identifying Your Future Possible Self
	Lesson 14	• Provide students with an opportunity to continue to work on the descriptions of their future possible selves. • Provide students additional practice in solving academic problems.	Chapter 3 Phase Three Chapter 4	• Identifying Your Future Possible Self • Solving Academic Problems
	Lesson 15	• Provide students practice in developing comprehension skills. • Introduce students to the decision-making process. • Provide students additional time to work on their future possible self-descriptions.	Chapter 2 Chapter 4	• Inspirational Stories • Comprehension Skills • Decision-Making Skills • Identifying Your Future Possible Self

Week	Lesson #	Learning Objectives	Chapter of Teacher's Manual	Activities/ Skills
4	Lesson 16	• Provide students with the opportunity to apply the decision-making process to their own lives.	Chapter 4	• Decision-Making Skills
	Lesson 17	• Review the general problem-solving and decision-making processes. • Provide students additional time to work on their future possible self-descriptions.	Chapter 4 Chapter 3 Phase Three	• Problem-Solving Skills • Decision-Making Skills • Identifying Your Future Possible Self
	Lesson 18	• Provide students with an opportunity to report on their future possible self-descriptions. • Introduce students to the concept that certain experiences, accomplishments, and schooling will probably be necessary for them to realize their future possible selves.	Chapter 3 Phase Three	• Identifying Your Future Possible Self • Articulating Necessary Experiences, Accomplishments, and Schooling
	Lesson 19	• Introduce students to the nature and power of mental imagery. • Provide students additional time to gather additional information about necessary experiences, accomplishments, and schooling.	Chapter 4 Chapter 3 Phase Three	• Imagery and Memory Skills • Articulating Necessary Experiences, Accomplishments, and Schooling
	Lesson 20	• Introduce students to the rhyming pegword technique. • Provide students additional time to gather information about necessary experiences, accomplishments, and schooling.	Chapter 4	• Imagery and Memory Skills: Rhyming Pegword • Articulating Necessary Experiences, Accomplishments, and Schooling

Week	Lesson #	Learning Objectives	Chapter of Teacher's Manual	Activities/ Skills
5	Lesson 21	• Present students with the familiar place technique. • Provide students additional time to gather information about their necessary experiences, accomplishments, and schooling.	Chapter 4	• Imagery and Memory Skills: Familiar Place • Articulating Necessary Experiences, Accomplishments, and Schooling
	Lesson 22	• Provide students with an opportunity to add to the Winner's Profile. • Provide students additional time to work on their necessary experiences, accomplishments, and schooling.	Chapter 3 Phase Three	• Constructing a Winner's Profile • Articulating Necessary Experiences, Accomplishments, and Schooling
	Lesson 23	• Have students report on their necessary experiences, accomplishments, and schooling.	Chapter 3 Phase Three	• Inspirational Quotes • Articulating Necessary Experiences, Accomplishments, and Schooling
	Lesson 24	• Introduce the concept of discrepancy analysis. • Have students begin the process of constructing a discrepancy analysis.	Chapter 3 Phase Four	• Completing a Discrepancy Analysis
	Lesson 25	• Provide students with additional time to construct a discrepancy analysis. • Provide students additional practice in developing comprehension skills.	Chapter 2 Chapter 3 Phase Four	• Inspirational Stories • Comprehension Skills • Completing a Dscrepancy Analysis

Week	Lesson #	Learning Objectives	Chapter of Teacher's Manual	Activities/ Skills
6	Lesson 26	• Provide students with an opportunity to report on their discrepancy analyses. • Provide students with additional practice in solving academic problems or engaging in decision-making or imagery and memory skills.	Chapter 3 Phase Four Chapter 4	• Completing a Discrepancy Analysis • Solving Academic Problems • Decision-Making Skills • Imagery and Memory Skills
	Lesson 27	• Introduce the concept of planning backwards. • Provide students additional time to work on their necessary experiences, accomplishments, and schooling.	Chapter 3 Phase Five Chapter 4	• Planning Backwards • Solving Academic Problems • Decision-Making skills • Imagery and Memory Skills
	Lesson 28	• Provide students practice in developing comprehension skills. • Provide students with time to begin planning backwards from their future possible selves.	Chapter 2 Chapter 3 Phase Five	• Inspirational Sories • Comprehension Skills • Planning Backwards
	Lesson 29	• Introduce students to the critical thinking and reasoning skill of analyzing errors. • Provide students with time to plan backwards.	Chapter 4 Chapter 3 Phase Five	• Critical Thinking and Reasoning Skills: Analyzing Errors • Planning Backwards
	Lesson 30	• Introduce more types of errors in thinking. • Provide students with additional time to plan backwards.	Chapter 4 Chapter 3 Phase Five	• Critical Thinking and Reasoning Skills • Planning Backwards

Week	Lesson #	Learning Objectives	Chapter of Teacher's Manual	Activities/ Skills
7	Lesson 31	• Introduce students to the concept of deductive thinking. • Provide students with more time to plan backwards.	Chapter 4 Chapter 3 Phase Five	• Critical Thinking and Reasoning Skills: Analyzing Deductive Conclusions • Planning Backwards
	Lesson 32	• Provide students with the opportunity to report on their backwards planning.	Chapter 3 Phase Five	• Planning Backwards
	Lesson 33	• Introduce students to the concept of making declarations about themselves.	Chapter 3 Phase Five	• Making Declarations
	Lesson 34	• Introduce students to the concept of taking small steps toward their goal. • Provide students with practice in developing comprehension skills.	Chapter 2 Chapter 3 Phase Six	• Inspirational Stories • Comprehension Skills • Taking Small Steps
	Lesson 35	• Introduce students to the concept of the "Inner Game of Success." • Introduce the concept of "inner dialogue." • Provide students with practice in analyzing deductive conclusions.	Chapter 4	• Self-Control and Self-Regulation Skills and Inner Dialogue • Critical Thinking and Reasoning Skills: Analyzing Deductive Conclusions

Week	Lesson #	Learning Objectives	Chapter of Teacher's Manual	Activities/ Skills
8	Lesson 36	• Provide students practice in developing comprehension skills. • Introduce students to the concept of "power of effort."	Chapter 2 Chapter 4	• Inspirational Stories • Comprehension Skills • Self-Control and Self-Regulation: the Power of Effort
	Lesson 37	• Introduce students to the concept of "power thinking." • Provide students additional time to work on their small steps.	Chapter 4 Chapter 3 Phase Six	• Self-Control and Self-Regulation skills: Power Thinking • Taking Small Steps
	Lesson 38	• Provide students practice in developing comprehension skills. • Provide students practice in analyzing deductive conclusions.	Chapter 2 Chapter 4	• Inspirational Stories • Comprehension Skills • Critical Thinking and Reasoning Skills: Analyzing Deductive Conclusions
	Lesson 39	• Introduce students to the concept of re-evaluating or changing one's plans. • Provide students with additional practice in solving academic problems.	Chapter 3 Phase Seven Chapter 4	• Inspirational Quotes • Re-evaluating Plans • Solving Academic Problems
	Lesson 40	• Introduce students to the concept of an aphorism. • Provide students with additional practice in solving academic problems.	Chapter 3 Phase Seven	• Creating Aphorisms • Inspirational Quotes • Solving Academic Problems

Week	Lesson #	Learning Objectives	Chapter of Teacher's Manual	Activities/ Skills
9	Lesson 41	• Examine the impact of the power thinking process. • Provide students additional time to work on their aphorisms. • Provide students additional time to work on essential skills.	Chapter 4 Chapter 3 Phase Seven	• Self-Control and Self-Regulation Skills: Power Thinking • Creating Aphorisms • Solving Academic Problems • Imagery and Memory Skills • Critical Thinking and Reasoning Skills • Problem-Solving Skills • Decision-Making Skills • Information and Memory Skills
	Lesson 42	• Provide students additional time to work on their aphorisms. • Provide students additional time to work on essential skills.	Chapter 3 Phase Seven Chapter 4	• Creating Aphorisms • Solving Academic Problems • Imagery and Memory Skills • Critical Thinking and Reasoning Skills • Problem-Solving Skills • Decision-Making Skills • Information and Memory Skills
	Lesson 43	• Provide students with the opportunity to share their aphorisms. • Provide students additional time to work on essential skills.	Chapter 3 Phase Seven Chapter 4	• Solving Academic Problems • Imagery and Memory Skills • Critical Thinking and Reasoning Skills • Problem-Solving Skills • Decision-Making Skills • Information and Memory Skills
	Lesson 44	• Provide students with time to evaluate themselves on the skills addressed during the Pathfinder Project. • Provide students additional time to work on essential skills.	Chapter 3 Phase Seven Chapter 6 Chapter 4	• Solving Academic Problems • Evaluating Success • Imagery and Memory Skills • Critical Thinking and Reasoning Skills • Problem-Solving • Decision-Making • Information and Memory Skills
	Lesson 45	• Provide opportunities for students to complete their self-evaluations. • Celebrate the completion of the Pathfinder Project.	Chapter 3 Phase Seven Chapter 6 Chapter 4	• Evaluating Success

Detailed Lesson Plans for the Nine-Week Course

Below, detailed lesson plans are presented for each of the 45 days in a nine-week course. Again, it is important to remember that this is a suggested sequence of activities that can be customized to your students' needs.

Lesson 1

Purpose of the lesson:

- *Help students understand the purpose and component parts of the Pathfinder Project.*

- *Help students understand the role of inspirational stories and quotes within the context of the personal project.*

- *Introduce students to a comprehension strategy.*

The first order of business is to introduce students to the Pathfinder Project and provide them with a sense of its nature and purpose. It is helpful to place several meaningful quotes (which are found in Chapter 9 of this Manual) around the classroom before you begin to explain the program to them. Show students the graphic representation of the component parts of the Pathfinder Project (Blackline Master A in Chapter 11). Explain to them that in this class they will be:

- Setting and working on a goal of their own choosing.

- Learning a process they can follow that will help them accomplish this goal over time.

- Learning essential skills that are necessary to function well in life.

- Studying what other people have done, what their goals were, what inspired them, and how they accomplished their goals.

- Learning a lot about themselves, their aspirations, and what inspires them to set and accomplish personal goals.

At this point you may wish to give each student his or her Student Notebook and help them see how the various sections in the Notebook relate to the component parts of the Pathfinder Project. (The Student Notebook is described in Chapter 7 of this Manual.)

Next, ask students to turn to the section in their Notebooks on inspirational stories. Discuss the concept of inspiration by describing a time when you were inspired by the actions of another person. Share with students why you think you were inspired, what you did as a result of being inspired, and the outcome of your actions. You may also wish to describe a time you were inspired, but did not act upon the inspiration.

Invite students to share various examples of inspirational people they have heard, read, or seen movies about. After several stories have been shared, explain to students that, while some stories they hear may be inspirational, they do not seem to have any personal relevance because the setting or the goal is so far removed from them. Because of this, some stories are interesting, but do not motivate us to action. A key reason inspirational stories are included in this program is that they collectively demonstrate a consistent pattern. Help students understand that realizing this pattern can help them reach their personal goals.

Explain that you will use a personal story about a young man named Todd to examine this pattern. (Todd's story is the first one in the Student Notebook.) Either read the story aloud to them or have them read the story silently, and then ask students to identify what they found meaningful. Give students Blackline Master B (found in Chapter 11), which identifies the general pattern. Have them fill it in with specifics from Todd's story, and share their completed sheets. Once students seem to understand how the specific parts of Todd's story parallel the general pattern, give them another story you have heard or experienced. Ask them to identify how the general pattern plays out in the new story by filling out Blackline Master C (also found in Chapter 11). Have students share what they have learned with one another in small groups.

Lesson 2

Purpose of the lesson:

- *Introduce students to the comprehension strategy.*

- *Introduce students to the academic problems that will be used throughout the course and explain their role in the program.*

Explain to students that, throughout the Pathfinder Project, they will be learning life skills to help them as they pursue various goals. One of these life skills deals with their capacity to read and comprehend information. Explain that they will learn how to answer and use various types of questions to increase their capacity to understand what they read.

Give an example of each of the three types of questions from Todd's story, and have students discuss how the three types differ. (Questions of each type are provided for each story in Chapter 8 of this Manual.) You may have to go back and review Todd's story to remind students of its content. Give them a copy of Blackline Master D (from Chapter 11), which provides the steps in the comprehension strategy. Briefly go over these steps with students, and then have them answer the questions in the spaces provided in their Notebooks at the end of Todd's story. Go over the answers and explain that you will revisit these kinds of questions as they read more stories.

Next, explain that another type of activity they will frequently be asked to engage in during the Pathfinder Project is to work "brain teaser"

problems that are academic in nature and fun to solve. Help them understand that, although these are not real life problems, they can learn something about real life problem solving from them. Because the answers are not readily available or easily solved, students will have a chance to observe how they react to difficult situations, and develop strategies and skills to help them persevere…even when things are difficult or the answers are not really obvious. These skills are essential to success in life.

Present students with the strategy for solving academic problems (Blackline Master E in Chapter 11). Go over the steps of the process using one of the various problems from the Academic Problems section in Chapter 10, then have them solve another academic problem. When they are done, discuss what they learned about this type of problem and about themselves as problem solvers.

Lesson 3

Purpose of the lesson:

- *Introduce students to the phases of the personal project so they can begin setting a personal goal.*

- *Introduce students to the notion of taking on something big in their lives—overcoming fear of failure.*

Explain to students that a major goal of the Pathfinder Project is to help them identify a personal goal, and begin to pursue that goal in a seven-phase personal project. By completing each of the seven phases, they will learn various life skills as well as a process they can use to accomplish their personal goals.

Ask students to turn to Phase One in their Student Notebooks, under the section, "My Personal Project." Explain that the intention of Phase One is to help them identify a personal goal. To begin Phase One, review Todd's story and provide some additional examples of people who have accomplished personal goals. Point out that the individual in each example took on something big in their lives—something that seemed difficult, if not impossible, for them to accomplish. Although their goal might not have been big in someone else's eyes, to them it was. Help students understand that these were ordinary people who achieved great things because they were deeply committed to or passionate about what they wanted to accomplish.

One of the major assumptions underlying the Pathfinder Project is that *everyone* has within them the desire and ability to do something extraordinary. Some people are fortunate enough to realize this potential while others are not. It all starts with belief in the possibility that we *can* do something extraordinary. However, what sometimes happens is that fear of failure paralyzes us, and we never move forward. Discuss whether students think the people in the examples were ever afraid they would fail, and how they might have overcome their fears.

Have students share their own stories about people who have accomplished things that seemed impossible at the time, and ask them to identify the fears these people might have faced. Discuss why and how they think fear of failure keeps us from accomplishing a goal.

Explain that a useful activity when setting a goal is to ask yourself, "What you would do if you knew you wouldn't fail?" This helps them think more clearly about what is deeply personal to them, and what they are passionate about. Point out that, sometimes, our strong desires are hard to identify because we don't even allow ourselves to think that they could happen.

Have students fill out Student Activity Sheet 1 in Phase One of their Student Notebooks and share their responses in small groups. While students are writing their responses, you should write your own; you should also take part in the sharing with the whole class.

Lesson 4

Purpose of the lesson:

- *Help students understand that if they are going to do something big, they must break patterns from the past.*

- *Provide students additional experience in solving academic problems.*

Explain that people sometimes do things that stop them from accomplishing their goals, and give various examples of such behaviors:

- Sometimes people tell themselves that they can't do anything right, and therefore they don't even try.

- Some people tell themselves that they can't accomplish anything because they have no money or resources.

- Some people say they want to accomplish a goal, but they continue to do other things of interest to them rather than take the first step towards their goal. That is, they tend to get sidetracked.

- Some people want to accomplish a goal, but they listen to others who tell them that they do not have the ability to accomplish their goal. Eventually, they give up.

Discuss the fact that we often have to break from patterns of the past to accomplish something big. As a self-analysis activity, have students select something from their list of "things they would do if they knew they wouldn't fail" (generated in Lesson 3) and use that item to complete Student Activity Sheet 2 (in Phase One of the Student

Notebook). Next, discuss the need to break old habits and patterns from the past when engaged in challenging tasks.

If time permits, review the academic problem-solving process, do more academic problems, and have students discuss or write about what they have learned regarding problem solving or about themselves as problem solvers in the Personal Reflections section of their Notebooks.

Lesson 5

Purpose of the lesson:

- *Help students identify a specific future accomplishment that taps into their dreams and strong desires.*

Begin the session with more quotes and short examples about people who have taken on big tasks.

Ask students to review the possibilities they generated by responding to the question, "What would you do if you knew you wouldn't fail?" Explain that it is time for them to select something to actually start working on by identifying some future accomplishment they would like to achieve. The accomplishment can be months or years in the future, and doesn't have to be a career-related goal (although this might be the most common selection). Students should be able to get a specific picture of what it would be like if they accomplished this goal. Remind them that they do not have to complete their personal goal by the end of this course; rather, they will be learning the process and skills they will need to get there at some future date.

Direct them to Student Activity Sheet 3 in Phase One of the Student Notebook. It asks students to identify:

- What they want to accomplish
- Where and how they will live

- Specific behaviors or activities they will engage in
- What they will look like
- The type of people they will be with
- How they will feel

Explain that the questions on the Activity Sheet are simply intended to help them think about what they might like to do in the future. They should answer these questions as specifically as they can at this time. Allow students sufficient time to complete the Activity Sheet, and fill in your own at the same time.

Invite students to share their responses, and have them discuss how overcoming fear of failure and breaking patterns of the past would relate to their projects.

This is the completion of Phase One of the personal project, so you may wish for students to record their reactions and thoughts in the Personal Reflections section of their Notebooks.

Lesson 6

Purpose of the lesson:

- *Provide students additional experience in developing comprehension skills.*
- *Introduce students to the concept of identifying a circle of support.*

Begin with some inspirational quotes about the importance of support. Then, tell students that they are now moving into Phase Two of the personal project, which addresses the need for and the various types of support they should elicit to reach their goals. Discuss the importance of support, help students see that support can come in a variety of ways, and explain that the next few activities will help them learn about eliciting support.

Have students read another story from Chapter 8 and answer the comprehension questions. Go over the comprehension strategy with them and discuss the answers to the questions. Also, discuss the type of support the person in the story needed to accomplish their goal.

Tell students that they will consider those people who currently provide support in their lives, how these people might offer support as they pursue their goals, what other types of support they might need, and who might be able to give that support.

Have students complete Student Activity Sheet 4 from the Phase Two section of their Notebooks, then discuss the nature of the support they currently have and what support they still need to elicit.

Lesson 7

Purpose of the lesson:

- *Introduce the concept of a heroes, role models, and mentors.*
- *Provide students additional experience in solving academic problems.*

Provide some quotations about the importance of heroes, role models, and mentors. Then explain that people who accomplish great things commonly have someone who inspired them and guided them along the way. Help students see the differences between a hero, a role model, and a mentor as described in Chapter 3. Explain that each of these kinds of people can provide support, albeit in different ways. Refer to the concept of a circle of support discussed in Lesson 6, and determine whether they have any heroes, role models, or mentors on their lists.

To help students further understand the role of heroes, role models, and mentors, provide examples you have heard about or examples from your own life. Then ask students to identify people who have been heroes, role models, or mentors to them.

Explain that, in this phase of their personal project, students will identify heroes, role models, or mentors to support them as they pursue their goals. Remind them that heroes and role models don't have to be people they actually know, but mentors are someone they actually have a chance to communicate with.

Have students complete Student Activity Sheet 5 from the Student Notebook. While they do so, identify possible mentors, heroes, and role models for your own project. Next, organize students into small groups and have them share the people they have selected, why they have selected them, and what they have learned about selecting people to support them as they pursue a goal.

If time permits, have students solve more academic problems.

Lesson 8

Purpose of the lesson:

- *Have students begin collecting information about their heroes, role models, and mentors.*
- *Provide students guidance in gathering and synthesizing that information.*

Begin the session by reviewing the importance of heroes, role models, and mentors. Explain to students that they will gather information on a specific person from their list of heroes, role models, and mentors and answer the following questions about them:

- Who is the person you have selected?
- Where and when were they born?
- Where are they now?
- What did they accomplish?

- What are some major obstacles they had to overcome along the way?

- How did they overcome these obstacles?

- Who helped them along the way?

- Why are they a hero, role model or mentor to you?

- What can you learn from this person?

Provide some time for students to select a specific person from the list they generated in Lesson 7. Help them understand that, by gathering information to answer the questions about these people, they will gain a clearer understanding of what they need to do to accomplish their personal goals. Also explain that they will learn where to find information, how to collect it, and how to organize it. To help them do this, brainstorm a list of the various ways they can collect information about their heroes, role models, and mentors. This list might include:

- Direct interviews

- Books

- Magazines

- The Internet

Have students identify the sources that are most likely to be useful to them, given the person they have selected.

Explain that that they will have a number of class periods to gather information on the person they have selected, and allow time for them to begin. You might also need to spend some time addressing various sources of information (see Chapter 4 for suggestions). As they collect information for each hero, role model, and mentor, have them organize it using Student Activity Sheet 6 (in Phase Two of their Notebooks).

Lesson 9

Purpose of the lesson:

- *Introduce students to the general problem-solving process.*

- *Provide students additional time to collect and gather information about their heroes, role models, and mentors.*

Present more quotations about the value of heroes, role models, and mentors, or some other aspect of the Pathfinder Project.

Point out that most people who have accomplished great things have had to solve many problems along the way. Explain that they have been solving some problems up to this point in class, all of which have been academic in nature. Discuss the differences between academic problem solving and solving problems in our daily lives. Have students provide an example of a problem they have experienced and how they solved it.

Present students either Blackline Master F or G (depending on the approach you choose), which contains the steps in the general problem-solving process. Discuss and exemplify the steps, and ask students how the example of the problem they previously shared relates to this problem-solving process.

Have students discuss some of the problems they are encountering as they pursue their goals. Have them identify the goal, the constraints that keep them from attaining the goal, the solutions they are considering, and the solution that would best serve them in accomplishing their goal. If there is time, continue gathering information on heroes, role models, and mentors.

Lesson 10

Purpose of the lesson:

- *Provide students additional time to collect and organize information about their heroes, role models, and mentors.*

- *Provide further information and practice in the general problem-solving process.*

Review the general problem-solving process with students. Go over and exemplify some of the steps that are particularly difficult, or that students have questions about. Ask students to identify a problem they are facing in their own lives, and apply some or all of the steps of the problem-solving process.

Provide additional experience in problem solving with some of the general problem-solving activities from Chapter 10. If time permits, have students continue gathering information on their heroes, role models, and mentors.

Lesson 11

Purpose of the lesson:

- *Provide students with the opportunity to present what they have learned about their heroes, role models, and mentors.*

- *Introduce the concept of the "Winner's Profile."*

Begin with more quotations and short examples from Chapter 9 of this Manual.

Explain that the purpose of this lesson is for them to share the information they have learned thus far about their heroes, role models, and mentors, and then to use that information to identify common characteristics. By comparing characteristics of their heroes, role models, and mentors, they will be able to construct a profile that describes the characteristics of successful people, referred to as the "Winner's Profile." Explain how they can use this profile as a pattern for conducting their own lives.

Ask some students to volunteer to informally present the information they have gathered about their heroes, role models, and mentors. Allow the other students to ask questions.

Then, organize the class into small groups to identify the common characteristics or traits among the various people studied which helped them achieve success. To facilitate this process, use Student Activity Sheet 7, depicted in Figure 6.2 below.

After the small groups complete their matrices, have each one report to the class. As a whole class, construct a "Winner's Profile" by identifying traits shared by all of the successful

Figure 6.2 Student Activity Sheet 7

Successful People	Trait 1	Trait 2	Trait 3	Trait 4
Person 1				
Person 2				
Person 3				
Person 4				

people studied. Put this on chart paper, and keep it displayed in the classroom. End the session by having students record (in the Personal Reflections section of their Notebooks) how they think the Winner's Profile might be of use to them as they work on their own personal goals.

Lesson 12

Purpose of the lesson:

- *Help students understand that not all support is equal, that some types of support are more useful than others, and that they should select support that will be most helpful to them.*

Begin the session by reviewing some of the points that were made about the importance of support. Point out that, from one experience to another, the type of support they might need could be different. Also, address the fact that sometimes when we think someone is supporting us, their actions may not, in fact, be helping us meet our goal. Throughout your discussion, help students understand the following:

- Sometimes people who are trying to support us tell us what we *want* to hear rather than what we *need* to hear.

- People who support us will continue to do so only if they see we are really trying.

- People are not really supporting us if they do things that we should be doing for ourselves.

- Different kinds of people give different types of support.

- When people give support in the form of advice, we always have the option to *not* follow it.

After the discussion about support, have students fill out Student Activity Sheet 8 in Phase Two of their Notebooks and share their responses with other members of the class. Then, as a group,

identify some generalizations about eliciting support and discuss what they have learned.

With Phase Two complete, you may wish to have students record their thoughts in the Personal Reflections section of their Notebooks.

Lesson 13

Purpose of the lesson:

- *Provide students additional experience in developing comprehension skills.*

- *Introduce students to the concept of creating a "future possible self."*

Begin with quotations emphasizing the importance of creating an image of yourself in the future.

Have students read another story from Chapter 8 and answer the comprehension questions. If necessary, go over the steps in the comprehension process.

Next, introduce the concept of a "future possible self." To do this, you might explain that psychologists have found that the act of imagining what life will be like in the future is not just idle daydreaming. In fact, it is important for us to envision the future. When we have an image of what life can be like, then we have something to work toward. Relate a story about the importance of imagining the future from your own life or the life of someone else. Discuss the degree to which students think the person in the story had pictured his/her future possible self, and what effect this might have had on accomplishing their goal.

Tell students that they will each create a future possible self relative to the goal they have taken on; point out that they began this process with the "what would you do if you knew you wouldn't fail" activity. Allow students some time to review their answers to the questions in this exercise (Student Activity Sheet 1).

Explain that, in the current activity, they will add more detail to their answers and create a written description of what they will be like and what life will be like in the future. Provide a model using the story of Todd (the first one in Chapter 8). Explain that when Todd was in high school, he might have written a description of his future possible self like the following:

I'm 25 years old, and I'm a Navy fighter pilot. I live in California, where I'm stationed. I'm in excellent physical condition as a result of my regular aerobics and weight training program, and my eyesight is 20/20. On a typical day, I get up early to exercise and then begin to prepare for the day's flights. I meet with my commander and with other pilots to plan missions when we're at sea, or to prepare for training flights. I write detailed notes to myself in a small manual that I carry with me on all my flights. Once the day's flights are planned, I begin to prepare the FA-18 for flight. Before I get into the cockpit, I go over every inch of the plane, checking to make sure that it is in perfect working condition. After each flight, I meet with the senior pilot to get feedback—for example, how well I landed on the aircraft carrier—so that I can continue to improve my skills. I'm proud of what I've accomplished so far and proud to be serving the United States, but I'm also pushing myself to accomplish even more in the Navy and to further hone my skills as a pilot.

Explain to students that it is now their turn to create a future possible self-description. To help them do this, refer to Student Activity Sheet 9 in Phase Three of the Student Notebook. Go over the various sections of the Student Activity Sheet and explain that it is intended to stimulate their thinking.

When students understand the requirements of the activity, allow them the rest of class time to work on their descriptions. Meanwhile, work on your own possible future self-description.

Lesson 14

Purpose of the lesson:

- *Provide students with an opportunity to continue to work on the descriptions of their future possible selves.*

- *Provide students additional practice in solving academic problems.*

Have students continue to work on their future possible self-descriptions. Once Student Activity Sheet 9 is completed, they should use that information as the basis for a written description of themselves. You might share the progress you have made on your own description and any issues that have arisen for you. You might also invite students to share and ask questions around their possible self-descriptions. If you sense that they need some type of group activity, present them with more academic problems from Chapter 10 or one of the activities for general problem solving from Chapter 10.

Lesson 15

Purpose of the lesson:

- *Provide students practice in developing comprehension skills.*

- *Introduce students to the decision-making process.*

- *Provide students additional time to work on their future possible self-descriptions.*

Begin the session by having students read another story from Chapter 8 and answer the comprehension questions. You might also want to review the comprehension strategy. Point out the decisions the person in the story had to make, and discuss whether they think some of them were harder to make than others.

Explain that we have to make decisions throughout our lives. Many of them are easy (like what movie to see) but some of them can be quite difficult (like whether to try out for a specific team, or what school to attend). Share some of the more difficult decisions you have faced in your life, and invite students to share some difficult decisions they have made. Explain that, when difficult decisions present themselves, it is best to have an explicit approach to decision making as opposed to approaching them in a haphazard way.

Present students with the steps to the decision-making process (either Blackline Master H or I, depending upon whether you elect to teach the simple or the more complex version of decision making). Demonstrate how the strategy can be used with real life decisions by showing how it applies to a decision you have made in the past, or one you are making at present. Model each step of the process and ask students to share what they are learning about decision making.

If there is time, allow students to work on their future possible self-descriptions.

Lesson 16

Purpose of the lesson:

- *Provide students with the opportunity to apply the decision-making process to their own lives.*

Start the session by reviewing the steps in the decision-making process. Have students generate and organize examples of difficult decisions they are trying to make as they pursue their goals. Give them time to apply the decision-making process to these issues in their lives. You may also wish to engage students in some of the practice activities for decision making from Chapter 10. When these exercises are completed, have students record their insights and reactions in the Personal Reflections section of their Notebooks.

If time permits, assign more academic problems from Chapter 10.

Lesson 17

Purpose of the lesson:

- *Review the general problem-solving and decision-making processes.*

- *Provide students with additional time to work on their future possible self-descriptions.*

Begin the class by reviewing the steps in the general problem-solving and decision-making processes. Break into small groups to discuss how problem solving and decision making are different, and how they are the same. Then discuss these conclusions as a whole group.

For the rest of the period, allow students time to continue their future possible self-descriptions.

Lesson 18

Purpose of the lesson:

- *Provide students with an opportunity to report on their future possible self-descriptions.*

- *Introduce students to the concept that certain experiences, accomplishments and schooling will probably be necessary for them to realize their future possible selves.*

Begin the session by asking for volunteers to read their future possible self-descriptions to the whole class, and allow others to ask questions. Next, break into small groups and ask the rest of the students to report in that setting.

Next, have a discussion with the whole class about the need to gather detailed information about the future you want to create if, indeed, it is to become a reality. Describe as an example the various experiences, accomplishments, and schooling you needed to become a teacher (e.g., good grades, a college degree, certification in your state, good interpersonal skills). Point out that students will most probably require specific experiences, accomplishments and schooling to realize their future possible selves.

Explain that the next activity in the project is to obtain specific information about what it will take to make the future they have described come true. Explain that Student Activity Sheets 10 and 11 are designed to help them identify the experiences, accomplishments and schooling necessary to accomplish their goals. Review the different information sources they might use and the strategies for gathering information as they address the questions in these activity sheets. Then allow the remainder of the period to work on the activity sheets.

Lesson 19

Purpose of the lesson:

- *Introduce students to the nature and power of mental imagery.*

- *Provide students with additional time to gather information about necessary experiences, accomplishments and schooling.*

Begin the session by explaining to students that human thinking occurs primarily in two forms: as words and as images. When they talk to themselves, it is an example of thinking in words. Often this inner dialogue is helpful in clarifying our thinking. However, it can also be somewhat harmful if what we are telling ourselves is negative. Explain to students that they will learn more about thinking with words later on in the project, but for now, they will be learning about how to think using images.

Explain how Albert Einstein used the power of mental images to create "thought experiments" (see Chapter 4 of this Manual). When students understand the nature and importance of thought experiments, involve them in some of the imagery practice activities found in Chapter 4. Have students share what they have learned about the nature and function of imagery.

During the rest of the session, allow students to gather information about their necessary experiences, accomplishments, and schooling.

Lesson 20

Purpose of the lesson:

- *Introduce students to the rhyming peg-word memory technique.*

- *Provide students additional time to gather information about their necessary experiences, accomplishments and schooling.*

Explain that you are going to teach students a way of using imagery to help them remember information that may want to store in a specific order. Begin by demonstrating the rhyming peg-word memory technique using Blackline Master J (Chapter 11) as a guideline. Have them practice the strategy on a list of ten items, and then discuss what they learned about using this particular memory technique. Explore how they might use this technique in other courses or classes they are taking, and remind them that if they add sounds, smells, feelings, and emotions to their images, they will better be able to recall the information.

Have students spend the rest of the period gathering information about their necessary experiences, accomplishments, and schooling.

Lesson 21

Purpose of the lesson:

- *Present students with the familiar place memory technique.*

- *Provide students with additional time to gather information about their necessary experiences, accomplishments and schooling.*

Begin the class by reviewing the importance of imagery and its role in helping recall information. Have students discuss their reactions to the memory strategy they learned the previous day, and see if they can still remember the list they memorized. If they cannot remember some of the items, ask what they might have done to improve their memory. Point out that, if they really want to remember information, they may need to add more detail to their mental images. This might include adding more physical sensations and emotions.

Explain that you are going to give them another memory technique that they might want to use: the familiar place technique. Describe the concept and have each student generate their own familiar place framework using Blackline Master K (from Chapter 11). Have them share their frameworks with other students, and then give them a list of items to store using their framework. Once they have mentally stored the items, have students write them down and then discuss how the framework helped them remember the list. Ask them to compare the use of this framework with the rhyming peg-word framework. Discuss which framework seemed easier for them, and under what circumstances they might like to use either technique.

Allow students the rest of the period to gather information on their necessary experiences, accomplishments, and schooling.

Lesson 22

Purpose of the lesson:

- *Provide students with an opportunity to add to the Winner's Profile.*
- *Provide students additional time to work on gathering information about their necessary experiences, accomplishments, and schooling.*

Begin the session by revisiting the Winner's Profile constructed in Lesson 11.

Explain that, since they have learned more about successful people, they might want to add characteristics to the Profile. Break into small groups to discuss what additional characteristics they might add to the original Profile, then update the Winner's Profile as a whole class.

Explain that they will be asked to report on what they have discovered about necessary experiences, accomplishments, and schooling when they meet next time, and allow students the rest of the period to gather information on these subjects.

Lesson 23

Purpose of the lesson:

- *Have students report on their necessary experiences, accomplishments, and schooling.*

Reaffirming the importance of creating a strong description of what the future will be like for you, and present a few quotations about the importance of creating a strong sense of the future.

Ask for volunteers to report on what they have discovered about necessary experiences, accomplishments, and schooling to the entire class. Then, organize students into small groups where they will report to one another. When students have completed the small group reporting, have a discussion with the entire class about how this new information might change their future possible self-descriptions. Allow time at the end of the period for students to record their thoughts and reactions in the Personal Reflections section of the Student Notebook.

Lesson 24

Purpose of the lesson:

- *Introduce the concept of a discrepancy analysis.*
- *Have students begin the formal process of constructing a discrepancy analysis.*

Begin the session by introducing the concept of a discrepancy analysis. Remind students that, to get where they want to go, they will have to acquire certain skills and accomplish certain things. Point out that they may already have some of these skills and may have achieved some of the requirements.

Next, explain what the term *discrepancy* means. According to the dictionary, a *discrepancy* is "a difference or inconsistency." No doubt, there will be some discrepancies between the experiences, accomplishments, and schooling required for students to accomplish their goals and the experiences, accomplishments, and schooling that they have already attained. Explain that one of the most powerful things they can do when identifying discrepancies is to be specific. Illustrate the point through a brief discussion about the discrepancies in your own future possible self-description.

Next, inform students that they will each perform a discrepancy analysis on themselves, and refer them to Student Activity Sheet 12 in the Student Notebook (depicted in Figure 6.3).

To demonstrate how the matrix should be filled out, provide one that you have completed for yourself. Walk them through your process of identifying discrepancies and determining how to alleviate them. Invite and address questions from students, then provide time to work on their own discrepancy analyses.

Lesson 25

Purpose of the lesson:

- *Provide students additional time to work on their discrepancy analyses.*

- *Provide students additional practice in developing comprehension skills.*

Begin the session by reading another story from Chapter 8. Have students answer the comprehension questions, and go over the answers. You might also wish to review the comprehension strategy with students at this point. Next, revisit the previous day's discussion regarding the discrepancy analysis and invite questions and insights from students. Discuss the discrepancies in the life of the person in the story, and explore how this person was able to

Figure 6.3 Student Activity Sheet 12

What experiences, accomplishments, and schooling will I need to become my future possible self?	What is my current status in this area?	What can I do now?	What will I have to do in the future?
1.			
2.			
3.			
4.			

overcome the differences. Allow the rest of the period for students to work on their discrepancy analyses.

Lesson 26

Purpose of the lesson:

- *Provide students with an opportunity to report on their discrepancy analyses.*
- *Provide students additional practice in solving academic problems or in engaging in problem solving, decision making, or imagery and memory skill activities.*

Briefly review the importance of a discrepancy analysis. Use your own discrepancy analysis to get things started, then invite volunteer students to share theirs with the whole class. Next, break the class into small groups to complete the activity and allow the rest of the students to share.

If there is additional time, present academic problems (see Chapter 10), practice activities for general problem solving (see Chapter 10), practice activities for decision making (see Chapter 10), or an imagery technique (see Chapter 4).

Lesson 27

Purpose of the lesson:

- *Introduce the concept of planning backwards.*
- *Provide students additional practice in solving academic problems, in general problem solving, decision making, or imagery and memory skills.*

Introduce the concept of planning backwards by revealing that students now have all the information necessary to develop a plan of action. Specifically, they have:

- identified something they are passionate about;

- identified a circle of support;
- identified a hero, role model, or mentor;
- created their future possible self-description;
- identified necessary experiences, accomplishments, and schooling; and
- completed a discrepancy analysis.

Explain that they can now begin to create a plan to achieve their personal goals, and point out that the most effective way to approach this is to plan backwards from their future possible self-descriptions. Illustrate with the following example from Todd's story:

> *Age 26, 1995: Earn my Navy wings*
>
> *Age 23, 1992: Complete primary flight school*
>
> *Age 22, 1991: Graduate from Officer Candidate School in the top of my class and get accepted into primary flight school*
>
> *Age 21, August 1990: Get accepted into the U.S. Navy's Officer Candidate School*
>
> *Age 21, June 1990: Graduate from the University of Colorado with a high GPA*
>
> *Age 20, 1989: Earn my private pilot's license*
>
> *Age 19, 1987: Transfer to the University of Colorado's engineering school*
>
> *Age 18, 1986: Apply for and get accepted to the state college*

Have students turn to Student Activity Sheet 13 (illustrated by Figure 6.4 on page 78), and explain that they will use this format to begin the process of planning backwards.

If time permits, present more academic problems (Chapter 10), general problem-solving practice activities (Chapter 10), decision-making practice activities (Chapter 10), or memory strategies (Chapter 4).

Lesson 28

Purpose of the lesson:

- *Provide students practice in developing comprehension skills.*
- *Provide students with time to begin planning backwards from their future possible selves.*

Begin with another story from Chapter 8. Have students answer the comprehension questions and go over the answers with them. Review the concept of planning backwards, and discuss how the person in the story might have planned backwards to accomplish his or her personal goal.

Explain that one of the key aspects of planning backwards is to estimate how much time it will take to accomplish certain things. Have students turn to Student Activity Sheet 13 in their Notebooks (depicted in Figure 6.4), and complete it using your own discrepancy analysis to illustrate.

Explain that the entry in the top row of the matrix should be the year of their future possible self-descriptions. The entry in the bottom row is the current date, and what they are doing now. The primary task is to fill in the rows below the top one with specific activities, accomplishments, and dates. Emphasize the fact that, as they begin to plan backwards, they might have to adjust their future possible self-descriptions (particularly in terms of when they might reach their goals). If you have a personal example of this fact, relate it to students. Invite questions to make sure that they are clear about the task. Then allow the rest of the period for the students to plan backwards.

Lesson 29

Purpose of the lesson:

- *Introduce students to the critical thinking and reasoning skill of analyzing errors.*
- *Provide students with an opportunity to work on their backward planning.*

Begin the session by explaining to students that sometimes, when they are trying to accomplish a goal, their thinking can become clouded and contain errors. These errors can lead them to make decisions that may impede progress toward their personal goals. They may even find that their heroes, role models, or mentors have errors in their thinking and, therefore, the advice they give may be based on faulty thinking. Help

Figure 6.4 Student Activity Sheet 13

Date	My future possible self-description becomes a reality
Date	Event
Date	Event
Date	Event
Date	Event
Today	

students understand that they should consciously look for errors in their own thinking and the thinking of others.

Present the steps in the process for analyzing errors described in Chapter 4 (listed in Blackline Master L1, which can be duplicated and presented to students). Explain and exemplify each step. Next, tell students that in order to use this process well, it is necessary to learn about common errors that people make. As they become aware of common errors in thinking, they can determine if they are falling prey to any of these mistakes.

Present Blackline Master L2, which depicts four categories of errors in thinking. Select one category and provide some examples of the kinds of errors that fall within that category. Once students have a sense of these types of errors, present some of the practice activities from Chapter 10. Explain to students that, as they continue to work on their personal projects, they should analyze their own thinking and the thinking of others to determine whether they are making any of these mistakes.

For the rest of the period, allow time for students to work on backwards planning.

Lesson 30

Purpose of the lesson:

- *Introduce more types of errors in thinking.*
- *Provide students additional time to plan backwards.*

Present more types of errors in thinking using Blackline Master L2 (from Chapter 11). Discuss and exemplify selected errors, and then give students some practice activities from Chapter 10.

For the rest of the period have students work on backwards planning.

Lesson 31

Purpose of the lesson:

- *Introduce students to the concept of deductive thinking.*
- *Provide students time to plan backwards.*

Present students with the concept of deductive thinking. Help them understand that we all use deductive reasoning every day when we apply a general situation to a new situation. Provide specific examples of when we reason deductively.

Explain that deductive reasoning, applied rigorously, employs logic that uses premises to form conclusions. Provide several examples of categorical syllogisms so students understand the component parts and see how the premises lead to a conclusion. Provide some practice analyzing categorical syllogisms using the exercises in Chapter 10.

Allow the rest of the period to work on backwards planning.

Lesson 32

Purpose of the lesson:

- *Provide students with the opportunity to report on their backwards planning.*

Begin with a review of the critical aspects of backwards planning. Invite students to share their backwards plans with the entire class. Then, have students spend some time writing what they have learned in the Personal Reflections section of their Student Notebooks.

Next, organize students into small groups to share what they have learned. When the small groups are complete, construct any general statements that can be made about backwards planning as a whole class.

Lesson 33

Purpose of the lesson:

- *Introduce students to the concept of making declarations about themselves.*

Explain to students that, in this phase of the personal project, they will make a personal statement or declaration about their goal. Help them to see that this is more than just sharing a prediction about what they want to accomplish. Rather, it is like making a promise to themselves and to others that they will continue to move forward to accomplish a personal goal. By making their declaration to other people, they ask these people to help hold them accountable for what they have said they will do. In a sense, declarations are a means of creating an additional support system. Point out that they are now prepared to make these declarations, since they have a goal and a plan in mind. Reinforce the importance of declarations through some relevant quotations (see Chapter 9).

Next, have them use Student Activity Sheet 14 to record some possible declarations and identify to whom they will make them. Then, invite students to make their declarations to the entire class and encourage them to make their declarations to the other people they have identified as soon as possible.

Congratulate students on completing Phase Five of their personal projects, and have them write what they have learned in the Personal Reflections section of their Student Notebooks.

Lesson 34

Purpose of the lesson:

- *Introduce students to the concept of taking small steps toward their goal.*

- *Provide students with practice in developing comprehension skills.*

Begin by reading another story from Chapter 8 and answering the comprehension questions. Point out that the person in the story did not accomplish his or her goal immediately; rather, he or she had to take "small steps." Provide some quotations from Chapter 9 as well as some examples of the importance of small steps from your own life. Next, provide time for students to identify a small step they will take relative to their goal using Activity Sheet 15 from their Notebooks. If necessary, organize students into small groups to brainstorm ideas.

Then, give each student a copy of Blackline Master M (which is a duplicate of Activity Sheet 15) to fill out with the same information, and an envelope to self-address. Have them place their completed forms (Blackline Master M) in the envelopes and seal them. Collect the envelopes, and explain that you will mail them back to the students exactly four weeks from this date. At that time, they will have a chance to see how much progress they have made in their small steps.

If time permits, provide students with additional practice in analyzing deductive conclusions by completing additional exercises in the categorical syllogism section of Chapter 10.

Lesson 35

Purpose of the lesson:

- *Introduce the concept of the Inner Game of Success.*

- *Introduce the concept of inner dialogue.*

- *Provide students with practice in analyzing deductive conclusions.*

Begin the lesson by presenting students with the concept that we constantly engage in an "inner game." Remind them of the earlier discussion in which they learned that we think in words and in images. Help them see that their inner games are related to the words, or inner dialogue, they engage in. That is, we often talk to ourselves as we think. The words we use in this dialogue can either help lead us to success or keep us from being successful.

Help students understand that they can control their inner thinking if they want to, and that the purpose of the next few lessons is to help them become more aware of their own inner games and the effect they have. If they become more aware of this dynamic, they can determine which parts of their inner dialogue they wish to continue and enhance, and which parts they want to stop and replace.

To help students understand this concept, provide some examples from your own life.

Next, have students complete the questions in Blackline Master N. They are:

- What are some things I say to myself about my future possible self that make me feel like working harder?

- What are some of the negative things I say to myself about my future possible self that make me want to quit?

- How can I change my negative inner dialogue?

While students are answering these questions, answer them for yourself. Then, ask for volunteers to share their answers with the class.

Provide some time for students to write in the Personal Reflections section of their Notebooks, then organize them into small groups to share their reflections about inner dialogue. Next, regroup as a whole class to identify and discuss some generalizations. Tell students that, in the next couple of lessons, they will learn some strategies to help them develop a successful "inner game."

During the remainder of the session, work on deductive reasoning practice activities found in Chapter 10.

Lesson 36

Purpose of the lesson:

- *Provide students practice in developing comprehension skills.*

- *Introduce students to the concept of the power of effort.*

Begin the session with another story from Chapter 8 and have students answer the comprehension questions. Discuss the tendency for people to explain success as a matter of talent versus a matter of effort. Help them see that, by telling themselves they need to try harder and also by picturing themselves doing it, they combine the use of inner dialogue with the power of mental imagery.

Next, ask students to identify an event or events when they tried hard in the face of adversity, and an event or events when they gave up. They might spend a few moments writing in the Personal Reflections section of their Notebooks to help recall these events.

Then, have students fill out Blackline Master O which is depicted in Figure 6.5 on p. 82.

Explain that the purpose of this activity is to identify a profile of the inner dialogue, bodily sensations, and mental pictures they have when they are willing to put a great deal of effort into a situation. When students have completed Blackline Master O, have them share their responses and awareness in small groups.

During the remainder of the period, present more deductive reasoning exercises from Chapter 10.

Lesson 37

Purpose of the lesson:

- *Introduce students to the concept of power thinking.*

- *Provide students additional time to work on their small steps.*

Revisit the discussion about the importance of effort. Explain that some people consciously make themselves think in a way that stimulates their effort. This is sometimes referred to as optimistic thinking. Provide quotations about optimism or optimistic thinking from Chapter 9.

Explain that the process of power thinking will help them become optimistic thinkers, and give them Blackline Master P (which contains the steps in the power thinking process). There are a number steps in this process you may wish to go over with students, including:

- The importance of Step One in developing a mental set for challenging tasks.

- The importance of setting explicit goals and monitoring progress toward them.

- The importance of identifying what we did well and what we did not do well, and then putting an incident behind us.

Engage students in a conversation about the relationship between the power thinking process and the small steps in their personal projects. When students have a basic understanding of the power thinking process, challenge them to use it the next time they are faced with a difficult task. Explain that you will provide an opportunity to report on their progress in a few days.

During the remainder of the period, provide time to work on their small steps.

Lesson 38

Purpose of the lesson:

- *Provide students practice in developing comprehension skills.*

- *Provide students with practice in analyzing deductive conclusions.*

Figure 6.5 Blackline Master O

When I Try Hard		When I Don't Try Hard	
What I say to myself		*What I say to myself*	
My mental picture		*My mental picture*	
My physical sensations		*My physical sensations*	
My emotions		*My emotions*	

Begin the session with a story from Chapter 8. Have students answer the comprehension questions, and go over the answers with them.

For the remainder of the period, practice analyzing deductive conclusions using exercises from Chapter 10.

Lesson 39

Purpose of the lesson:

- *Introduce students to the concept of re-evaluation, or changing one's plans.*
- *Provide students with more practice in solving academic problems.*

Begin the session with quotations from Chapter 9 about the legitimacy of changing or re-evaluating plans. Help students understand that, even with the best of plans, we often find that we need to re-evaluate what we are doing once we have started. This might be because some unexpected things have happened (e.g., a small step took longer than anticipated, additional steps emerged that had not been previously considered). Emphasize this point by providing examples of times in your life when you had to change your plans, or even your goals.

Have students return to Student Activity Sheet 9 to review the descriptions of their future possible selves. Point out that they wrote those a number of weeks ago and, since then, they have learned some new information that might change their descriptions. Also, have students re-read their backward plans (Student Activity Sheet 13) to see whether they still apply. Next, direct their attention to Student Activity Sheet 16 and have them record any changes they would like to make in their plans. When they have completed this, break into small groups and to discuss the changes they have made.

If time permits, do some more academic problems from Chapter 10.

Lesson 40

Purpose of the lesson:

- *Introduce students to the concept of an aphorism.*
- *Provide students with more practice in solving academic problems.*

Explain that you will ask students to design an aphorism, which is a "short saying embodying a truth or astute observation." Point out that, throughout the personal project, you have been providing aphorisms from other people in the form of inspirational quotes. Discuss the impact that these quotes may have had thus far. You may wish to ask students to review the quotation section of their Notebooks and select certain quotes that were meaningful to them personally.

Help students understand that aphorisms are statements that "come from the heart"—statements people make because something has affected them profoundly. Explain that their aphorism should be a reflection of what they have observed or some truth that they have come to understand.

Direct students to Student Activity Sheet 17 in their Notebooks, which asks them to create four aphorisms. Explain that they don't necessarily have to create four aphorisms, but they should try to generate at least two. Allow students some time to work individually or in small groups and then engage them in more academic problems from Chapter 10.

Lesson 41

Purpose of the lesson:

- *Examine the impact of the power of thinking process.*
- *Provide students additional time to work on their aphorisms.*
- *Provide students additional time to work on other essential skills.*

Review the power thinking process (Blackline Master P). Remind students that they were to try the process upon encountering a challenging task. Ask for volunteers to report on their findings, and then have a discussion with students about the importance of controlling their thinking.

Allow time for students to work on their aphorisms.

Also, provide time to engage in more exercises and activities involving one or more of the following:

- Deductive thinking
- Errors in thinking
- Academic problems
- General problem solving
- Decision making
- Memory techniques

Lesson 42

Purpose of the lesson:

- *Provide students with time to work on their aphorisms.*
- *Provide students additional time to work on essential skills.*

Allow time for students to work on their aphorisms and to engage in more exercises and activities involving one or more of the following:

- Deductive thinking
- Errors in thinking
- Academic problems
- General problem solving
- Decision making
- Memory techniques

Lesson 43

Purpose of the lesson:

- *Provide students the opportunity to share their aphorisms.*
- *Provide students additional time to work on essential skills.*

Organize students into small groups and ask them to share their aphorisms with each other. Then, as a whole class, discuss the effect that sharing aphorisms had on them personally, and the effect that it might have had on other students in the class. Help students see that when aphorisms are expressed, they can be meaningful to others. Ensure that students make the connection between their aphorisms and the inspirational quotes that have been used throughout the personal project.

Also, provide time to engage in more exercises and activities involving one or more of the following:

- Deductive thinking
- Errors in thinking
- Academic problems
- General problem solving
- Decision making
- Memory techniques

Lesson 44

Purpose of the lesson:

- *Allow students time to evaluate themselves on the skills addressed during the Pathfinder Project.*
- *Provide students additional time to work on essential skills.*

Review the various categories of knowledge and skill that have been addressed throughout the Pathfinder Project.

If you have been providing systematic feedback on these categories using the rubrics in Chapter 5, have students construct a "summary score" or "final score" for each element evaluated. Otherwise, have them complete Student Activity Sheet 18 in their Notebooks (which represents a much more general evaluation).

Have a conference with each student during which you review their self-evaluations and compare them with yours. While you are conferencing with individual students, allow the remainder of the class to read another story or engage in activities and exercises involving:

- Deductive thinking
- Errors in thinking
- Academic problems
- General problem solving
- Decision making
- Memory techniques

Lesson 45

Purpose of the lesson:

- *Provide opportunities for students to complete their self-evaluations.*
- *Celebrate the completion of the Pathfinder Project.*

Continue conferencing with students about their evaluations.

While you are conferencing with individual students, allow the remainder of the class to read another story or engage in activities and exercises involving:

- Deductive thinking
- Errors in thinking
- Academic problems
- General problem solving
- Decision making
- Memory techniques

End the period with a celebration of success!

A Three- to Four-Week Course

If you wish to present the Pathfinder Project in a shorter format, perhaps three to four weeks, it is probably best to address the seven phases of the personal project as described in Chapter 3, along with selected stories and quotes as described in Chapter 2. The sequence of presentation for these aspects would be the same as depicted in the nine-week course; however, less time can be allowed for each aspect.

A Semester-Long Course

The Pathfinder Project fits quite nicely into a semester-long course. In addition to allowing more time between the seven phases of the personal project, you can include the following supplemental activities:

Movies

There are a number of feature-length movies that can be used to exemplify various aspects of the Pathfinder Project. Of course, permission should be obtained from parents before movies are used, and only movies with appropriate ratings should be shown.

A list of movies you might consider follows. *Again, we caution that parental permission should be obtained before any movies are shown.* Also, students' maturity level must be carefully considered when selecting fims.

1. Brian's Song

This movie is about Chicago Bears' football players Brian Piccolo and Gale Sayers. Roommates and rivals, these two rookies soon become best friends because of their competitive natures and complementary personalities. When Piccolo is stricken with cancer, Sayers is inspired to reach his athletic potential, eventually becoming one of the best running backs ever to play in the National Football League.

2. Ghandi

This movie is a panoramic look of the life of Mohandas K. Gandhi, who introduced the doctrine of nonviolent resistance to the colonized people of India. Gandhi's unwavering commitment to nonviolent resistance enlists millions of native Indians and ultimately wins India its freedom from British rule.

3. Glory

This film draws from the letters of Robert Gould Shaw, the 25-year-old son of Boston abolitionists. Shaw volunteered to command the 54th Regiment of the Massachusetts Volunteer Infantry, comprised totally of African-American men, during the Civil War. Their training and battle experience leads them to a final assault on Fort Wagner in South Carolina, where their heroic bravery turned bitter defeat into a symbolic victory, bringing recognition to black soldiers and turning the tide of the war.

4. Hoosiers

This movie tells the true story of the Hickory Huskers, an underdog basketball team from a tiny Indiana high school with 64 students. Even though the team and its new coach have a rough start, they eventually make it to the state championship game where they beat a team from a high school with an enrollment of 1,500.

5. It's a Wonderful Life

George Bailey grows up in the small town of Bedford Falls, dreaming dreams of adventure and travel, but circumstances conspire to keep him enslaved to his home turf. Frustrated by his life and haunted by an impending scandal, George prepares to commit suicide on Christmas Eve. A heavenly messenger arrives to show him a vision: what the world would have been like if George had never been born.

6. Mr. Holland's Opus

Mr. Holland is an aspiring composer and musician. He takes a job teaching music at a local high school to save money while he composes his music. But when his wife becomes pregnant, Glenn Holland must put aside his dreams. Over the course of his life, he learns the importance of teaching and contributing to others.

7. October Sky

This true story about Homer H. Hickam, Jr., begins in 1957 with Russia's historic launch of the *Sputnik* satellite. While Homer sees Sputnik as his cue to pursue a fascination with rocketry, his father casts fear and disdain on Homer's pursuit of science. Homer eventually wins a prestigious science competition and ends up working for NASA as an engineer.

8. Places in the Heart

Places in the Heart is a look at life in Depression era Texas. Recently-widowed Edna Spalding struggles and fights to keep her family together by raising cotton. She enlists the help of a drifter named Mose who knows the ins and outs of growing cotton. Because Mose is black, the locals make it rough on them. She perfectly conveys the determination of a woman facing tremendous odds. She simultaneously shows a strong front and a touching vulnerability while facing setback after setback.

9. Remember the Titans

Set in Alexandria, Virginia, in 1971, this fact-based story begins with the integration of black and white students at T. C. Williams High School. The integration effort is most keenly felt on the school's football team, the Titans, where bigoted tempers flare when a black head coach is appointed and his victorious predecessor reluctantly stays on as his assistant. The players represent a hotbed of racial tension, but the players ultimately become a championship team and life-long friends.

10. The Rookie

The Rookie is about Jimmy Morris, who has boyhood dreams of playing major league baseball. However, he incurs an injury that seems to end his dream, so he becomes a high school science teacher and baseball coach in a small, rural Texas town. His high school players marvel at his ability when they observe him pitching batting practice, and encourage their 35-year-old coach to give professional baseball a second try—a recommendation he does not take seriously. However, when he challenges his team to begin winning, they turn his challenge into a bet: if they win, he will again try out for professional baseball. The high school team does win, and Jimmy Morris must keep his end of the deal by trying out for professional baseball. To his amazement, he is signed to a professional contract and within a matter of months is a major league relief pitcher.

11. Rudy

Rudy Ruettiger is a blue-collar kid. His father worships Notre Dame football, but would never dare to dream that any of his sons could be a part of the team. The film is about Ruettiger's ceaseless commitment toward that goal, despite tremendous obstacles in the form of physical stature, educational requirements, dismissive coaches, poverty, his father's envy, and endless delays. This film conveys the message that the battle is its own reward.

12. Stand and Deliver

Based on a true story, this inspiring movie features a high school teacher who motivates a class of East L.A. barrio kids to care enough about mathematics to pass an advanced placement calculus test. The film concerns itself with assumptions and biases held by mainstream authorities about disadvantaged kids, and the teacher's efforts to keep his students coolheaded enough to prove the "experts" wrong.

13. To Kill a Mockingbird

Atticus Finch, the small-town Alabama lawyer and widowed father of two, gives an impassioned defense of a black man wrongfully accused of the rape and assault of a young white woman. While his children, Scout and Jem, learn the realities of racial prejudice and irrational hatred, they also learn to overcome their fear of the unknown as personified by their mysterious, mostly unseen neighbor Boo Radley.

Guest Lecturers and Field Trips

Guest lecturers quite naturally fit into the Pathfinder Project. Specifically, as students identify their heroes, role models, and mentors, they might contact individuals who are willing to speak to the class. These individuals might also have access to facilities and resources directly related to the personal projects of individual students.

A Language Arts Course

The Pathfinder Project can be offered as a traditional language arts course that focuses on writing. Such a course would closely align with Macrorie's I-Search approach to teaching composition (Macrorie, 1988). In describing his approach, Macrorie notes:

> For many decades high schools and colleges have fostered the 'research paper' which has become an exercise in badly done bibliography, often an introduction to the art of plagiarism, and a triumph of meaninglessness—for both writer and reader. (Macrorie, 1988, p. 4)

Macrorie's alternative to the research paper is the I-Search paper. As Macrorie explains:

> Teachers around the country and I have been challenging students to do what we call I-Searches—not Re-Searches, in which the job is to search again what someone has already searched—but original searches in which persons scratch an itch they feel, one so marvelously itchy that they begin rubbing a finger tip against it and the rubbing feels so good that they dig in with a fingernail. A search to fulfill a need, not that the teacher has imagined for them, but one they feel themselves. (Macrorie, 1988, p. 14)

One of the critical features of the I-Search paper is that, instead of selecting a topic, students are encouraged to have the topic select them. While he uses different terminology, Macrorie is essentially telling students to identify a topic about which they are passionate. Interestingly, many of the examples of I-Search papers Macrorie presents are written by students exploring possible futures for themselves.

Macrorie's approach is particularly strong in providing guidance to collect information from direct interviews, which corresponds nicely with the identification of heroes, role models, and mentors in the personal project.

In short, there are a number of writing assignments within the personal project that can be used as the basis for a composition course in the genre of Macrorie's approach to composition.

An After School Program

The Pathfinder Project can be presented as after school program of varying duration ranging from three weeks to a full semester. The sequence of events for these venues would follow the descriptions above.

A Home Study Course With Parents

Even though the descriptions and directions in this chapter assume that the Pathfinder Project will be presented in the context of a course or program offered in school under the direction of a teacher, it can also be used in the home by parents and children. In such cases, the parent or parents take on the role of the teacher following the directions and discussion provided for teachers. It is strongly recommended that parents participate directly with their children by engaging in a personal project of their own. Additionally, parents and children should do the practice activities and exercises together discussing answers, confusions and insights.

CHAPTER 7
THE STUDENT NOTEBOOK

As described throughout the previous six chapters, the Student Notebook is an integral part of the Pathfinder Project. It contains four sections which are briefly described here. These sections are entitled: 1) Stories, 2) My Personal Project, 3) Quotations, and 4) Personal Reflections.

Stories

The first section of the Student Notebook contains the same inspirational stories found in Chapter 8 of this manual. As described in Chapter 2 of this manual, students read these stories throughout the Pathfinder Project. As they do so, they are asked literal, inferential, and self-analysis questions. Chapter 8 of this manual provides you, the teacher, with a number of each type of question for each story. You may select those you find the most appropriate and useful for your students. The Student Notebook does not contain the questions. Rather, it simply contains blank lines where students record their responses to the selected questions you ask.

My Personal Project

The second section, entitled My Personal Project, is the heart of the Student Notebook. As described in Chapter 3 of this Manual, the personal project contains seven phases each of which involves one or more specific activities. This section of the Student Notebook contains the 18 numbered Student Activity Sheets that correspond to the activities in each phase. The activities for each phase are as follows:

Phase One: Identifying a Personal Goal to Pursue

Student Activity Sheet 1: Overcoming Fear of Failure

Student Activity Sheet 2: Breaking from Patterns of the Past

Student Activity Sheet 3: Identifying a Future Accomplishment or Goal

Phase Two: Eliciting Support

Student Activity Sheet 4: Identifying a Circle of Support

Student Activity Sheet 5: Identifying Heroes, Role Models, and Mentors

Student Activity Sheet 6: Learning about Your Hero, Role Model, or Mentor

Student Activity Sheet 7: Constructing the Winner's Profile

Student Activity Sheet 8: Understanding the Nature of Support

Phase Three: Gathering Information about the Goal

Student Activity Sheet 9: Identifying Your Future Possible Self

Student Activity Sheet 10: Articulating Necessary Experiences and Accomplishments

Student Activity Sheet 11: Articulating Necessary Schooling

Phase Four: Discerning Discrepancies between Current and Future Self

Student Activity Sheet 12: Completing a Discrepancy Analysis

Phase Five: Creating a Plan

Student Activity Sheet 13: Planning Backwards

Student Activity Sheet 14: Making Declarations

Phase Six: Moving into Action

Student Activity Sheet 15: Taking Small Steps

Phase Seven: Evaluating the Effectiveness of Your Actions

Student Activity Sheet 16: Re-evaluating Plans

Student Activity Sheet 17: Creating Aphorisms

Student Activity Sheet 18: Evaluating Success

Quotations

The quotations section of the Student Notebook is a place where students record quotations that are personally meaningful to them. As quotations are systematically presented to students throughout the Pathfinder Project, students select those that strike them as related to their projects and their lives, record these quotations, and explain why they are personally meaningful. Finally, when students are asked to create aphorisms of their own during Phase Seven on Student Activity Sheet 17 of the personal project, they use the quotations recorded in their Notebooks as a reference.

Personal Reflections

The Personal Reflections section of the Student Notebook is the place where students record the insights, awarenesses, and questions that arise as they progress in their personal projects and other activities. Students may write in the Personal Reflections section at the urging of their teacher and at their own discretion. In effect, this section of the Student Notebook serves as a personal journal.

CHAPTER 8
INSPIRATIONAL STORIES

This chapter contains 13 stories to be used throughout the Pathfinder Project, as described in Chapter 6. Chapter 2 describes how comprehension skills might be taught and reinforced while using the stories.

Nine questions follow each story: three literal comprehension questions, three inferential comprehension questions, and three self-analysis questions. The Student Notebook (described in Chapter 7) includes all 13 stories, along with spaces to answer the questions. However, the questions themselves are not provided. This allows you, the teacher, to select the questions you wish to use, or you can even add questions of your own design.

The questions you select or design should be written on the whiteboard and read to students. When identifying the number and type of questions to use, consider factors such as the amount of time you wish to spend on the questions, the complexity of the questions, your students' level of interest and maturity, and so on.

When students have had adequate time to write the answers to the questions in their Student Notebooks, discuss the answers they have constructed and the reasoning behind these answers.

The 13 stories in this chapter are presented in a recommended sequence. However, this sequence is only a recommendation—feel free to change the order to meet your needs.

Todd Marzano

*I*n high school, Todd Marzano wasn't the worst of students, but he wasn't the best either. He earned As in metal shop and physical education, but only Cs and an occasional B in other classes. Todd's real passion was top-fuel dragsters, racecars that could go from zero to over 200 miles per hour in a matter of seconds. He spent lots of time at the speedway watching them race, and daydreamed about someday being on the crew of a national champion dragster—or maybe even driving one.

In the middle of his junior year of high school, Todd announced that he wasn't going to college. "What's the point?" he said. "I don't really like school, but I do like working on cars. I'll be a mechanic. I'll like what I do and I'll make good money. Maybe someday I'll get to work on a racecar." It was a perfectly logical plan.

A perfectly logical plan that changed the day he went to see the movie *Top Gun*. The film was about a Navy fighter pilot who was selected to go to an elite school—Top Gun—where only the "best of the best" were admitted. It had great scenes filmed from the cockpit of a real F-14. Todd was mesmerized as he watched. Flying a jet fighter at over 1,000 miles per hour made racing a car—even a top-fuel dragster—look tame.

Top Gun changed Todd's daydreams. Instead of imagining himself as a racecar driver, he began to see himself as a Navy fighter pilot. "What a life that must be," he thought, "flying off an aircraft carrier in a supersonic jet. What would it be like to do that?"

For a while he didn't dare tell anyone. But finally at dinner one night, he mentioned to his father and stepmother that he had been thinking about becoming a pilot. As soon as the words were out of his mouth, he wanted to take them back. He was embarrassed that he had said anything to anyone. To his surprise, however, his parents actually encouraged him. "Give it a try," they said. "You can do it." That night, for the first time, Todd began to think seriously about the possibility of becoming a fighter pilot. If someone else thought it was possible, maybe it really was. What would it take?

Todd soon discovered that his first challenge would be academic. He found out that the Navy wanted people with engineering degrees, and to earn one, he would have to get into a very good college. Both were big steps. Nonetheless, he set his sights on one of the best engineering programs in the country at the University of Colorado at Boulder. Because he lacked certain prerequisite courses, Todd couldn't get into CU right away. He could, however, get into an open-enrollment college in Denver. Then, if his grades were good enough, he'd be eligible to transfer after a few years.

During his time at the college in Denver, Todd found out everything he could about the academic and physical requirements for the Navy's pilot training program. On the physical side, one big obstacle was his vision. Todd's eyesight was decent, but the Navy required perfect 20/20. So Todd came up with a plan. He saved his money and purchased an eye exercise program to improve his vision. Though it was physically uncomfortable to do the exercises, Todd never missed a session and actually improved his eyesight beyond the Navy's requirement. On the academic side, Todd approached his classes with a totally different attitude than he had in high school. He threw himself into his work, studied diligently, and managed his time to the minute. After two years of college in Denver, he had done so well that he applied to and was accepted by the University of Colorado at Boulder's engineering school—exactly what he had hoped for.

Four years later he graduated with honors, earning a degree in aerospace engineering. Along the way he was inducted into a highly prestigious engineering honor society *and* earned his private pilot's license, receiving a score of 100 on the Federal Aviation examination—a feat that surprised even his instructor.

Todd was one of only about a half dozen candidates from Colorado accepted into the U.S. Navy's Aviator Officer Candidate School, or AOCS, the first step in becoming a fighter pilot.

When Todd left Colorado to attend AOCS in Pensacola, Florida, he knew he would face great obstacles. About 50% of the young men and women accepted into the program dropped out within the first two months, and many others were asked to leave. He promised himself only one thing: that he would not give up, no matter what happened. They could kick him out, but he would never quit.

As a result, Todd put 100% of his effort into everything he was required to do. Nothing could dampen his resolve. Not the long hours in the classroom, not the intense physical training that left him exhausted, not the fatigue he felt from sleeping just six hours per night. He wasn't deterred by the drill instructor's constant yelling or the fact that he missed his home and family some 2,000 miles away. His determination paid off. He graduated from AOCS as one of the top officer candidates and was commissioned into the Navy as an ensign.

The next step was flight school in Corpus Christi, Texas, where the biggest decision about his future would be made. Not all Navy pilots were asked to fly jets. In fact, to fly jets, Todd would have to finish in the top 20% of his class during the first phase of flight school, called Primary Flight School. The other 80% of the pilots would be assigned to fly propeller aircraft or helicopters. Though they were neat aircraft, Todd had joined the Navy to fly jets; that was his goal.

During Primary Flight School, Todd had his share of discouraging days—days when he just couldn't try any harder, days when he wondered if he really was good enough. But he stuck to his plan, determined to give 100% to everything, no matter what happened. Again, his persistence paid off. He not only finished in the top 20% of his class, but at the *very top* of his class.

Todd was assigned to fly jets. He packed his bags and left for training in Meridian, Mississippi.

The first day Todd flew a jet fighter was like a dream. He had a hard time believing that he was actually in the cockpit of a multimillion-dollar airplane. It was even better than he had imagined. He could fly upside down, or point the nose of the plane straight up and fly right through a cloud. But what he liked most was flying low to the ground—500 feet off the ground—at 500 miles per hour. At that speed and altitude, trees were nothing but a green blur.

After a year of instruction, Todd was ready for the most challenging test faced by new Navy fighter pilots: landing on an aircraft carrier (a special type of ship designed expressly for this purpose). Todd knew that sometimes even pilots who had performed extremely well up to that point in their training still couldn't master the art of landing a jet on the back of a ship. The carrier's "runway" was only 300 feet long, and the jets came in at 150 miles per hour. It seemed impossible.

The big day came and Todd flew his jet out to sea, 100 miles off the coast of San Diego. As he prepared for this last and most difficult test, Todd thought about just how far he had come. He wasn't watching a movie about a Navy fighter pilot; he *was* a Navy fighter pilot—almost.

He lined his plane up behind the carrier. He was amazed at how small the carrier looked and how quickly he was coming down—2,000 feet, 1,000, 500, 300—he knew the eyes of every sailor on the ship were on him, and he knew that he had no margin for error. Four feet too high or too low, and he would fail. In another instant, he was just off the water, and then—blam—he felt the hook at the back of his plane catch one of the four cables at the back of the ship, just the way he'd been taught. His plane went from 150 miles per hour to zero in less than two seconds, jarring every bone in his body. And he had done it. He had passed the final test.

In the next phase of Todd's career, he experienced more than he had ever hoped for. After receiving his Navy wings of gold, he was assigned to fly a $36-million F/A-18, the newest jet in the Navy. He served on board the USS Kitty Hawk, the USS Carl Vinson, the USS Stenis, and was engaged in combat in the Persian Gulf and Afghanistan. But the greatest thrill of his life was still to come.

Because of his superb record as a fighter pilot, Todd was one of only a handful of outstanding pilots selected to go to Top Gun school for additional special training. In September of 1999, Todd graduated from the school that takes only "the best of the best." The movie he had seen, the dreams he had dreamed, had become his life.

(Story by Shae Isaacs)

Literal Comprehension Questions:

1. What are some of the major events that lead Todd to become a Navy fighter pilot?

2. What did Todd do to ensure that his eyesight was good enough to be accepted by the Navy?

3. Describe the process involved in landing an airplane on an aircraft carrier.

Inferential Comprehension Questions:

1. What do you think might have been one of Todd's lowest or scariest moments in his efforts to become a fighter pilot? Explain your thinking.

2. From Todd's perspective, what do you think was his greatest triumph? Explain your thinking.

3. Why do you think the movie *Top Gun* was so inspirational to Todd? Explain your thinking.

Self-Analysis Questions:

1. Imagine that you are Todd, and you know that you have to get into and graduate from a good college to even be considered for the Navy's flight school. But, at age 17, you don't have the necessary grades to get into college or the money to pay for college once you are accepted. What are some of the ways you might consider solving this problem?

2. Todd was inspired by the movie *Top Gun* about a Navy fighter pilot. What movie has inspired you and made you dream of things you might be able to accomplish? What are some of the things the movie has made you think of doing? What is there about the movie that has inspired you?

3. At first, Todd was afraid to tell anyone about his dream to be a Navy fighter pilot. What are some dreams you have that you are reluctant to tell anyone about? Why do you think you are hesitant to share these dreams?

Jeanette Mitchell

At the end of every school year, Jeanette Mitchell's class would take a field trip to a popular amusement park in St. Louis, Missouri, and every year, Jeanette and the other black children would spend the entire day waiting outside with a nun. "Black children were not allowed into Forest Park Highlands," Jeanette recalls. "I remember hiding in the bushes and thinking 'I don't want to be this color.'"

Growing up in the 1950s, Jeanette was aware that other people were defining her by her skin color. The prejudice of the day ran deep and, though Jeanette didn't like it, it carved deep into her self-esteem. Yet something in Jeanette kept fighting and eventually won. In the course of her lifetime, she has overcome others' false images and proven herself to be a highly-accomplished professional and community leader.

"My mother was the one who implanted in me the idea that there is always a way." Janie Reed instilled in all six of her children the importance of education, even though she herself had not finished high school. "My mother was the crossing-guard, the neighborhood babysitter, and the daycare worker—always helping us to better our lives," says Jeanette. Not surprisingly, it was her mother who enrolled Jeanette in the well-respected Catholic school system, starting in second grade.

Jeanette's Catholic high school, Rosati-Kain, was a very good school. However, as a product of the times, it was not immune to subtle and not-so-subtle forms of racism. "I remember once wearing a brand new sweater my mother had bought me," says Jeanette. "Another girl—a white girl—had misplaced hers and the nuns accused me of stealing it! I was pulled out of class and sent to the principal's office. They called my mother and she straightened them out, but nobody ever apologized to me."

Despite the prejudice she saw around her, Jeanette tried to stand up for herself and for what she believed was right—like the time the high school administration decided to make the seniors wear their school uniforms an extra month. "It wasn't fair and we staged a walkout," says Jeanette. "Later, when they asked me if I had been part of it, some of the girls denied it, but I owned up." It was this kind of inner strength that would help Jeanette become a leader.

After graduating from high school, Jeanette moved to Milwaukee. Soon after, she enlisted in the Army, hoping it would help her get the education she desired. She was based in the Deep South—Fort Anniston, Alabama—where prejudice against blacks was even greater than in St. Louis. In Anniston, department stores had special back door entrances for blacks and restaurants hung signs that said, "WHITES ONLY."

"I was at the Woolworth's food counter one day with my platoon, both black and white," says Jeanette, "but the waitress wouldn't serve the black members. Our white friends refused to pay until she did." Even so, the blacks were forced to eat at the end of the counter.

It wasn't easy to fight against such outrageous humiliation. Once, while waiting for a train, a white man spit on the ground in front of Jeanette, simply because she asked him what time it was. "At that point I almost gave in; I almost decided just to accept myself as inferior."

Jeanette's military career and her plans for further education were cut short by her decision to get married. She left the Army and the South and settled with her husband in Chicago. By age 23, Jeanette had three children and moved back to Milwaukee. Parenting sidelined her plans for getting an education, but not the necessity of earning a living. So Jeanette got a job with the phone company—Wisconsin Bell.

Though her marriage didn't work out, her career blossomed. Determined to provide well for her children, Jeanette moved from being an operator, to a clerk, to a service representative. "At the time, it was the highest paid job for women in the phone company."

During her early years at Wisconsin Bell, Jeanette had several important mentors. Their encouragement, her own hard work, and a new openness to blacks in the workplace as a result of the Civil Rights movement allowed her to move up the corporate ladder. In time, she was encouraged to become a manager. "I was a little skeptical. I wondered if I was being promoted because now it was fashionable to promote blacks," says Jeanette. But her mentors assured her of her competence and convinced her it was the right move. Slowly, Jeanette's confidence grew. She began seeing her face in company advertisements and brochures. "I started to recognize that I could achieve in a business environment and pave the way for other blacks."

After many years of working and raising children, Jeanette had the opportunity to fulfill an old, but not forgotten, dream when a weekend program opened at Alverno College. "I was the kind of person who watched college classes on television and actually sent in the homework," she recalls. After watching her sister attend Alverno for one year and nervously wondering if she could do it too, Jeanette enrolled, attending classes on Friday nights and all day Saturday and Sunday. She was 36 years old.

"Alverno was the best thing that ever happened to me," says Jeanette. At Alverno, Jeanette began to develop a sense of purpose and a personal identity—not an identity defined by others. It was a time of tremendous personal growth. "For four years these questions were always in front of us: Who are you? What's meaningful for you? What's fun? How are you going to contribute to your community?"

In 1982, Jeanette and her three children all graduated, the kids from high school and Jeanette from Alverno with a degree in business.

The little girl who once had hidden in the bushes outside the amusement park feeling helpless was about to take on the town.

"After college, I began to think about power and about how things got done in my city," says Jeanette. I became fascinated with politics and civic issues." Supported by a program called Future Milwaukee, Jeanette began to hone her leadership skills. "I interviewed one of our City councilmen and thought, 'I think I could do that job.'" She decided that someday she would run for office.

Six months later, "someday" arrived. A position on the local school board opened up. "It combined all my interests—education, kids, and politics."

The area she would serve was 85 percent white. "I was told a black person could not win. At one point I was advised to leave my photo off my campaign materials, which I didn't." Instead, Jeanette went door-to-door, making connections with her constituents and building her credibility. People listened to her and liked her. "I won. Not by a lot of votes, but I won," she says.

Jeanette served on the school board for eight years, including three years as president. She credits two of the board members for helping her develop her leadership skills. "I learned what it really takes to make something happen in the community."

Throughout her years on the school board, Jeanette continued to work for the phone company, which supported her school board involvement and also sponsored her to complete an executive MBA program at the University of Wisconsin, Milwaukee. "It was a training reserved for those on track toward being a vice-president," she says proudly. By now Jeanette was a district manager, the highest-ranking black woman in the company.

But the company was shifting. As part of the federal break-up of the phone company, Wisconsin Bell was one of five smaller phone companies absorbed into the regional giant, Ameritech, headquartered in Chicago. Jeanette realized that the telephone company's values were shifting as it underwent reorganization. Her own heightened awareness of equity issues, after years of community service and her school board tenure, made Jeanette question what others at Ameritech accepted. "I began to wonder why there weren't more blacks and women in top-level positions."

In 1994, after 30 years of service, Jeanette retired from the phone company and took a position as a program officer for a local foundation. "I got to give money to good causes; it was the best job ever."

Later, she completed a doctorate in Leadership at Cardinal Stritch University, which then offered her her current job: Executive Director of the Cardinal Stritch University Leadership Center. Now, on a daily basis, she helps bring concepts of leadership, learning, and service to nonprofit organizations, businesses, and educators, and helps them look for ways to make a difference in the community.

Jeanette Mitchell has learned the importance of knowing who you are, even when others don't see it or try to tell you otherwise. "I want to tell people—especially young people—that they don't need to let other people define them. Deep inside, everyone knows who they truly are and what his or her mission is in life. It's important to figure out who you are and to live and work true to that. And always keep in mind that education and learning really do open doors."

(Story by Shae Isaacs)

Literal Comprehension Questions:

1. What strong belief did Jeanette's mother instill in her?

2. Why was Alverno College the best thing that ever happened to Jeanette?

3. Why was Jeanette so excited about the position on the school board?

Inferential Comprehension Questions:

1. Growing up, Jeanette faced a great deal of racial prejudice. However, something within her made her keep fighting. What do think it was that made her react this way? Where do you think this strength came from? Explain your thinking.

2. Why do you think the nuns at Jeanette's high school assumed that she had stolen the missing sweater? Explain your thinking.

3. When Jeanette was promoted to the position of manager at the phone company, she wondered whether she was being promoted because it was "fashionable to promote blacks." What do you think Jeanette meant by this? Explain your thinking.

Self-Analysis Questions:

1. As a child Jeanette remembers thinking that she "didn't want to be this color." What is something about you that you wish were different? How do you think your life would change if you were different?

2. How do you think you would have reacted to the prejudice Jeanette faced as a girl? Why do you think you would have reacted this way?

3. At Alverno College the following questions were always in front of Jeanette: Who are you? What's meaningful for you? What's fun? How are you going to contribute to your community? How would you answer these questions for yourself?

Coach Shawn

The new head coach of the boys' basketball team stood in front of a gym full of players and parents and talked about his goals for the season. "Winning is important, but it isn't everything," said the coach. "What really makes a difference in your life is being a good person first, and a dedicated student second. Basketball, while fun and important, comes third."

The team—50 young men in all—listened carefully. Their new coach had begun playing basketball at this very school. He'd gone on to play Division I basketball in college, done a brief stint in the NBA, and then played pro ball in the international leagues for six years. They had seen some of his game films and admired his graceful and powerful moves on the court. They couldn't help believing that if this determined young African-American man could succeed, maybe they could, too.

And nobody believed it more than Coach Shawn. At age 11, Shawn had written that he wanted to travel and see the world—a goal that seemed far away and unattainable because his parents had divorced and his mom was struggling to support her three kids. Shawn felt pretty invisible in his family, and wasn't an outstanding athlete at that point either. In fact, he wasn't an outstanding anything. He wasn't a great singer, a stellar student, or a super popular kid in school. He was sickly, skinny, and angry. Shawn was afraid not only that he wasn't special, but that he wasn't going to be anybody at all.

So what turned his life around? Two things: a mentor who believed in him and supported him, and the confidence and strength that came from his own hard work and determination.

Shawn's mentor, Kate, came into his life when he was 13 years old. "That meeting turned out to be life changing for me," says Shawn. "I needed someone on my team, and I needed that person right away. My grades weren't good, I had lots of absences at school, I had broken my hand in a fit of rage, and I had pending court dates for some run-ins with the law."

Kate, a neighbor, noticed that Shawn seemed lost and sad. She thought she might be able to help him with his school work now and then. But it soon became apparent that Shawn needed more than an occasional meeting to work on spelling or math. As one crisis after another occurred in his family, Kate became the one adult Shawn could always count on. At the time, Kate had no idea how important her support would turn out to be for Shawn; nor did she realize how knowing Shawn would change her own life. "I just knew that if he didn't get support, he might be lost," recalls Kate. Over time, Kate took on a parental role with Shawn, providing love, support, food, clothing, and shelter.

"If Kate hadn't come along, I would have ended up in prison or dead," Shawn says. "She helped me imagine a future that would be worth sticking around for."

Kate made a point of introducing Shawn to successful, independent, and happy people—men and women of all races—to give him positive role models. When Shawn took an interest in art and drafting, Kate bought him his first drafting board. When he began venting his frustration by punching things, Kate bought him a punching bag. When he began developing an interest in basketball, she bought him his first pair of real basketball shoes. At one point, Kate even transformed her living room into a mini-gym, replacing its pristine white wicker furniture with a basketball hoop so Shawn could practice the moves of the NBA stars he admired.

After several visits to doctors and dentists, Shawn's malnutrition and dental problems improved. He began to grow stronger physically. With regular sleep and attention to homework, Shawn's grades and attendance improved, too. Kate and Shawn spent some time in court dealing with past incidents and putting them to rest. They read books together about Nelson Mandela, Harriet Tubman, and Dr. Martin Luther King, Jr., black heroes whose lives illustrated the importance of integrity, of being a trustworthy person, of keeping commitments, and of doing the right thing. With Kate's coaching, Shawn began to change his attitude and to gradually create a dream for his future.

By the time he was 14, Shawn had developed a real interest in basketball. Kate encouraged him and drove him across town daily so he could play ball with other young black men his age. "Most of them had been playing since they were in grade school or even earlier. I felt like I was playing catch up," Shawn explains. "I wasn't the tallest, the strongest, or the fastest, but I was determined to get better." The harder he worked, the stronger, smarter, and faster he became.

As a sophomore, Shawn made the junior varsity squad and, as a result, found himself spending even more time on the court practicing. He watched and learned from the varsity players, and soon was asked to suit up for varsity games as well.

His junior year, Shawn changed high schools. The coach at his new school was a caring, strong, and knowledgeable man who helped Shawn develop his skills both on and off the court. A great role model, Shawn's new coach inspired him to think about becoming a high school teacher and coach himself.

That same year Kate insisted that Shawn take his ACTs and SATs early, even though he didn't want to, so he'd have time for additional study and re-tests if necessary. "I was mad at Kate for making me take the tests then," recalls Shawn. "I couldn't understand what the big deal was; nobody on my team was taking their ACTs and SATs that year." But taking the tests early turned out to be key. Shawn realized he had to focus more seriously on his studies and, fortunately, he had the time. His improved grades and second round test scores gave him a real edge when college scouts came to check out future players at his school. "I learned that, while basketball skills are important, scouts are looking for players who also have good attitudes, are highly coachable, and are good students," says Shawn. "The scouts know that basketball skills alone are not enough to make a successful college player. They know that you have to have the grades and study skills to keep you in school and on the team."

After considering a variety of offers, Shawn chose an in-state junior college to start his college career. The smaller setting made a comfortable transition from high school to college. His college coach demanded hard work and self-discipline from his players, and Shawn grew as a result. He became a real student of his game and a diligent student in class as well, earning the best grades of his life. He began to make life choices that were "right" though not necessarily "easy."

His junior year, Shawn transferred to a Division I university. "I was happy to be on the team, but I struggled at first," Shawn said. "I finally realized that it was my own attitude that was keeping me from getting the playing time I so desperately wanted. And I knew that only I could change my attitude." When he did, the transformation was remarkable. Shawn became a significant force on the team, both as a player and a team leader. "My skills and confidence grew. I was strong and smart on the court, and I enjoyed playing again," Shawn says.

After college, Shawn played briefly with the NBA, but soon found himself playing professional basketball in the international leagues. "I was fortunate to be able to enjoy a six-year pro career that took me to 25 countries on five continents. I got a firsthand look at the world that most people only dream of. I spent time on the magnificent Great Wall of China, and I felt the sadness of a concentration camp in Germany. Through my travels, I met people with a wide variety of cultures and histories," Shawn says. "My view of the world and its people changed forever."

It was a gift. One for which he'd worked hard.

After six years abroad, Shawn decided it was time to head home. There were other dreams he wanted to fulfill. He knew the value of having a mentor, and he wanted to share his skills and experiences with other young people. "I wanted to coach and teach, so I was excited to learn that the school where I first played basketball was looking for a new boys' head basketball coach. I was thrilled when I got the job. It's been hard but rewarding work ever since. Both coaching and teaching require every bit of energy, patience, and creativity I have. But I wouldn't trade it for the world."

And what about Shawn's mentor? Kate couldn't be more proud. "It's a joy to watch Shawn work so hard with his students and players," Kate said. "He cares about them, he wants them to succeed, and he knows that he can play a powerful role in their growth."

Shawn credits Kate for giving him needed support, direction, and inspiration. That, coupled with his own hard work and determination, changed Shawn's life.

"I was very fortunate to meet Kate when I did and to have her guidance over the years," says Shawn. "Because I know from my own experience how much difference a mentor can make, I'm now willing to spend my time and effort helping other young kids coming up. A kid gains so much from a dedicated mentor, but I would tell adults who are considering mentoring that they will get back even more from inspiring a young person to be their best.

"Kids who are out there hoping for a mentor, should realize that the person who can help them may be very different from them. Kate is white, grew up in a small town, and works in a corporate environment. On the surface, she didn't seem like someone who could teach me about basketball or how to grow up to be a man of integrity and character. But she was just the person I needed. So don't wait for your favorite sports star to be your mentor. Look around at the people you know, the ones you respect, trust, and admire, and those who have your best interests at heart. Then let them know that you'd appreciate some of their time and advice. I think you'll be pleasantly surprised at their reaction. But remember, once someone agrees to help you, you have to be sure that you're doing your part to help yourself. Listen to what your mentor says, follow up on their advice, and work hard. Show them—and yourself—you're worth their time and effort. You are."

(Story by Shae Isaacs)

Literal Comprehension Questions:

1. Why did Kate buy Shawn a punching bag?

2. What was the outcome of Shawn's taking the SAT and the ACT?

3. What qualities does Shawn recommend you look for in a mentor?

Inferential Comprehension Questions:

1. Why do you think Shawn didn't realize that he was interested in basketball until he was 14? Explain your thinking.

2. Why do you think Kate took such a strong interest in Shawn? Explain your thinking.

3. What do you think it means that Shawn became a "real student of the game of basketball?" Explain your thinking.

Self-Analysis Questions:

1. Kate supported Shawn even though it seemed like there was nothing for her to gain. Who is there in your life who supports you this way? Why do you think they do this?

2. When you are an adult you might someday return to your school, just like Shawn did. What are some things you think you might tell the students at your school? Why would you tell them these things?

3. When Shawn first started playing organized basketball at age 14, he felt like he was playing "catch up" because the other young men had started at much younger ages. Where in your life do you feel you are playing catch up? Why do you think you feel this way?

Joan Mazak

*O*n a sweltering August morning, a six-foot tall yellow chicken waddled up to the Mazak family's suburban townhouse and rang the doorbell.

"Is Jennifer home?" it asked when Joan Mazak opened the door.

The "KIMN Chicken," as it was known around town, was a local radio mascot. Actually a man dressed up in a chicken costume, the KIMN Chicken's normal duties included showing up at ribbon cuttings, shopping mall openings, football games, and other public places to promote the station. But today the KIMN Chicken was doing something a bit out of the ordinary; he was visiting a very sick little girl—Joan Mazak's eight-year-old daughter, Jennifer—who had made a special request to meet him.

"It was the highlight of her life," recalls Joan. "The KIMN Chicken hung out with Jennifer all day. They walked around the neighborhood. All the other kids wanted to touch him but he would only let Jennifer. He was her special friend, and that made her so proud. When he left, he gave her a little stuffed chicken, which she hung onto until she died."

Sadly, Jennifer did die, three weeks later. But the visit by the KIMN Chicken, which brought her such unexpected pleasure, inspired Jennifer's parents and a group of their friends to launch the Make-A-Wish Foundation of Colorado, an organization that grants wishes to children suffering from life-threatening or terminal illnesses.

A divorced mother of two girls, Joan Mazak's life revolved around the care of her oldest daughter, Jennifer, who had been born with biliary atresia, a serious liver condition. Because she had to devote most of her day to Jennifer, Joan had long since given up any thoughts of having a career. At the drop of a hat, Joan may have to rush her daughter to the hospital. That meant the car always had to be filled with gas, the refrigerator always had to be filled with food, and there always had to be a place lined up where Joan could drop off her other daughter in case she had to remain at the hospital with Jennifer. It was a hectic and emotionally-draining existence.

By the time she was eight years old, little Jennifer had been hospitalized 84 times and undergone 17 surgeries. While they prolonged her life, the surgeries reached the limit of their effectiveness. The only hope was a liver transplant. In 1982, that process was experimental, expensive, and political. "You had to fly to Philadelphia just to qualify," says Joan. "If you did, they sent you home with instructions to raise a quarter of a million dollars and to find a Lear jet you could borrow in the event a donor was found." And finding a donor was like finding a needle in a haystack.

Joan's parents moved in to help her, which freed Joan to take a part-time job in the evening tending bar at a local hotel. She'd care for Jennifer all day, run to the hotel at 4:00, work until 8:00, and run back home. "It was easy money," says Joan. And she was meeting people. Although she didn't know it at the time, a number of her co-workers would later end up helping her start Make-A-Wish.

When the media learned of Jennifer's need for an immediate transplant, they jumped on the story. The publicity from radio and television stories raised both awareness in the community, and money. Donations poured in and Lear jets appeared. A friend asked Joan what Jennifer would like if she could have any wish in the world, and they came up with the idea of a visit from the KIMN Chicken.

But in spite of the outpouring of goodwill, Jennifer's little body gave out before the Mazak family could reach its goal of obtaining a liver donor. She died on September 10, 1982.

Understandably devastated, Joan survived this low period in her life by taking one day at a time. When she could focus again, she began thinking about the nearly $50,000 that had been raised for Jennifer's liver. What should she do with the money?

A few months earlier, she and Jennifer had watched a show on television about a small company in Phoenix that granted wishes for terminally ill children. "We both thought it was kind of neat," recalls Joan. Now Joan wondered if she could start something similar in Denver with the unused funds. She talked with her ex-husband, Jennifer's father (with whom she had an amicable relationship). She also tossed the idea around with her pals at the hotel.

Her friends encouraged Joan to contact the original, and at the time the *only*, Make-A-Wish Foundation in Phoenix. With the organization's blessing, Joan hired a lawyer to draw up the necessary papers and bylaws for a non-profit organization. She made several people from the hotel the Foundation's first Board of Directors—a waiter, the maitre de, an accountant, an administrative assistant, and a salesperson. Joan became President and her ex-husband, Vice President. Thus, the Make-A-Wish Foundation of Colorado was born. "I thought we'd put in about one day of work a month, maybe grant two or three wishes a year, and that our original funds would probably last us a lifetime," laughs Joan.

Initially, Joan and her partners took their time getting publicity, afraid that two or three wish requests might come in at once and they wouldn't know what to do. Their first wish was a fish wish.

"There was a little boy who was dying of cancer, and all he wanted to do was catch a fish," recalls Joan. As chief wish-granter, it was Joan's job to coordinate the wish. She got everybody to pitch in. The Public Service Company donated $10,000 and a helicopter to fly the boy and his family from the town of Bennett to Lake Dillon. The Bennett Fire Department drove the boy to the helicopter in their fire truck, with sirens blaring. The warden at Lake Dillon stocked the lake so full of fish there was no way the little boy would not catch one. Still, it was her first assignment and Joan and was nervous. "I was so worried it might not work that I wanted to hire a scuba diver to go down and put a fish on his hook," recalls Joan. But it worked just fine, and in the end the boy caught several fish. "That's all he wanted," says Joan.

In the early years of Make-A-Wish, Joan worked from her home. When a wish came in, she'd scramble to get it together as quickly as possible. Still deeply saddened by the loss of her own daughter, Joan found that focusing on making someone else happy took her mind off her own troubles. The Foundation granted all kinds of wishes, from visits to Paris to visits with grandma, from new bedroom furniture to new entertainment centers, even trips to Disney World!

When she wasn't busy coordinating wishes, Joan was learning the ins and outs of running a non-profit organization. "I learned mostly by making mistakes," she says. One of her most memorable mistakes occurred just after Make-A-Wish had moved into its first office, five years after its creation. The so-called office amounted to a closet-sized space with a donated copier that worked sporadically, a card table, two chairs, and a telephone. The Board had just voted to officially hire Joan and to pay her a small salary, which meant she could quit bartending and focus all of her energy on the Foundation.

"One day we got a call from a group of little old ladies who had held a bake sale and wanted to donate the proceeds to Make-A-Wish," says Joan. "They insisted I drive across town and have my picture taken with them. I figured the donation would be about $20.00, so I tried to convince them just to mail it to me. After a while they got kind of ticked off and decided to drive to her office themselves. They told me to *be sure* to have a camera ready. When they got there, they handed me a check for $18,000!"

"That was my very first lesson with donors, a lesson I've never forgotten," says Joan. "Now I never say 'no' to meeting with anyone."

Having an office helped the young Foundation show the community that it wasn't just a fly-by-night venture. So did the inception of the Make-A-Wish parent company. Ever since the Phoenix Make-A-Wish was profiled on television, people like Joan had been inspired to start similar organizations in their own states. Now they joined forces, and Joan was asked to be one of the founding members of the national board.

"Rubbing shoulders with Rhoades scholars and other bright people on the national board, many of whom had a lot more education than I did and knew a lot about running non-profits, really built my self-esteem. It made me feel important, sometimes too important," she admits. "One of my personal lessons has been that even when you're enjoying success and doing good work, it's important to keep things in perspective."

Though Joan has been in the wish-granting business now for over 20 years, she's still surprised when people come to her for advice on starting and running a successful non-profit. "I didn't have a formal education in this field," says Joan, "and I spent the first ten years wondering if I could really do it. But I was very lucky and I never gave up. So that's the advice I give: Hang in there! Every time I had a question I went to the library or found someone to ask. You can, too. And today, with the Internet, there are even more ways to learn on the job. Don't give up."

It's funny. Sometimes the worst thing in your life can lead to the best thing in your life. That's what Joan Mazak says about Make-A-Wish. She still identifies with grieving parents and is reminded of Jennifer each time she meets a sick child. But she cautions parents not to forget the other *living* children in their family. "It's easy to do when you are wrapped up in your own sadness and the suffering of one child. Actually, everyone in the family is going through a tough time."

Today, Make-A-Wish Foundations across the country grant some 11,000 wishes for sick children and their immediate families each year. Nearly 200 are granted by the Denver chapter, where Joan now works with a staff of ten. "When we started Make-A-Wish, there was no such thing as an organization dedicated to making people happy," says Joan. "We changed that."

(Story by Shae Isaacs)

Literal Comprehension Questions:

1. Who were some of the people on the first Board of Directors for the Make-A-Wish Foundation of Colorado?

2. Where did Joan get the money to start the Make-A-Wish Foundation of Colorado?

3. What was the first wish that came in to the Make-A-Wish Foundation of Colorado, and how was it granted?

Inferential Comprehension Questions:

1. How do you think Jennifer Mazak felt about her visit from the KIMN Chicken? Explain your thinking.

2. What do you think is meant by the statement, "Finding a donor was like finding a needle in a haystack?" Explain your thinking.

3. What do you think made Joan happy about fulfilling people's wishes? What parts of fulfilling people's wishes might have made Joan sad? Explain your thinking.

Self-Analysis Questions:

1. Joan said that sometimes the worst thing in your life can lead to the best thing in you life. What is something negative in your life that has lead to something positive? How did this happen?

2. For a long time, Joan was so upset by the death of her daughter that she could not concentrate on anything else. This is a natural and understandable reaction to a tragedy. What has happened in your life that made it difficult for you to concentrate on anything else? How does it make you feel to realize that your reactions are natural and understandable?

3. The Make-A-Wish Foundation is about granting wishes. If you could grant a wish to someone, who would it be and what wish would you grant? Why did you pick this particular person and this particular wish?

Allor Ajing

The thugs in Sudan who kidnapped Allor Ajing when he was 14 couldn't have cared less about his future. "They got on the bus, waving guns and shouting," says Allor. "They made the women and the old men get off. I thought about my mother, my younger brothers, and my sister. I was afraid they would kill me and my family would be left alone."

Allor's country, Sudan, in northeastern Africa, has been embroiled in civil war since before Allor was born. "It's a tough life," says Allor. "There are no jobs and few opportunities for smart kids." The Sudanese government is a military dictatorship led by the National Islamic Front, a fundamentalist religious group. Military service is required, and rounding up men by kidnapping is a relatively routine military procedure.

Allor and the other men "recruited" on the bus that day were taken to a government-run military training camp in Khartoum, the capital city. Their heads were shaved and they were put through rigorous physical training. "We did pushups until we cried with pain, but if you stopped they would beat you or starve you. Other times we were forced to stand outside and stare at the sun for hours," recalls Allor.

It didn't take long for Allor to begin dreaming about running away, although he knew it would mean risking his life. Worse, he would be putting his family in serious danger.

Escape wasn't the only thing Allor dreamed about. He also dreamed of finding his father, who had fled Sudan because he was wanted by the government. Allor's father had instilled in him the importance of education. "My father taught me that the way to improve yourself and help others was through education. He told me stories about my great-grandfather who had been a king in south Sudan and had helped many people. I wanted an education."

After two months in the camp, Allor and four other young men decided to attempt an escape. On a night when the camp leaders were meeting, Allor and his friends scaled a fence in darkness and ran to a nearby road. They secretly hopped on the back of bus traveling toward Khartoum, hoping the driver hadn't spotted them. "We couldn't ride the bus the normal way because if the driver figured out what we were doing, he would just drive us back to the camp—and collect a reward from the government."

Allor was able to get to his home city of Omdurman and visit his mother, although they both knew he couldn't stay. His safety was far from certain, and his journey had only begun. As they feared, military officials showed up in Omdurman shortly after the escape and interrogated Allor's mother in an effort to discover his whereabouts. They beat her and even sliced off a piece of her ear, but she refused to talk.

Although it took time working odd jobs where nobody knew him, Allor eventually earned enough money to acquire a passport and take the train to Aswan, Egypt, and later a ship up the Red Sea to the capital city of Cairo. His memories of arriving in Cairo aren't pleasant. "I will never forget the bad smells," he says. "There was trash piled high, the bathrooms were filthy, and many people did not clean their teeth. It made me sick to my stomach."

By now, Allor was 16 years old which, by American standards, is still very young (barely old enough for a driver's license and maybe a first job). But Allor's life experiences made him seem much older. He still dreamed of a better life, of freedom, and of making something of himself through education.

In Cairo, Allor met up with other refugees from South Sudan who helped him locate his father. Together, they came up with a plan to get the rest of the family out of Sudan. It worked! The family was reunited.

But living in Egypt was far from ideal. "Every day we would worry what was going to happen," says Allor. "There was so much prejudice. We weren't liked or welcomed. People called us terrible names, and other kids would splash my clean clothes with nasty water." Allor says he drew strength during this time from his religious faith, and through the Sudanese church his family joined. "I thought about Moses and the years he spent living in Egypt before he led the Israelites to freedom," he recalls. "It was tough."

Allor enrolled in Egyptian schools, which required him to pay a higher tuition because he was Sudanese. To afford school, Allor had to work. And to work, he had to learn Egyptian Arabic, which was quite different from his native Sudanese Arabic. But Allor did what he had to do, because he was determined to stay in school.

In situations like the one Allor's family faced, where it is too dangerous to return home, refugees can apply to live legally in other countries. It's a lengthy process with no guarantees, but it was a chance Allor's family decided to take. Not long after they had been reunited in Egypt, they decided to apply as refugees to live in the United States of America.

The application process involved formal interviews with U.S. officials where family members retold their harrowing stories. Allor had to recount why he escaped from Sudan, how he ended up in Egypt, and why he wanted to go to America. In spite of the fact that the interviews were friendly, Allor and his family worried almost constantly. What if they were not accepted? What would become of them? It was nearly a year before they received the good news.

On August 25, 2000, Allor and his family arrived in Denver, Colorado, in the United States of America. "We were so happy," Allor recalls. "It was one of the greatest days of our lives. I was so tired from the trip, but I still woke up early and just looked outside at the houses. We were free."

Once in the United States, Allor immediately enrolled in 11th grade at Wheat Ridge High School. He was 17 years old. "At first everybody stared at me," he says. "But then they started asking questions. What's your name? Where are you from?"

Still, it was a while before Allor could keep up his end of the conversation. "I had studied British English in fifth grade in Sudan," he says, "but not like I would ever have to speak it." All that English sounded like wind blowing in one ear and out the other. Unsure of this new language, Allor said very little at first. "I didn't want to use the wrong words and embarrass myself." His guidance counselor helped him get started in English classes for second language learners and, after a few weeks, he decided the best way to learn to speak American English was to hang out with his new friends and try talking the way they did. It was. In his spare time, Allor practiced reading. Later he worked as a newspaper delivery person and at an automobile emissions testing station, which also helped improve his English.

In May 2002, Allor achieved a dream that he had held close since his days as a young boy in Sudan: he graduated from high school. That fall, he began classes at a local community college. He intends to transfer to a four-year university, and possibly pursue a degree in mechanical engineering. He hopes someday to design cars, but for now, his focus is simple. "I want to finish school and do the best I can," says Allor.

Someday, if it's ever peaceful, Allor says he may visit Sudan. But he's not in a hurry. "I like it here," he says, flashing a broad smile. His advice to other young people? "Listen to your parents. Remember: you can accomplish whatever you want; don't put failure in your mind. But finish school for sure. School is everything."

(Story by Leticia Steffen)

Literal Comprehension Questions:

1. Why did Allor and his four friends who were trying to escape from the army ride on the back of the bus?

2. Why did Allor's father flee from Sudan?

3. Why was Allor tentative when he first started to use English at Wheat Ridge High School?

Inferential Comprehension Questions:

1. What are some ways Allor at age 16 was different from the typical 16-year-old in the United States? Explain your thinking.

2. Why do you think there was a great deal of prejudice in Egypt against the Sudanese? Explain your thinking.

3. Why to you think Allor believed so strongly in getting an education? Explain your thinking.

Self-Analysis Questions:

1. How would you have reacted to the way Allor was treated in the military? Why do you think you would have reacted this way? What does this tell you about yourself?

2. The United States was a refuge for Allor and his family. A refuge is a place that provides safety and opportunity. Sometimes a refuge is a place; sometimes it can be a person. What place or what person do you consider to be a refuge in your life? Why?

3. If you were Allor and were giving advice to other kids, what would you say to them? Why would you give this advice?

Polly Baca

*T*he first time Polly Baca realized her family was "different" she was in church. It was a lovely spring day when the Baca family arrived at the small church in Greeley, Colorado. Outside, several young girls in pretty white dresses prepared to march into the flower-filled sanctuary. Three-year-old Polly was enchanted. She urged her parents to take a seat in the center section so she could stand on the kneeler for the best view. But no sooner had they sat down than an usher rushed over and quickly moved the family to a more "appropriate" spot: a side pew, with a limited view, with the other Mexican and Mexican American families.

At the time, few of the parishioners in that small northern Colorado church would have questioned the usher's actions. Prejudice against people with Mexican blood, many of whom had lived in the area for generations, ran deep. No Mexican, least of all a girl, could ever amount to much; everybody knew that. But Polly Baca would prove them wrong. Dead wrong. In the course of her long and fascinating career, Polly would be a State Senator, work in the White House—twice, and make extraordinary political and civic contributions for women, Hispanics, and other minority communities.

This is her story….

Jose Manuel Baca was just a boy when his family lost its farm near Roy, New Mexico. To survive, they became migrant farm workers, moving from farm to farm, caring for and harvesting sugar beets, potatoes, and onions. They performed backbreaking labor, were paid next to nothing, and lived in miserable conditions. It was a rough life—so rough that only five of Jose Manuel's fourteen siblings lived into adulthood.

By the time Jose Manuel married, he had become a seasonal farm worker. This meant that he and his family lived in one place and worked the crops of a particular farm. In exchange, they received a small percentage of the farm's profits and were given housing, which were frequently tiny, dirt-floored shacks or poorly-built wooden firetraps. Jose and his wife, Leda, worked the fields and raised three daughters: Fernie, Polly, and Bettie.

As a young girl, Polly developed a strong personal faith that countered some of the pain of growing up amidst poverty and prejudice. "We only went to church on Sundays, but I talked to God all the time," says Polly. "I believed He wanted me to change the way people treated Mexican Americans by demonstrating, through my life, that we were bright and capable." Throughout the years, Polly would hold tight to the belief that this was her mission.

In grade school, Polly instinctively understood that if she worked hard and did her best every day, the future would somehow take care of itself. In high school, she resolved to get a college scholarship. Her parents encouraged her, even though some of their friends thought it was ridiculous to send a girl to college. "After all, they're just going to go off and get married. Why waste all that money?" said one of her parents' friends. But Polly's hard work and dedication paid off. During her senior year, she was awarded a full scholarship to any Colorado state-funded college.

Although Polly believed she had a mission—to change the way people treated Mexican Americans—she didn't have the first clue how to accomplish it.

Colorado State University in Fort Collins widened Polly's horizons, exposing her to new ideas and new people. A professor who observed her interest in politics encouraged her to change her major from physics to political science. It was a decision that opened many doors for Polly, beginning when she was 19 years old with an internship on the 1960 presidential campaign of young Democratic Senator John F. Kennedy. During the campaign, Polly had the opportunity to meet many of the Kennedy operatives who came through Colorado. One of them, Carlos McCormick, would connect Polly to her first job in the "big leagues."

After graduating from college, Polly tried without success to find a job in Colorado. She even considered becoming a nun, but knew she wouldn't be happy living a cloistered life. What to do, then? Without a clear destination, Polly decided to continue her education and began to study for a Masters degree in teaching, thinking that she would work hard and be ready when the first step of her "mission" presented itself.

Just a few months into her graduate school career, Carlos McCormick from the Kennedy campaign tracked Polly down. A friend of his had two positions open with a labor union in Washington, D.C., and was looking for bright, young college graduates to fill them. When she got the call asking her to interview for the position, Polly's first reaction was to say no. She found that she couldn't.

"I hung up the phone and started to sob. I didn't want to go. My housemother said that I didn't have to go if I didn't want to—but I knew that I did. This kind of opportunity did not present itself very often— *especially to young Mexican American women*."

Polly interviewed, was offered the job, and accepted it. In December of 1962, at age 21, she left Colorado for Washington D.C. She had never before been on a plane, train, or a ship. In fact, she had never traveled east of Cincinnati, Ohio, never eaten in a fancy restaurant, and didn't know a soul in the Nation's capital.

All that was about to change.

In the early years of her career in Washington, Polly worked nonstop, developing job skills that would serve her for years to come. She also witnessed key moments in history. When Martin Luther King delivered his famous "I Have a Dream" speech, Polly was there. Later, she was nearly injured in the riots that followed King's assassination. She attended the inauguration of President Lyndon Johnson after President Kennedy was assassinated in Dallas. Everywhere she went she met interesting people, including leaders in the budding farm workers' movement: Cesar Chavez, Dolores Huerta, and Luis Valdez. Their work connected Polly with her roots and reaffirmed her deepest desire: to help Mexican Americans in the Southwest.

After four and a half years with the labor movement, Polly moved to a position in the White House; however, she was soon convinced to go to work instead for the presidential campaign of Senator Robert F. Kennedy. On June 6, 1968, at the Ambassador Hotel in Los Angeles, she witnessed another historic moment. "I was not far from the senator when he was assassinated, which left an indelible mark on my emotional and mental psyche," Polly remembers. "It was the first time I truly recognized how fragile life is and how important it is to live in the present moment and to live each day to the fullest."

Saddened by the death of her hero and disillusioned with politics, Polly—now 27—decided to leave Washington. It wouldn't be the last time she made that decision.

After several weeks of traveling in Mexico and Central and South America, Polly was ready for the next phase of her work life. Her first stop back in the United States was the 1968 Democratic Convention in Chicago. Midway through the week-long convention, she participated in a peace demonstration. She decided to take a break and had just entered a hotel—and was thus, safe—seconds before the now infamous moment when the police charged the protesting crowd. The experience shook her, but at the same time helped her make an important decision: it was time to follow her heart. "I was convinced that I had to get focused on my original mission and try to change the way people treated each other."

Her idealism led her to a job with a small but committed group of Mexican American activists based in Phoenix who had recently founded the organization that eventually became the National Council of La Raza. The work of the NCLR was exciting and challenging. They were on the forefront of the Chicano movement and were involved in every Southwest regional activity aimed at helping Mexican Americans. "We were committed to the cause, loved what we were doing, and were convinced we would succeed despite the challenges we faced."

During the same period, Polly fell in love with one of her colleagues, Miguel. Their relationship raised eyebrows in the very Catholic, Mexican American community of the Southwest, because Miguel had once been a priest. To avoid scandal, Polly and Miguel kept their relationship, and later their marriage, a secret. But when Polly became pregnant, the marriage was impossible to deny. To make matters worse, the marriage was in trouble at this point. Polly and her husband separated, and she moved with their one-month-old baby back to Denver amid a barrage of rumors. "At the tender age of 30," she says, "my political epitaph had been written: no young Mexican woman could do what I had done and ever expect to survive politically."

But that was not to be Polly's reality. "That's when I learned that making mistakes and failing doesn't mean *you're* a failure. YOU are the ONLY person who can determine your success or failure," says Polly.

Family and friends remained loyal to her. Before long, colleagues in Washington offered Polly a contract job, advising her to bring her baby along. So Polly headed back to the East Coast with baby Monica in tow. "We made a bed for Monica in a file cabinet until someone brought in a baby carriage. When I had special meetings to attend, staff members would pitch in and look after her," says Polly.

With that contract completed, Polly was offered a special assignment for the Democratic National Committee that involved much travel in the Southwest, coupled with long hours in Washington. On one occasion, Polly was working late at DNC headquarters at the Watergate Office Building when she heard a strange noise in the hallway. "I went out to look, but no one was there," recalls Polly. "The next morning, our comptroller asked if I had seen or heard anything during the night. Someone had broken into the DNC offices and tried to get into the treasurer's file cabinet where the petty cash was kept. Only after a second break-in that later became known as *Watergate* did we realize that the first break-in was probably when the Watergate burglars placed telephone bugs in selected DNC phones."

No matter where Polly went that election year, she was never far from power plays and political intrigue. To survive, she had to learn how to make ethical decisions—to do the *right* thing, even when it wasn't the *easiest* thing. At times that meant turning down lucrative business offers or prestigious positions. It also meant coming to terms with her work and personal life, which were pulling her in two different directions.

After carefully weighing many options, Polly returned to Colorado. Her mother had been caring for Monica for several months, and Polly wanted to care for her child herself—and try to reconcile with her husband, Miguel.

It was a tough transition. Polly returned to Colorado without a job, yet she still felt strongly called to her mission. She began to think about running for public office, and eventually set her sights on becoming the Democratic nominee for State Representative. "When I said I was interested, I was reminded that there had never been a woman or a minority elected to a partisan office in the history of Adams County. I was determined to change that." And change that, she did. She won the election and became the only Mexican American woman in the country to win a seat in a State House in 1974.

The election propelled Polly into the national spotlight. At the time, she had no idea that someone would be sharing the spotlight with her in a very dramatic way.

Polly and Miguel had been trying to repair their marriage, and began living together again. Soon, Polly was expecting another baby. "It wasn't unique enough that I was the only Mexican American woman in the State Legislature," reflects Polly. "I had to be the first woman to be in legislative session *while* she was pregnant."

The legislative session lasted well beyond its typical April ending into May, and all the way through June. The legislature finally adjourned on July 1st at 6:00 p.m. Polly's son, Miguelito, was born the following afternoon.

Polly served four years as a State Representative, and then went on to serve eight years in the State Senate, its first minority woman member. During that time she also served as the Vice Chair of the Democratic National Committee.

Being a legislator and a single parent was challenging, but having a supportive mother helped enormously. During that time, Polly also searched for a church where she felt comfortable, and credits a wise Catholic priest for helping her reconnect with her religion. "Father Charles Chaput taught me that having a spiritual direction is important throughout your life in whatever you do."

But for each life there are many seasons, according to Polly. "And in 1986, my public life season was coming to an end." Her second term in the Colorado Senate was up, and she decided to run for the United States House of Representatives. Although she put forth an extraordinary effort, Polly lost the primary. It was a crushing defeat.

Exhausted and terribly disappointed, Polly knew from her own past experience that failing didn't mean *she* was a failure. Still, the defeat stung.

In time, Polly set about looking for work to renew her spirits. She found it in a rewarding job at the Colorado Hispanic Institute, where she developed a leadership program—*Visiones*—emphasizing multicultural understanding. "I began to recognize that if you love what you're doing, are helping others, and having fun, you'll succeed," says Polly.

In 1991, opportunity knocked once again on Polly's door. She accepted long-time friend, Hillary Clinton's, request to co-chair her husband's presidential campaign in Colorado. As a direct result of her work on the Clinton campaign, Polly was offered and accepted a position as Special Assistant to President Clinton for Consumer Affairs and Director of the U.S. Office of Consumer Affairs.

So it was back to live in Washington, D.C.—again.

But this move was different. Far away from friends and family, even with an exciting and meaningful job in Washington, Polly felt lonely. "Having reached the peak of my career, I discovered one of the most important lessons of my life," says Polly. "Having your loved ones close to you is essential to happiness."

After much soul searching, Polly returned once again to Colorado in 1994.

Back in Colorado, Polly has accepted one new challenge after another, working for multicultural understanding in a variety of roles. She has served as GSA Regional Administrator for the Rocky Mountain Region, worked as a private consultant, done volunteer work, and is currently the Executive Director of the Latin American Research and Service Agency (LARASA).

Polly credits a deepening spiritual life for helping her navigate increasingly complicated work and personal situations. Her advice to young people: "You are unique. There is no one else like you—so live your life to its fullest. Don't worry about the past—it's gone. Focus on doing your best *today*—at this moment in time. Then the future will take care of itself. "

(Story by Shae Isaacs)

Literal Comprehension Questions:

1. What event made Polly realize that her family was "different?"

2. What decision did Polly make in college that opened many doors for her?

3. What are some of the important moments in history that Polly witnessed?

Inferential Comprehension Questions:

1. Polly relied on her "spiritual life" to get her through many rough times. What do you think Polly meant by her spiritual life? Explain your thinking.

2. After Polly received the telephone call asking her to interview for the job in Washington, D.C., she sobbed. Why do you think she reacted this way? Explain your thinking.

3. What do you think Polly meant by the phrase, "You are the only one who can determine your success or failure?" Explain your thinking.

Self-Analysis Questions:

1. Polly was the first Mexican-American woman to do a number of things. What are some things that you would like to be the first person to do? Why would these accomplishments be important to you?

2. Polly believed that failing at something does not make you a failure. In fact, you can fail at a specific task and still learn a great deal from the situation. What have you failed at and learned a lot from? What did you learn?

3. Polly believed that she had a "mission" or "purpose" in life. Do you believe you have a mission or purpose in life? If so, what is it? If you don't believe in a mission or purpose, why not?

Paul Martin

Growing up in Massachusetts with a hot-tempered father, Paul Martin channeled his energy into hockey and other sports—when he wasn't busy getting in trouble. But it wasn't until he lost his lower left leg in a car accident, at age 25, that he took responsibility for his own happiness and began to discover his real potential as an athlete.

Paul's father, a union pipefitter, instilled both love and fear into his children, rarely hesitating to discipline with a quick smack to the head—and sometimes worse. Paul's adventurous nature and his tendency to act first and think later only added to the tensions that brewed in the Martin household. "At the time, I didn't think a lot about the consequences of my actions; if something sounded fun, I'd just do it."

But at 15, when he and some friends wrecked a car they had taken out for a joy ride, the lid blew off. Paul's dad punished him severely—too severely. "I loved my dad," says Paul, "but he was terrifying and somehow I knew I shouldn't be that scared of my own father."

Social Services agreed. At Paul's request, they allowed him to move into a foster home. Paul liked his foster mother. She was tough on him when necessary, but fair. Eventually, even his relationship with his father improved, though they limited their time together.

Paul had always enjoyed sports. He loved football. He'd been playing hockey since he was ten years old, and was an excellent high school player. In fact, Paul daydreamed about being a professional athlete. But daydream was all he did: he didn't set goals, make plans, or take any action to move his life in that direction.

After high school, Paul enrolled at the University of Lowell, where he felt that he didn't fit in. "At that point, I wasn't very interested in school," he says. With the hopes of becoming a pilot, he tried out the Air Force Reserve Officers Training Corps (ROTC). The day he was yelled at for having a wrinkled shirt—and yelled back—quickly ended his pre-military career. He quit college after three months.

Uncertain what to do with his future; Paul got a job as an ironworker. For the next two years he worked incredibly hard. It was tough physical labor and he learned a lot about himself, including how strong and resilient he was. The work ultimately inspired him to try college again. "I wanted to be able to have a job where, at the end of the day, my back and hands didn't ache."

With renewed purpose, Paul completed a degree in mechanical engineering, graduating in the top third of his class. He landed a job in sales with Lincoln Electric, a company that designed and sold welding equipment. But six months into a seven-month training program at Lincoln, he was in a serious car accident.

Following dinner with friends and a few too many beers, Paul fell asleep at the wheel. He awoke just as his car sailed over a ridge on an interstate highway, into the blinding lights of a fire truck and ambulance parked where an earlier accident had occurred. Paul tried to swerve but couldn't manage it quickly. He slammed into the fire truck and his body flew from the car, but his left leg lodged in the door jam.

Nine days later, doctors amputated his mangled left leg above the knee. As he lay in the hospital, Paul wondered how he could ever have a normal life as an amputee. Would he be a freak? Would he ever get a date? But unexpectedly, he wasn't sad. On his first day home from the hospital, he recalls getting out of the shower, looking at himself in the mirror, and actually smiling. "One less leg, one less anything, I realized that having all your parts isn't what makes you happy."

Paul adapted surprisingly quickly to life with one artificial leg. He continued to work for Lincoln and became something of a star in the sales office. When the opportunity to move to a position in New York City opened up, Paul went for it. But the new job left him feeling empty.

Paul began to hunt for something more rewarding and was increasingly drawn back to his earlier passion for sports. He began running in Central Park on the weekends, and had a new prosthetic leg built to suit his more athletic lifestyle. Before long he competed in and won his first track and field event for amputees. He started swimming at the local YMCA and bicycling near his home in New Jersey. Gaining strength in the three sports that make up a triathlon—running, swimming, and cycling—he set his sights on competing in one. But it was the New York City marathon that would transform him and clinch his commitment to sports.

On a chilly November morning in 1995, Paul was one of the thousands of runners pounding the pavement, bounding over bridges, and dodging potholes along the 26-mile course which extends through the five boroughs of New York City. He finished in about four and a half hours, exhilarated and overwhelmed. "The power, the possibility, the potential ... after the marathon I felt limitless!" Paul recalls. Then and there he promised himself he would dedicate himself to sports. "Money from a paycheck never felt as good as crossing the finish line."

One month later he took off to pursue his dream of becoming a world class athlete.

Wanting to add skiing to his growing repertoire, Paul moved to Winter Park, Colorado, a ski town high in the Rockies, where he began training. He set his sights on competing in the 1998 Paralympic Winter Games in Nagano, Japan. When he wasn't skiing, he continued to train and began to compete seriously as a runner and a triathlete. In the early days of his new-found "career," he supported himself by a growing number of professional sponsorships, "and credit cards for awhile," he admits.

Unfortunately, after all that training, a broken shoulder prevented him from competing at Nagano. He was terribly disappointed, but by this time, Paul had learned to focus on what he *could* do instead of what he *could not*. So he went looking for an opportunity to take his mind off his loss. Fate assisted. At a triathlon competition, Paul found himself seated next to Jim Howley, the founder of the Transcontinental Triathlon for Life, an event that raises money for physically challenged kids. As a result of their fortuitous meeting, Paul was added to the team making the formidable cross-country trek.

After three years, Paul left Winter Park and relocated to Boulder, Colorado, where he continued to distinguish himself in the world of elite athletes. In 1997 he was named the U.S. Olympic Committee Disabled Athlete of the Year. He added cycling to the list of events he regularly competed in and, in 2000, he made it to the Paralympic Summer Games in Sydney, Australia, as a member of the cycling team.

Perhaps Paul's most demanding event is the Hawaiian Ironman Triathlon. Held in a tropical climate where temperatures and the humidity can soar into the high 90s, Paul faces off with a field of able-bodied competitors in a grueling test of strength and endurance involving a 2.4 mile swim, 112 mile cycle, and 26.2 mile run. In his first Hawaiian Ironman Triathlon in 1998, he set a goal of completing the course in 12 hours. He finished at 11 hours, 55 minutes. Since then, he has competed annually in this and other triathlon events around the world.

Paul's dream has become a reality. Every year he adds new competitions and new victories to an already impressive list of accomplishments. He attributes his success not to extraordinary talent, but to total commitment—keeping his goals foremost in his mind and arranging his life to support those goals.

"When life gives you lemons, make lemonade" aptly describes Paul Martin's ability to turn a problem into an opportunity. He's even done it with jail time! One winter, due to a series of cross country misunderstandings, an unpaid ticket for having a non-working headlight in New York ballooned into a ticket for driving with a suspended license in Colorado, which carried a mandatory five-day jail sentence. Paul used the unexpected "retreat" to do 2,500 pushups and to set a big goal: he committed to writing a book about his life.

That book, *One Man's Leg*, was published in October 2002. Now, in addition to training and competition, Paul travels the country promoting his book and sharing the lessons he's learned with young people and adults alike.

"I lost my leg due to my own irresponsibility," says Paul, "but a month later I made the decision to make the most of my situation and, on top of that, to be happy. After all, I could still laugh, I could still think, I could still love and be loved. It seemed to me I was as whole as I had ever been."

(Story by Leticia Steffan)

Literal Comprehension Questions:

1. What happened that made Paul's father punish him so severely?

2. What happened that made Paul want to dedicate himself to sports?

3. After Paul's leg was amputated, what are some of the sports he competed in?

Inferential Comprehension Questions:

1. How did Paul's relationship with his dad affect his personality and his way of approaching life? Explain your thinking.

2. Why do you think Paul yelled back at the ROTC officer who criticized him for having a wrinkled shirt? Explain your thinking.

3. What do you think Paul meant by the statement, "Having all your parts isn't what makes you happy?" Explain your thinking.

Self-Analysis Questions:

1. How would you react if you lost your leg in an accident like Paul did? Why do you think you would act this way? What does this tell you about yourself?

2. Paul once had to spend five days in jail. To make use of the time, he set a goal to do 2,500 push-ups while there. Identify a time when you were in a situation that looked like it was going to be a waste of time. What did you do or what could you have done to make that time productive? If you did something productive, how did it make you feel? If you didn't do anything productive, why not?

3. Paul ultimately took responsibility for the many negative things that happened to him in his life. Identify some negative things that have happened to you. To what extent are you in some way responsible for those negative things? What made you responsible for those things happening? If you think you are not responsible in any way, why not?

Marta Gabra-Tsadick

*I*n August 1991, Marta Gabre-Tsadick safely entered her homeland of Ethiopia for the first time in 17 years, even though she had been working for its people for decades. Marta and her husband, Demeke, are the founders of Project Mercy, a humanitarian organization that helps refugees, which they started after they narrowly escaped Ethiopia during a brutal communist takeover in the 1970s. The very events that threatened her life and her family's survival strengthened Marta's resolve, inspiring her to help others who were still suffering.

Ethiopia is one of the oldest kingdoms in the world. Situated in eastern Africa, across the Red Sea from Yemen and Saudi Arabia, Ethiopia is the only African nation that has never been colonized, with one exception: the Italians. When Marta was a young child, the Italians occupied Ethiopia for five years under Mussolini's spreading fascist regime. Her family's home in the western province of Welega was torched and her father was forced into hiding, leaving Marta and her mother to resettle in the Ethiopian capital of Addis Ababa. Her mother found work as a nurse in a missionary hospital and, as a firm believer in education, saw to it that Marta received the best schooling possible. At 13, when Marta finished her elementary studies, the mission hospital hired her and began training her as a nurse. Who could have imagined that she would soon meet a man who would profoundly affect the course of her life: the Emperor Hailie Selassie.

As was common in Africa, the Emperor Haile Selassie came into power by virtue of his family tree. He descended from a long line of kings and rulers who had controlled Ethiopia for centuries. Well loved by his people, he sought to modernize Ethiopia. Selassie had traveled widely and had observed the progress being made in Europe and the West. He realized that the well-being of his beloved country lay largely in the education of its children, and he constantly kept an eye out for bright, high-spirited young people who he believed held the future of Ethiopia. He often used his influence and resources to help such young people acquire an education abroad, hopeful that they would return to Ethiopia and offer their services to the betterment of their country.

One day, the Emperor and his wife made a visit to Marta's hospital, where she had the honor of meeting them. Perhaps the Emperor saw in Marta the spark of the hope he had for Ethiopia's future; perhaps it was her lively spirit. Whatever it was, their meeting was the beginning of a friendship based on their mutual commitment to helping Ethiopia. Their connection remained solid for decades until the Emperor met his death at the hands of a military "Derg" many years later. But, we're getting ahead of the story.

"I respected this man and all that he stood for," says Marta. "I respected his love for our people."

At the age of 15 Marta entered into an arranged marriage with a Norwegian missionary named Peter Myhre. Within two years they had two sons and, by the time the second child was born, Marta discovered they were deeply in debt. Peter had been spending his own salary plus borrowed money to educate and care for destitute children. Worried, Marta decided that she had better be able to support the family herself, if necessary. So she set out to get an education. She began making inquiries about schools in America, and about visas, cram courses in English, and work-study programs. Her persistence paid off. She found a college in New Mexico, and later one in Colorado, where she could get the education to enable her to stand independently on her own two feet.

In August of 1953, when she was in her early 20s, Marta sent her two sons to live with her mother and left for the United States to further her education. She arrived with the equivalent of a fifth grade education, and returned home to Ethiopia five years later with a high school diploma, a college degree in Elementary Education, and the ability to earn a living.

This was a good thing. For shortly after her return, her husband Peter died, leaving Marta as the sole supporter of herself and their two sons—and with enormous debts. In need of a good job, Marta went to see her old friend, the Emperor Haile Selassie.

The Emperor gave Marta a job in Ethiopia's Office of Foreign Affairs, where she worked for the next ten years, eventually advancing to a position as Minister of Asian Affairs. During that time, Marta married Demeke Tekle-Wold and they had two sons.

In 1968, Marta was appointed to the Ethiopian senate where she became the first female senator. Marta served in the senate for six years; but political turmoil was brewing in her beloved Ethiopia, and it was only a matter of time before it would come to a head.

Since coming to power in 1930, Emperor Haile Selassie's progressive ideals had often been at odds with Ethiopia's old-fashioned ways and its royalty, who resisted his vision of a modernized Ethiopia. But in the early 70s, a new threat to the Emperor gradually surfaced. Ethiopian students who were being educated overseas came home, bringing to a country that had long been under the rule of royalty new ideas like "democracy" from America and "Marxism" from Eastern Europe and the USSR. Against this background, communist ideals took root and were used by students and the military to fuel distrust of the Selassie government and gradually erode its power.

Marta saw it coming. In 1972 she resigned from the senate and moved her family out of Addis to Dire Dawa. She warned the Emperor about the imminent danger she perceived. By that time, however, he was surrounded by advisors who were protecting him from seeing the political realities.

In 1974, a powerful military "Derg" began arresting and executing anyone they believed to be a threat to their socialist ideals, including landowners, wealthy families, and over 60 members of the Selassie government. The Derg took control of Ethiopia and placed Emperor Haile Selassie under house arrest. He died a year later under mysterious circumstances.

Later that year, Marta and Demeke secretly returned to Addis to offer their condolences to the families of the men who had been murdered, many of whom had been Marta's friends and mentors. But while in Addis, they learned that they, too, were marked for arrest. With no other choice, Marta and Demeke decided to risk everything and flee Ethiopia for Kenya.

It was an arduous six-day trip, nearly fatal to the family and the lowest point in her life, says Marta. Out of water in the desert, her sons grew very ill and were on the verge of losing consciousness due to dehydration. Marta made the agonizing decision to take water out of the radiator of their Land Rover and give it to the boys. The water had an orange color to it she could not strain out, and she was terrified it would hurt or even kill her sons. But they were desperate for hydration, so she gave it to them anyway. Thankfully, they survived.

In Kenya, which borders Ethiopia to the south, agents of the Derg were on the lookout for Ethiopians on the run. Marta and her family had to move on quickly. Through connections they had with the

Kenyan government, they were able to get to Greece where, after seven months, they received word that a church in Indiana was willing to sponsor their move to the United States.

They arrived in the United States in the summer of 1976 and, once here, realized a purpose for their survival. They knew that they could give a true account of the recent takeover in Ethiopia and share the desperate situation of the many refugees. "Our escape took place just at the beginning of a major exodus. Thousands fled," Marta recalls. Now, in the safety of a country far from the turmoil, she was concerned for other refugees and became determined to help them in any way possible.

A year later, in 1977, Project Mercy was born. Originally established to help Ethiopian refugees, over the years it has expanded to serve other African refugees as well. Project Mercy has sent food, clothing, educational supplies, and money to help those who have fled war and famine and are living in Ivory Coast, Guinea, Djibouti, Kenya, Liberia, Malawi, and Sudan.

The civil and economic strife from which Marta and Demeke escaped worsened under the new regime and made it only too easy for neighboring countries to stir up trouble along Ethiopia's borders. It wasn't until 1991, when the communist government was toppled and the beginnings of democracy were established, that Marta and Demeke were able to travel safely to their homeland. After 17 years of caring for people who had fled, Project Mercy could send help directly into Ethiopia.

The focus of that work has been in Yetebon, a rural area 80 miles southwest of Addis Ababa. Here, at the invitation of community elders, Project Mercy has established a system of clean water delivery, built new all-weather roads, provided skills-training for both adults and children, and opened a school for 700 students from kindergarten to 8th grade. A new hospital is currently under construction.

At 73, Marta revels in the happiness she sees in the eyes of Ethiopian children. She says it reminds her that "we can find joy and happiness with whatever we have, and even with what we do not have."

Marta credits her ability to endure and will to succeed to her strong religious beliefs, her mother (whom Marta describes as "a woman of wisdom"), and her husband, Demeke, who has been a constant and powerful influence. "We are totally and completely of one mind," she says.

Marta's unusual life has exceeded her dreams, and along the way there have been many lessons. She advises others to "respect and love everyone, until they prove you wrong." And don't fear work. "Think big!" she says. Marta stresses the importance of listening to elders, and not dismissing their ideas until a better one comes along.

"Don't get discouraged when one door of opportunity closes. Have faith," says Marta. Her survival and success have come by always knocking at the next door.

(Story by Leticia Steffen)

Literal Comprehension Questions:

1. How did Emperor Hailie Selassie come to power in Ethiopia?

2. Marta arrived in the United States in 1953 and spent five years there. During that time, what advances did she make in her education?

3. To what does Marta attribute her ability to endure hardship and persevere?

Inferential Comprehension Questions:

1. Marta was married at age 15 to a Norwegian missionary. It was an "arranged marriage," which means that her parents selected the man she was to marry. How do you think Marta felt about this arranged marriage? Explain your thinking.

2. Why do you think Marta revels in the joy she now sees in the eyes of Ethiopian children? Explain your thinking.

3. What do you think a military Derg is? Explain your thinking.

Self-Analysis Questions:

1. Marta was hunted a number of times. While you have probably never been hunted as Marta was, have you ever been in a situation where you feared for your own physical or emotional safety? Describe that situation. How did you react to it?

2. Both Marta and Emperor Haile Salessie were strongly commited to the improvement of Ethiopia. Have you every had a strong commitment to something? Describe what it was. How did that commitment influence your behavior?

3. Marta was a great believer in the importance of education. What is your opinion about the importance of education? How does that opinion affect what you do or do not do in school? How might your behavior change if your opinion of school changed?

Ben Wentworth

*I*n high school, Ben Wentworth graduated 61st out of a class of 62. He had a permanent seat in detention and was voted most likely NOT to succeed his senior year. To say that school didn't agree with Ben would be an understatement.

Today, the same Ben Wentworth is a highly respected educator. He has created amazing tools for learning, including a planetarium that enables blind students to "see" stars, moons, and comets with their fingers. He has garnered numerous awards for his fine teaching, including the prestigious Disney American Teacher award in two different categories.

It's taken Ben a good part of his life to unravel some of his own mysteries. Why was school so difficult for him as a kid? Today he has the answer, and he uses that information to help kids with similar problems, kids who don't fit in . . . in other words, kids like him.

Growing up on a large dairy farm in Vermont, Ben spent much of his boyhood roaming the forests. There he could be absorbed easily for hours, hunting for frogs' eggs, building tree houses, or just wandering along the stream.

But school was a different matter. Stuck in a classroom, Ben found it painfully hard to concentrate and harder still to sit quietly. Much later, Ben would discover he had Attention Deficit Hyperactivity Disorder (ADHD) and a reading disability, two conditions commonly identified and treated in childhood today. But in Ben's case they slipped under the radar, leaving him to tumble through school, a mystery to himself and a problem for everyone else.

Many of Ben's teachers saw him as disruptive, unfocused, and a big discipline problem. In a way, they were right. But the symptoms of ADHD weren't something Ben could control, and his teachers' assessment hurt Ben's sensitive feelings. Occasionally he had a teacher who saw through his increasingly tough shell, but more often than not his teachers misread the signs and just made him feel worse.

When Ben was 12, half of his family's 80 milk cows were struck with a deadly fever and they were forced to sell the dairy farm. Ben dreaded the move. "The farm was the one place I felt accepted," he remembers.

His troubles followed him to his new school in upstate New York, where he had a very formal math teacher. "In her class, there was only one right way to do something and I rebelled," says Ben. "I tried as hard as possible to fail and succeeded at maintaining a perfect 'F' for the entire year."

But in order to get out of eighth grade, Ben needed to pass the state math test. In spite of himself, he had absorbed the material and tied for the highest grade in the class. "That grade didn't mean as much to me as the red-faced look on my teacher's face when she told me," Ben recalls.

Acing that test turned out to be an unexpected boon for Ben's self esteem. He may have done it for spite, but the experience gave him confidence that he was smart and that he could succeed if he put his mind to it.

In his junior year, Ben became interested in science. Even without cracking a book he did pretty well in class (a fact that did not go unnoticed by his teacher, who encouraged Ben's curiosity). Ben began building small, solid fuel rockets. He conducted experiments with size and pressure to see how far he could get them to fly without blowing them up.

Ben's fascination with science would play a big part in his later life, but in high school, with an undiagnosed reading disability and ADHD, studying continued to be a challenge. When he finally graduated, at the bottom of his class, Ben closed the door on school forever.

Or so he thought.

Ben enlisted in the Air Force. After basic training, he was sent to study electronics for a year and then stationed at Whiteman Air Force Base in Missouri. There he met his future wife, Judy, a student nurse.

The routines of military life agreed with Ben. The structure helped him focus and he developed more self-acceptance. He and Judy married, and her support gave him an added anchor.

It was the mid-1960s and the Vietnam War was in full action. In December 1966 Ben was assigned to Clarke Air Force Base in the Philippines as part of a mobile communications group directly supporting activities in Vietnam. "I became increasingly uncomfortable with the way the American government was handling the war," says Ben. "What I saw was only partially reported, and it was tinted toward what America wanted to hear." His disillusionment was so strong that Ben even considered giving up his American citizenship and moving to Australia. "I didn't like what America was doing, but eventually I realized I had a better chance of changing things by staying and working from the inside."

For the first time in his life, Ben began to think seriously about education. Going to college might help him to succeed personally and enable him to have an effect on the kinds of things the war had made him think about.

In 1969, Ben left the military and started college at the University of Missouri-Columbia. With his new perspective and motivation, plus the support of a wise college advisor, Ben earned high grades and began to shape his future. In his second year, Ben's career goal crystallized: he wanted to teach. Through teaching, Ben felt, he could have the impact on society that he envisioned. He believed that, through tolerance and understanding, he could help kids who appeared on the surface to be doing it all wrong.

Ben eventually combined his desire to teach with his long-time interest in science by becoming a high school science teacher.

Later he specialized in teaching students with severe visual problems, and moved to a school for the deaf and blind. There he became known for his talent at putting science concepts into touchable forms that non-sighted students could use to experience things like the sun's shadow, the Earth's rotation, seasons, and time. "I teach the way I wish I'd been taught," says Ben.

But there was still a missing piece in the puzzle of Ben: his own ADHD. It was finally diagnosed when Ben took his daughter in to be tested. The physician noted that Ben, now in his early 40s, exhibited classic symptoms (which tests confirmed). Later, while working on a master's degree in Special Education, his reading disability was also uncovered. Both discoveries helped Ben to understand his rocky past and to get a handle on his life as never before. With proper medication Ben was able to focus, which in turn allowed him to learn skills he hadn't been able to learn as a child, a young man, or even as an adult.

Today Ben's insight into ADHD from his own life experience is part of what makes him a great teacher. He still identifies with troubled kids. He knows what it feels like to struggle.

"I want people to understand that even with something like ADHD you can excel. The idea that an ugly duckling can turn out to be a swan isn't just a fairytale. It's the truth.

"We all learn and behave just a little bit differently from each other. I teach my students to believe in themselves and I don't let them get away with saying 'I can't.'"

Ben's outstanding teaching has been rewarded with a TAPESTRY grant to develop an innovative astronomy program for the blind. He has received two Disney American Teacher Awards and been recognized as an Outstanding Earth Science Teacher. He's been named the Colorado Aerospace Education Teacher of the Year 2002 by the United States Air Force Association-Aerospace Education Foundation. He has consulted with NASA on the Hubble Telescope Braille Book, *Touch the Universe*.

And, as an adult, Ben has never once been sent to detention.

(Story by Leticia Steffen)

Literal Comprehension Questions:

1. Why was Ben's family forced to sell their dairy farm?

2. What did Ben discover about himself that explained why he had such a hard time in school?

3. What are some of the awards Ben received as an adult?

Inferential Comprehension Questions:

1. Why do you think that the farm was the only place where Ben felt accepted? Explain your thinking.

2. Why do you think Ben tried as hard as he could to fail the mathematics course taught by the very formal teacher? Explain your thinking.

3. How might Ben have felt when he learned that he had ADHD? Explain your thinking.

Self-Analysis Questions:

1. Ben tried to fail his math course. Identify something at which you have tried to fail or, at least, something at which you did not try very hard to succeed. Why do you think you acted this way? How would things have been different if you had tried harder to succeed?

2. As an adult, Ben was able to figure out why he had acted certain ways and why he had done certain things in the past. What have you discovered about yourself that explains why you have acted certain ways or done certain things?

3. Ben enjoyed learning, but he did not enjoy school. What are some things you like learning about outside of school? What is there about these things that you like? How could you bring one of these things or a part of one of these things into your studies at school?

Lily Walters

No one really knows why bad things happen. But Lilly Walters believes that there are few accidents in life, even the "accident" that happened to her when she was ten.

Summer in rural California is as fresh as a bucket of strawberries. One sunny afternoon, Lilly and two friends were enjoying a ride on the back of a forklift that Lilly's father had rented to move hay for their horses. Going down a small hill, the rig's steering gear broke. It teetered precariously. Lilly's father tried to keep the forklift upright, nearly pulling his arms from their sockets. But the huge machine flipped, knocking him unconscious, breaking the arm of one of the neighbor children, and pinning Lilly underneath. The other child, unhurt, kept his wits and ran for help.

Lilly survived, but lost most of her left hand.

"She had just started taking piano lessons. I kept thinking of all the things Lilly would not be able to do," admits her mother.

The accident and its consequences were difficult to accept but, as fate would have it, the people she met and the events that followed the accident began to lead Lilly in new directions and transform her into someone who could help others.

Lilly returned to the hospital frequently after the forklift accident for various surgeries. On her eighth visit, she shared a room with a teenage girl named Tony, who had a fiery spirit that outshone her deformed body. "I've been waiting for you," said Tony when Lilly and her mother arrived. Tony's optimism and enthusiasm impressed Lilly, who was surprised to learn that Tony had polio and went to a special school for the handicapped. "But you aren't handicapped," blurted Lilly's mother.

"Right," said Tony. "You aren't handicapped as long as you can help someone else." Tony told Lilly about her schoolmate who was born with no arms or legs. "She helps us by teaching us typing, using a wand between her teeth," Tony explained.

The idea of typing struck a chord with Lilly's mother, a writer, who believed that typing was an important skill. Inspired, she immediately contacted IBM to obtain one-hand touch-typing charts for her daughter. When Lilly was finally able to return to school—her left hand still bandaged—she brought the charts. The principal allowed her to study one-hand typing with the typing teacher during lunch.

Soon Lilly could touch-type all her homework at the respectable speed of 50 words per minute. Not only that, she shared her new skill with her English teacher, whose right arm had been made useless by polio. Lilly found helping her teacher extremely satisfying. As Tony had predicted, as long as Lilly could help others she did not feel handicapped.

One day, not long after Lilly returned to school, her sixth grade teacher read aloud a poem called "Touch of the Master's Hand." At the time, anything about hands grabbed Lilly's attention. The poem's message touched her deeply. Thirty years later, when she was working on a one-hand typing manual for children, the poem surfaced seemingly out of nowhere. This time, Lilly decided to learn more about its author, Myra Brooks Welsh, and discovered that Myra came from a musical family and loved to play the organ. When severe arthritis forced her to stop playing, Myra channeled her musical soul into poetry, which she would type slowly, using the eraser end of two pencils held in her badly disabled hands.

Myra's story gave Lilly new inspiration.

As an adult, singing became one of Lilly's passions. In the midst of preparing for a particularly grueling community theater performance, she developed a sore throat and went to her family doctor. After sitting in the waiting room for over an hour, a frustrated Lilly grabbed a phone book and found a throat specialist nearby who could see her immediately. When she arrived at the new doctor's office, she was startled when the nurse on duty asked about her hand.

"What I need to know is how it has affected you life," said the nurse. "I just had a baby girl and her hand is like yours. I need to know how it has affected your life," the nurse repeated.

Lilly considered the question. Never in the 25 years since her accident had anyone ever asked so bluntly about her hand. "It has affected my life, but not in a bad way," she answered. "I do many things that people with two normal hands find difficult. I type 75 words a minute, I play guitar, I have ridden and shown horses for years, I even have a Horsemaster Degree," she continued. "I'm involved in musical theater, I'm a professional speaker, and I do television shows four or five times a year.

"Your daughter does not need to have a problem, but a lot of that will depend on what you teach her," Lilly advised. "She'll figure out she's different, but you need to teach her that different is wonderful. Normal means average. What's so fun about that?"

Just then the doctor came in to examine Lilly's throat. He wanted to anesthetize it and put a probe down it. No thanks, Lilly decided. She walked out. The next day her throat was completely well.

Lilly believes that many things in life happen for a reason, and that unseen forces play a part in shaping our destiny. The events of her life have inspired her to reach out to others, in part through her writing and speaking. She is the author of six books on public speaking and a best-selling one-handed typing manual. She is a professional speaker and seminar leader, as well as a speaker bureau executive who represents thousands of presenters, from celebrities, to local heroes, to business speakers.

(Story by Shae Isaacs)

Information for this story was used with permission from "Angels Never Say Hello!" by Dottie Walters © 2000, "Those Touched By The Master's Hand" by Lilly Walters © 2000 and "Why Do These Things Happen?" by Lilly Walters, which is included in "A 2nd Helping of Chicken Soup for the Soul" © 1995 by Jack Canfield and Mark Victor Hansen.

Literal Comprehension Questions:

1. How did Lily lose most of her left hand?

2. Why did Lily's mother react to the accident by saying that Lily "had just started taking piano lessons?"

3. How did Lily answer the nurse's question about how the loss of her hand affected her life?

Inferential Comprehension Questions:

1. What do you think Tony meant by the statement, "You aren't handicapped as long as you can help someone?" Explain your thinking.

2. Do you think Lily's father blamed himself for the loss of his daughter's hand? Why or why not? Explain your thinking.

3. What do you think Lily meant when she said, "Normal means average. What's so fun about that?"

Self-Analysis Questions:

1. Lily found inspiration from people who were doing remarkable things but were less fortunate than she. Think of someone you know whom you consider to be less fortunate than you. Are they a source of inspiration to you? Why or why not?

2. Lily believed that even bad things sometimes happen for a reason. Do you also believe this? Why or why not?

3. Is there something that makes you feel "handicapped in some way?" How could you think differently about this?

Dave Liniger

At age 20, Dave Liniger was a scrawny, hardworking young father with big dreams and little confidence. A poorly paid Air Force sergeant anxious to provide well for his family, Dave supplemented his military paycheck by delivering newspapers, pumping gas, and selling tickets at a movie theatre. But when he stumbled into a new career, and later found a mentor who helped him develop self-confidence, Dave discovered a passion that enabled him to live out his dreams and, at the same time, help others find theirs.

Not only that, he got rich too.

Growing up on a farm in Marion, Indiana, Dave learned the value of hard work. "My father taught me to start early and work long hours," says Dave. "As soon as I could, I got every part-time job possible, from mowing lawns to cleaning up the sheet metal shop—anything that kids did back in Indiana." But Dave's daydreams took him far beyond the corn and soybean fields of his small town. He was fascinated with movies about Tarzan, cowboys, soldiers, and adventurers. He often imagined what it would be like to live the lives he saw played out on the big screen. Dave saw himself flying around the world in a hot-air balloon and big game hunting in the heart of Africa. Though his dreams seemed farfetched for a farm boy, they inspired him to keep moving forward, even when times were tough.

Dave started college at Indiana University when he was 17. At the time, he couldn't see the connection between his dreams and the business courses he was enrolled in. After only three semesters he dropped out, but not before meeting a beautiful young woman whom he soon married. Dave enlisted in the Air Force, and the young couple moved to Davis Monthan Air Force Base in Tucson, Arizona. Dave still dreamed of big adventures, but a new responsibility set in before he had time to get his dreams off the ground: he became a father. Suddenly, Dave was a family man. "I decided I had better grow up and figure out how to run my life," he says.

Hard work was second nature to Dave, who worked three part-time jobs in addition to his military duties. He made a decent living, but nothing spectacular until one day he stumbled upon a book that introduced him to a clever way of making money. It was written by a postal service worker who, in his spare time, bought "fixer-uppers"—homes in need of repair that could be bought cheap, fixed up, rented for a while, and then sold for a profit. The idea inspired Dave and he decided to try it for himself. He bought his first house for $10,000, made improvements, and sold it eight months later for an astonishing $14,000. "I was amazed. I made more money off one house than I did from three part-time jobs and my full time military paycheck."

Dave was onto something. He set a goal of owning 21 single-family homes by the time he was 21 years old, and he made it. Along the way, he decided to get his own real estate license; that way, he could save part of the commission he was currently paying an agent each time he bought a property. Armed with a license, Dave started dabbling in the sales end of the business as well. But selling took a kind of confidence in dealing with people that Dave didn't have at the time.

"Back then, real estate agents were these older, gray-haired guys in suits. There I was with my military crew cut, skinny, and so young-looking the police would stop me just to see if I had a driver's license. I drove a beat-up VW Bug with no air-conditioning—in Phoenix! I didn't have confidence that I could really do the job."

Dave tried selling houses for six months without success. Discouraged and ready to quit, he half-heartedly attended a talk by a motivational speaker, Dave Stone, at the ritzy Mountain Shadows Country Club in Scottsdale. Stone was unlike anyone Dave had ever heard before. A real estate agent himself, Stone exuded confidence. He understood what motivated people and the psychology of sales. While Stone spoke, Dave's mind raced. "I kept thinking, gosh, if I understood the real estate business the way he does and could be as convincing, I'm sure I could get some business." At the break, Dave ran up to Mr. Stone and told him what he was thinking. He also told Stone he had been working in real estate sales for six months without listing a single home or making a single sale.

Stone advised him to quit.

Was it just a strategy to make Dave try harder, or did Stone mean it? It didn't matter. Dave was convinced that if he could learn Stone's method, he could succeed. Something in Dave had awakened. On the way home, he stopped at the grocery store to purchase a half-gallon of milk.

"In the checkout line I overheard this young woman talking to her father about selling his house. I said, 'Excuse me, but are you talking about real estate?' She explained that her father needed to move from Tempe, Arizona to Albuquerque, New Mexico. 'Well sir,' I said, 'Do you know anything about title insurance or mortgages or closings?' He looked at me and muttered something in Spanish. 'He really doesn't understand much English,' his daughter said."

At that moment Dave knew he could help. "I offered to sell his house for him and we went over to see it that very night. It was a 'fixer-upper'—I knew about those. I listed the house that night and immediately had two full price offers. The next morning, I took the young woman and her fiancée out and sold them a house by lunch. They referred me to two other couples and I sold them houses, too. So, basically, in two days, I had listed one house and sold four. I never looked back."

Dave became good at sales, very good. By the time his military stint was up in Arizona, he had established himself as a successful real estate agent. He moved his family to Denver, Colorado, and got work easily. But he had begun thinking about starting his own business. He had a radical idea which, if it worked, would shake up the conservative real estate industry. He decided to give it a shot.

The idea was to start a company that would let the agents keep 100% of the commissions they made, rather than splitting them 50-50 with the managing organization. In this model, agents would have a voice in running the office and share the actual expenses of doing so. The idea was very controversial at the time.

With profits from his own pocket plus a handful of investors, Dave started RE/MAX in 1973. Almost immediately the country went into a recession. His partners' investments collapsed. With several offices already opened and managers hired, Dave found himself with no financial backing, no experience running a business, and with established real estate companies dead set against him.

"Right away we ran into a real buzz saw," he chuckles, looking back.

The first couple of years were pretty bleak for RE/MAX. "The harder we tried, the more money we owed, and the fewer people would come to work for us," recalls Dave. Still, the agents who did come to RE/MAX found that the model of sharing office costs while keeping their full commissions really worked. "The agents were thriving," says Dave, "and we tried to learn from them. We asked, how do we make this business better? What can we do for you that we're not doing? What are we doing right? What are we doing wrong?" With the agents' help and Dave's determination, the tide eventually turned. Satisfied homebuyers and real estate agents spread the word about the fledging company, much to the aggravation of the older, established firms.

"They waged a constant crusade to drive us out of business. I guess I had enough military in me to fight back."

Dave's hard work and perseverance, although essential to the RE/MAX start-up, were not enough. "I needed the courses I should have had when I was in college—economics, marketing, franchising, legal implications of all the businesses we were running." So Dave sought education any way he could get it, attending seminars with his mentor, Dave Stone, reading every business book he could get his hands on, going to real estate conventions, and taking training courses.

At the same time Dave was launching RE/MAX, another historic change was occurring in the real estate industry: women were getting into the business. Prior to the 70s, there had been virtually no women in real estate. But by the time RE/MAX started, a growing number had become successful agents with smaller companies. The two largest firms clung to the past and would hire women only as secretaries or receptionists. This pool of talented women was hitting the glass ceiling and RE/MAX offered them the right opportunity at the right time. "By our fifth year in business we had 289 agents, and about 70 percent were female. The two biggest companies in town didn't have one woman apiece in sales."

And the rest, as they say, is history. The following year, over 200 men who saw the direction the industry was moving joined RE/MAX, giving the company 500 agents. "We had paid off our bills and cleaned up our debt. That year we were the number one real estate company in the Denver metropolitan area," says Dave. RE/MAX had taken over a market that had been dominated by two old line companies for over 50 years.

Since those early days, RE/MAX has grown tremendously. Today, it is the largest privately owned real estate franchising company in the world with over 80,000 agents and more than 4,500 offices in 42 countries.

And what about Dave's childhood dreams of being an adventurer? Many of those have come true as well. His lifestyle has afforded him the opportunity to take up flying, skydiving, ballooning, hunting, fishing, and boating. He is a NASCAR driver and team owner, owns a private, 18-hole golf course used by charitable organizations, and recently built a museum, *The Wildlife Experience*, dedicated to wildlife conservation.

"I never lost my childhood vision," says Dave. "I think its okay to daydream. I think its okay to put yourself in different positions and imagine what it would really be like if you could grow up and be what's in your dreams. If your vision is strong enough, it will help you over the hurdles of getting there. Without dreams, there's nothing to achieve."

(Story by Shae Isaacs)

Literal Comprehension Questions:

1. What were some of Dave's dreams as a boy?

2. What inspired Dave to buy his first house?

3. What were some problems Dave faced when he first started REMAX, his real estate company?

Inferential Comprehension Questions:

1. Why do you think Dave Liniger was so strongly influenced by Dave Stone? Explain your thinking.

2. Using women as real estate agents was one of the "innovations" that made REMAX so successful. Why do you think that, up until that time, women were not commonly employed in real estate? Why do you think women were so successful in real estate when given the opportunity in REMAX? Explain your thinking.

3. How do you think Dave feels now about his life and what he has accomplished? What do you think makes him feel the best? Explain your thinking.

Self-Analysis Questions:

1. Dave Liniger was once told by Dave Stone, a man he greatly admired, to get out of the real estate business. However, he stayed in the business and became enormously successful. How do you think you would have reacted if you were told the same thing? Why do you think you would have reacted this way? What does this tell you about yourself?

2. One of the keys to Dave's success was his strong belief in "hard work." Do you believe that you can be successful in whatever you choose if you work hard enough? What are you working hard at right now? Why? What are you *not* working hard at? Why?

3. Dave finally earned enough money to do just about anything he wanted. What would you do if you had unlimited money and resources? Why?

Dian Megarry

Nestled at the foot of the Rocky Mountains, 65 miles south of Denver, sits the city of Colorado Springs. Here, in the shadow of Pike's Peak, Dian Megarry and his wife Jan run a school for martial arts: the Rustic Hills branch of the Universal Kempo Karate School. At 43, Dian is a second-degree black belt. It's hard to believe that when he was seven years old, Dian Megarry was pronounced legally dead.

As a boy, Dian was medically fragile. He wore braces on his legs from the knees down and spent much of his young life in the hospital. Given his "weak constitution," every time he contracted a common childhood illness he would get tonsillitis as well.

It was a bout of croup—similar to whooping cough—that triggered the tonsillitis that swelled his glands to the point Dian couldn't breathe. His family rushed him to the hospital, but it was too late. He lay in the emergency room "dead" for 23 minutes.

But during that time, Dian was not dead. Rather, he experienced a profound sense that his life was precious and very important. Dian recalls: "The feeling returned to my arms and legs and suddenly my eyes popped open. I heard an orderly nearby shout, 'Somebody get a doctor. This boy isn't dead!'"

It was this "near death" experience that Dian says changed his life.

Dian's physical problems weren't small. He spent a year in recovery after his near death experience. He grew stronger physically and mentally; in fact, for a few years he was just about normal. But when he was 12, Dian's world began literally fading away. He was diagnosed with Stargart's disease, a disease of the vision system. At first his sight loss was mild but it grew worse until, by the age of 30, all he could make out was a bit of shadow and light—with one eye. In addition, he developed a moderate hearing loss in his right ear and a mild hearing loss in his left.

If he couldn't rely on his body, Dian decided to strengthen his mind. He studied hard in high school, aced the ACT college admission test, and attended the University of Northern Colorado where he earned a double degree in Elementary and Special Education.

After graduation, Dian moved to Utah, where he got additional certification in gifted and talented education at Brigham Young University. He began teaching elementary school, but soon realized his ambitions lay elsewhere. "I enjoyed teaching," says Dian, "but I didn't want to teach in a regular school anymore, so I just resigned. I had no job and I wasn't sure what I wanted to do. I just knew this wasn't quite it."

It was a bold move, but it paid off. Dian found work as an aide at the Utah School for the Blind and began studying at the University of Utah for a graduate degree to teach the blind and visually impaired. In one of his classes, he met and began dating Jan Wright, who he would later marry. At 32, the boy who had been born cripple, pronounced dead at seven, and gone nearly blind and partly deaf, finally felt things were going his way.

But a memory from the past still haunted him.

When Dian was 18, he and his guide dog had been attacked by a group of boys who wanted money. "They told me to hand over my wallet, which I did, but there was only a dollar in it. That made them really mad. They went berserk. They kicked my dog and started punching me. Then one of them pulled out a knife."

The attack landed Dian in the hospital—again—with a broken nose, broken ribs, and cuts under both his arms that required 250 stitches. His injured dog lay nearby.

"I was angry," says Dian, "really angry. I decided this was *never* going to happen to me again."

Though he recovered from his injuries, Dian never forgot the experience and was determined to find a way to be physically able to defend himself—even with his limitations.

In 1993, Dian and Jan moved to Colorado Springs. By day, Dian taught at the Colorado School for the Deaf and Blind; by night, fueled by his memory of the attack, he and Jan began to study martial arts. They were drawn to a form of karate called Universal Kempo, a combination of self-defense and awareness. Universal Kempo teaches students to deal instantly and effectively should a dangerous situation arise. It also increases endurance, strength, muscle tone, and mental alertness.

It was a fit for Dian and Jan. Eventually they took over the karate school, doubled its enrollment, and even started an after school program teaching martial arts to deaf and visually impaired kids. Today, as a martial arts instructor, Dian tries to pass along to his students his traits of willpower and "can do" attitude. "I tell them all the time, there's not going to be somebody standing over you the rest of your life telling you what to do. You've got to do it yourself. And they *can* learn to do things for themselves. I know it's hard, but I have a lot of faith in people's abilities."

An inspiring mentor to his young students, Dian credits his own mentors for helping him along the way. "Sometimes that's more important than anything else—a mentor saying, 'You *can* do this.' In our arrogance, we forget that we didn't get where we are by ourselves. It took other people to help us get there. Having mentors in my life who have reinforced that I can do whatever I put my mind to has made a big difference."

At age 40, Dian's body presented him with its toughest challenge to date. He suffered a grand mal seizure. Once again, Dian hovered near death. An abnormal EEG revealed brain damage, likely the result of that long ago day when his tonsils swelled and cut off precious oxygen. The seizures continue and have increased in severity since then, and Dian admits it's a challenge. "But when it's really tough," he says, "my spirit rises up and I realize I can't do anything about it, so I deal with it. If it happens, it happens."

Dian's experience during the 23 minutes he hovered between life and death still inspires him to be the best he can be. He recently tested for—and earned—his second-degree black belt, a feat that required him to draw on all of his reserves. As he prepared for the test, he recalled the advice of his karate teacher. "There's no such thing as a disabled black belt," he told Dian, "so don't whine about it. It's unbecoming to you. Just do it."

(Story by Leticia Steffen)

Literal Comprehension Questions:

1. What happened to Dian during the time he was pronounced legally dead?

2. What happened that made Dian want to become an expert in the martial arts?

3. What were the physical challenges Dian faced throughout his life?

Inferential Comprehension Questions:

1. Why do you think Dian did not like teaching at a "regular" school? Explain your thinking.

2. What do you think were some of Dian's greatest challenges when becoming a black belt? Explain your thinking.

3. Dian said that, during his "near death experience," he didn't want to come back to life. What do you think he meant by this? Explain your thinking.

Self-Analysis Questions:

1. Dian developed the belief that he shouldn't worry about things he can not control. Would you agree or disagree with Dian's belief? Why? What are some things you are currently worried about that you cannot control?

2. Dian's mentor told him, "there is no such thing as a disabled black belt so don't whine about your disability." What are some things you whine about? What good things has your whining produced? What bad things has your whining produced?

3. When Dian was beaten up for the one dollar in his wallet, he decided that this would never happen to him again. That decision lead him to eventually become a black belt in karate. What negative experience inspired you to take action?

Legson Kayira

No matter how impossible a goal may seem it can be reached. Legson Kayira—once an indigent wanderer in Africa with a dream, now a successful professor and author—can attest to this.

In October 1958, Legson was a teenager in Africa with a big dream: to travel to the United State for an education. For his 3,000-mile journey from East Africa to Cairo, Egypt, Legson brought enough food for five days, a small ax, a blanket, and his two prized books—the Bible and "The Pilgrim's Progress." His supplies quickly dwindled, but not his determination. This is his story.

Growing up in East Africa, Legson, like many of his peers, often felt oppressed by poverty. He used poverty as an excuse for not doing his best at his studies and for not trying to accomplish more with his life. But his life began to change when missionaries working in his home town of Karongo in Nyasaland gave Legson books with stories of Abraham Lincoln and Booker T. Washington. The stories of these men sparked something inside Legson that made him want to make something more of himself. Their stories brought glimmers of hope to his life.

Abraham Lincoln became Legson's hero. The story of Lincoln's rise from poverty to presidency and his fight to help free the slaves inspired Legson immensely. Legson also deeply admired Booker T. Washington, a former slave who became a great American reformer and educator.

Legson realized he wanted to make a difference in the world and help humankind, just as these two men had done. To accomplish that, Legson knew he needed an education, and he knew the best place to get a good education was in the United States. At the time, Legson had no money and no idea of what, exactly, college *was*; he simply had an idea and the determination to make something better of himself.

But his trek across Africa proved more difficult than he had expected. After five days, he was out of food, nearly out of water, had no money—and he had only traveled 25 miles! "I will not stop until I reach America," Legson told himself. "Or until I die trying." So he continued.

At one point, Legson contracted a fever and became gravely ill. But kind strangers gave him a place to rest and treated him with herbal medicines, helping Legson get back on his feet and continue his journey.

After 15 months, Legson had crossed 1,000 miles and reached a large city, Kampala, Uganda. There, Legson worked odd jobs to earn money for his journey, but he spent most of his time at the library reading as many books as he could. Among other things, Legson picked up a directory of American colleges and universities.

In its pages, an illustration of Skagit Valley College in Mount Vernon, Washington, caught Legson's eye. The stately, friendly-looking institution with its lovely fountains and lawns was set beneath a blue sky and surrounded by mountains. The setting reminded Legson of the peaks surrounding his home in Nyasaland and inspired him to write the dean of the college, explaining his situation and requesting a scholarship. Legson's letter proved to be so moving that the dean granted him admission, offered him a scholarship, and gave him a job to pay for room and board.

Now, all Legson needed was a passport, a visa, and transportation to Cairo. Just as the rest of his amazing journey had fallen into place, these obstacles were also overcome. The missionaries who gave Legson the inspirational books that formed his dream also helped him get a visa and passport. And students at Skagit Valley College, along with citizens from the local town, heard Legson's amazing story and sent $650 to cover his airfare to America.

In December 1960, Legson arrived at Skagit Valley College. With his two treasured books in hand, Legson walked proudly onto the campus to begin his studies. He pursued his dream even beyond graduation, becoming a professor of political science at Cambridge University in England and a widely respected author.

Despite his humble beginnings, Legson Kayira held tight to his dream, and refused to let obstacles make him give up. His life is a testament to the fact that, with determination, even the most impossible dreams can come true.

(Story by Shae Isaacs)

Literal Comprehension Questions:

1. What did Legson bring with him for his 3,000 mile trip from East Africa to Cairo?

2. What did Skagit Valley College remind Legson of?

3. After he graduated from college, what did Legson go on to do?

Inferential Comprehension Questions:

1. Why do you think Legson and his boyhood friends used poverty as an excuse for not doing well their studies? Explain your thinking.

2. At what point do you think Legson was most discourged? Explain your thinking.

3. How do you think the citizens from the town near Skagit Valley College heard about Legson? Why do you think they wanted to help him? Explain your thinking.

Self-Analysis Questions:

1. Legson explained that, as a boy, he and his friends used poverty as an excuse not to try to accomplish more. What excuses prevent you from trying to accomplish more at school?

2. Legson wanted to make a difference in the world—to make the world a better place. What difference do you want to make in the world? Why?

3. Legson simply would not give up on his dream to get an education in the United States. What have you been unwilling to give up on? Why?

CHAPTER 9
QUOTATIONS

This Chapter contains over 900 quotations intended to be used on a systematic, even daily basis with students as a motivational tool throughout the Pathfinder Project (see Chapter 2). Students select quotations that are of interest to them and record them in the appropriate section of their Student Notebooks. (See Chapter 7 for a discussion.) Additionally, in the final phase of the personal project, students are asked to create their own aphorisms representing what they hold true about life and about themselves as a result of engaging in the personal project. (See Chapter 3 for a discussion.)

There are far more quotations in this chapter than you will need for the Pathfinder Project, so select those that will be the most relevant to your students. You may also decide to use quotations from other sources. Those listed here are organized into categories:

Taking on Big Things

Changing Plans

Declarations and Powerful Statements

The Power of Dreams and Aspirations

Optimism

Heroes, Role Models, and Mentors

The Future

Taking Small Steps

Understanding the Nature of Support

Miscellaneous

Taking on Big Things

Aesop	*"Plodding wins the race."*
George E. Allen	*"People of mediocre ability sometimes achieve outstanding success because they don't know when to quit. Most men succeed because they are determined to."*
Julie Andrews	*"Perseverance is failing nineteen times and succeeding the twentieth."*
Anonymous	*"Every worthwhile accomplishment, big or little, has its stages of drudgery and triumph; a beginning, a struggle and a victory."*
Anonymous	*"The man on top of the mountain did not fall there."*
Aristotle	*"It is the mark of an educated mind to be able to entertain a thought without accepting it."*
Author Unknown	*"Don't expect to find life worth living; make it that way."*
Author Unknown	*"If you find a path with no obstacles, it probably doesn't lead anywhere."*
Author Unknown	*"It's not who you are that holds you back, it's who you think you're not."*
St. Teresa Avila	*"Learn to self-conquest. Persevere thus for a time, and you will perceive very clearly the advantage which you gain from it."*

Roger Bannister	*"The man who can drive himself further once the effort gets painful is the man who will win."*
Henry Ward Beecher	*"The difference between perseverance and obstinacy is that one comes from a strong will, and the other from a strong won't."*
Josh Billings	*"Be like a postage stamp. Stick to one thing until you get there."*
Bill Bradley	*"Ambition is the path to success. Persistence is the vehicle you arrive in."*
Claude M. Bristol	*"It's the constant and determined effort that breaks down all resistance and sweeps away all obstacles."*
H. Jackson Brown	*"In the confrontation between the stream and the rock, the stream always wins—not through strength but by perseverance."*
James Buckham	*"Every trial endured and weathered in the right spirit makes a soul nobler and stronger than it was before."*
Carol Burnett	*"When you have a dream you've got to grab it and never let go."*
Leo Burnett	*"When you reach for the stars, you may not quite get them, but you won't come up with a handful of mud, either."*
Eric Butterworth	*"Nothing stops the man who desires to achieve. Every obstacle is simply a course to develop his achievement muscle. It's a strengthening of his powers of accomplishment."*
Thomas Fowell Buxton	*"The longer I live, the more I am certain that the great difference between the great and the insignificant, is energy— invincible determination—a purpose once fixed, and then death or victory."*
Dale Carnegie	*"Flaming enthusiasm, backed by horse sense and persistence, is the quality that most frequently makes for success."*
Dale Carnegie	*"Most of the important things in the world have been accomplished by people who have kept on trying when there seemed to be no help at all."*
Rosalynn Carter	*"You have to have confidence in your ability, and then be tough enough to follow through."*
Chinese Proverb	*"The gem cannot be polished without friction, nor man perfected without trials.*
Sir Winston Churchill	*"Success is not final, failure is not fatal: it is the courage to continue that counts."*
Calvin Coolidge	*"Nothing in the world can take the place of persistence. Talent will not; nothing is more common than unsuccessful men with talent. Genius will not; unrewarded genius is almost a proverb. Education will not; the world is full of educated derelicts. Persistence and determination alone are omnipotent."*

Leonardo da Vinci	*"Obstacles cannot crush me. Every obstacle yields to stern resolve. He who is fixed to a star does not change his mind."*
Russel W. Davenport	*"Progress in every age results only from the fact that there are some men and women who refuse to believe that what they know to be right cannot be done."*
Eugene Debs	*"The most heroic word in all languages is revolution."*
Richard M. Devos	*"If I had to select one quality, one personal characteristic that I regard as being most highly correlated with success, whatever the field, I would pick the trait of persistence. Determination. The will to endure to the end, to get knocked down seventy times and get up off the floor saying, 'Here comes number seventy-one!'"*
Frederick Douglass	*"Without a struggle, there can be no progress."*
Thomas A. Edison	*"Genius is 99 percent perspiration and 1 percent inspiration."*
Thomas A. Edison	*"When I have fully decided that a result is worth getting I go ahead of it and make trial after trial until it comes."*
Edward Eggleston	*"Persistent people begin their success where others end in failure."*
Albert Einstein	*"In the middle of difficulty lies opportunity."*
George Eliot	*"Failure after long perseverance is much grander than never to have a striving good enough to be called a failure."*
Walter Elliott	*"Perseverance is not a long race; it is many short races one after another."*
Ralph Waldo Emerson	*"All great masters are chiefly distinguished by the power of adding a second, a third, and perhaps a fourth step in a continuous line. Many a man has taken the first step. With every additional step you enhance immensely the value of you first."*
Ralph Waldo Emerson	*"Nothing great was ever achieved without enthusiasm."*
Ted W. Engstrom	*"The rewards for those who persevere far exceed the pain that must precede the victory."*
William Feather	*"Success seems to be largely a matter of hanging on after others have let go."*
Ella Fitzgerald	*"Just don't give up trying to do what you really want to do. Where there is love and inspiration, I don't think you can go wrong."*
Bertie C. Forbes	*"History has demonstrated that the most notable winners usually encountered heartbreaking obstacles before they triumphed. They won because they refused to become discouraged by their defeats."*

Henry Ford	*"One of the greatest discoveries a man makes, one of his great surprises, is to find he can do what he was afraid he couldn't do."*
Thomas Fuller	*"An invincible determination can accomplish almost anything and in this lies the great distinction between great men and little men."*
Newt Gingrich	*"Perseverance is the hard work you do after you get tired of doing the hard work you already did."*
Johann Wolfgang von Goethe	*"What does not kill me makes me stronger."*
Dag Hammerskjold	*"Never measure the height of a mountain until you reach the top. Then you will see how low it was."*
Ernest Hello	*"The man who gives up accomplishes nothing and is only a hindrance. The man who does not give up can move mountains."*
Herodotus	*"Some men give up their designs when they have almost reached the goal while others, on the contrary, obtain a victory by exerting, at the last moment, more vigorous efforts than ever before."*
Conrad Hilton	*"Success seems to be connected with action. Successful men keep moving. They make mistakes, but they don't quit."*
William E. Holler	*"You can do what you want to do, accomplish what you want to accomplish, attain any reasonable objective you may have in mind— not all of a sudden, perhaps not in one swift and sweeping act of achievement—but you can do it gradually, day by day and play by play, if you want to do it, if you work to do it, over a sufficiently long period of time."*
Ernest Holmes	*"Never limit your view of life by any past experience."*
Oliver Wendell Holmes	*"Every calling is great when greatly pursued."*
Ellen Hubbard	*"The greatest mistake you can make in life is to be continually fearing that you will make one."*
I Ching	*"Perseverance alone does not assure success. No amount of stalking will lead to game in a field that has none."*
Pope John Paul I	*"If someone had told me I would be Pope one day, I would have studied harder."*
Samuel Johnson	*"If your determination is fixed, I do not counsel you to despair. Few things are impossible to diligence and skill. Great works are performed not by strength, but perseverance."*
Michael Jordon	*"Obstacles don't have to stop you. If you run into a wall, don't turn around and give up. Figure out how to climb it, go through it, or work around it."*

Kitty Kelley	*"Once I decide to do something, I can't have people telling me I can't. If there's a roadblock, you jump over it, walk around it, crawl under it."*
Mary-Claire King	*"I think there are two keys to being creatively productive. One is not being daunted by one's fear of failure. The second is sheer perseverance."*
Billie Jean King	*"Champions keep playing until they get it right."*
Melissa Lima	*"All respect comes from persisting to completion."*
John Locke	*"Fortitude is the guard and support of the other virtues."*
Henry Wadsworth Longfellow	*"Perseverance is a great element of success. If you only knock long enough and loud enough at the gate, you are sure to wake up somebody."*
Orison Swett Marden	*"All who have accomplished great things have had a great aim, have fixed their gaze on a goal which was high, one which sometimes seemed impossible."*
George Matheson	*"We conquer—not in any brilliant fashion—we conquer by continuing."*
Rene McPherson	*"You just keep pushing. You just keep pushing. I made every mistake that could be made. But I just kept pushing."*
Dr. A. B. Meldrum	*"Bear in mind, if you are going to amount to anything, that your success does not depend upon the brilliancy and the impetuosity with which you take hold, but upon the everlasting and sanctified bulldoggedness with which you hang on after you have taken hold."*
Harry Millner	*"All progress occurs because people dare to be different."*
Christopher Morley	*"Big shots are only little shots who keep shooting."*
F. W. Nichol	*"When you get right down to the root of the meaning of the word 'succeed,' you find that it simply means to follow through."*
Friedrich Nietzsche	*"On the mountains of truth you can never climb in vain: either you will reach a point higher up today, or you will be training your powers so that you will be able to climb higher tomorrow."*
William Penn	*"Patience and diligence, like faith, remove mountains."*
Persius	*"He conquers who endures."*
Peter's Principle of Success	*"Get up one time more than you're knocked down."*
Pablo Picasso	*"Give me a museum and I'll fill it."*
Plutarch	*"Perseverance is more prevailing than violence; and many things which cannot be overcome when they are together yield themselves up when taken little by little."*
Prince	*"Can you imagine what I would do if I could do all I can?"*

J. Herman Randall	*"Any individual can be, in time, what he earnestly desires to be, if he but set his face steadfastly in the direction of that one thing and bring all his powers to bear upon its attainment."*
Admiral Hyman Rickover	*"Good ideas are not adopted automatically. They must be driven into practice with courageous patience."*
Jacob A. Riis	*"I'd look at one of my stonecutters hammering away at the rock, perhaps a hundred times without as much as a crack showing in it. Yet, at the hundred and first blow it would split in two, and I knew it was not that blow that did it, but all that had gone before."*
James Whitcomb Riley	*"The most essential factor is persistence—the determination never to allow your energy or enthusiasm to be dampened by the discouragement that must inevitably come."*
John D. Rockefeller	*"I do not think there is any other quality so essential to success of any kind as the quality of perseverance. It overcomes almost everything, even nature."*
John-Roger and Peter McWilliams	*"Nothing succeeds like persistence. The common denominator of all successful people is their persistence."*
Franklin Delano Roosevelt	*"When you get to the end of your rope, tie a knot and hang on."*
Theodore Roosevelt	*"Far and away the best prize that life has to offer is the chance to work hard at work worth doing."*
Sadi	*"A little and a little, collected together, becomes a great deal; the heap in the barn consists of single grains, and drop and drop make the inundation."*
George Santayana	*"Fanaticism consists of redoubling your efforts when you have forgotten your aim."*
Robert C. Savage	*"You can measure a man by the opposition it takes to discourage him."*
Robert H. Schuller	*"Most people who succeed in the face of seemingly impossible conditions are people who simply don't know how to quit."*
David Joseph Schwartz	*"All great achievements require time."*
Seneca	*"It is not because things are difficult that we do not dare; it is because we do not dare that they are difficult."*
Eric Sevareid	*"Tenacity is a pretty fair substitute for bravery, and the best form of tenacity I know is expressed in a Danish fur trapper's principle: 'The next mile is the only one a person really has to make.'"*
Minnie Richard Smith	*"Diamonds are only chunks of coal that stuck to their jobs, you see."*

Sylvester Stallone	*"I believe there's an inner power that makes winners or losers. And the winners are the ones who really listen to the truth of their hearts."*
Ben Stein	*"There is no sudden leap into the stratosphere... There is only advancing step by step, slowly and tortuously, up the pyramid towards your goals..."*
Harriet Beecher Stowe	*"When you get into a tight place and everything goes against you, till it seems as though you could not hang on a minute longer, never give up then, for that is just the place and time that the tide will turn."*
Janet Erskine Stuart	*"The great thing and the hard thing is to stick to a thing when you have outlived the first interest and not yet the second which comes with a sort of mastery."*
Anne Sullivan	*"Keep on beginning and failing. Each time you fail, start all over again, and you will grow stronger until have accomplished a purpose—not the one you began with perhaps, but one you'll be glad to remember."*
Tom Robbins	*"To achieve the impossible, it is precisely the unthinkable that must be thought."*
Brian Tracy	*"Your decision to be, have and do something out of the ordinary entails facing difficulties that are out of the ordinary as well. Sometimes your greatest asset is simply your ability to stay with it longer than anyone else."*
Mao Tse-tung	*"Once all struggle is grasped, miracles are possible."*
Mark Twain	*"The miracle, or the power, that elevates the few is to be found in their industry, application, and perseverance under the prompting of a brave, determined spirit."*
Vincent Van Gogh	*"Great things are done by a series of small things brought together."*
Vivekananda	*"Take up one thing and do it, and see the end of it, and before you have seen the end, do not give up. Those who only take a nibble here and a nibble there will never attain anything."*
Denis Waitley	*"As long as we are persistence in our pursuit of our deepest destiny, we will continue to grow. We cannot choose the day or time when we will fully bloom. It happens in its own time."*
John Wanamaker	*"One may walk over the highest mountain, one step at a time."*
Isaac Watts	*"Do not hover always on the surface of things, nor take up suddenly with mere appearances; but penetrate into the depth of matters, as far as your time and circumstances allow, especially in those things which relate to your profession."*

Edwin Percy Whipple	"The universal line of distinction between the strong and the weak is that one persists; the other hesitates, falters, trifles, and at last collapses or 'caves in.'"
Ella Wheeler Wilcox	"There is no chance, no destiny, no fate, that can circumvent or hinder or control the firm resolve of a determined soul."
John R. Wooden	"Do not let what you cannot do interfere with what you can do."
Ernest L. Woodward	"So great has been the endurance, so incredible the achievement, that, as long as the sun keeps a set course in heaven, it would be foolish to despair of the human race."
Yoda	"Do or do not. There is no try."

Changing Plans

Saint Peter of Alcantara	"The trouble is that everyone talks about reforming others and no one thinks about reforming himself."
Muhammad Ali	"A man who views the world at 50 the same as he did at 20 has wasted 30 years of his life."
Ed Allen	"To change is difficult. Not to change is fatal."
Lisa Alther	"That's the risk you take if you change: that people you've been involved with won't like the new you. But other people who do will come along."
Maya Angelou	"If you don't like something, change it. If you can't change it, change your attitude. Don't complain."
Dr. Robert Anthony	"When it becomes more difficult to suffer than to change ... you will change."
Dr. Robert Anthony	"When you blame others, you give up your power to change."
Aristotle	"Change in all things is sweet."
Elaine N. Aron	"While it is wise to accept what we cannot change about ourselves, it is also good to remember that we are never too old to replace discouragement with bits and pieces of confidence and hope."
Marcus Aurelius	"Observe constantly that all things take place by change, and accustom thyself to consider that the nature of the Universe loves nothing so much as to change ... The Universe is change."
Richard Bach	"In order to live free and happily you must sacrifice boredom. It is not always an easy sacrifice."
James Baldwin	"Not everything that is faced can be changed, but nothing can be changed until it is faced."
W. L. Bateman	"If you keep on doing what you've always done, you'll keep on getting what you've always got."

Arnold Bennett	*"Any change, even a change for the better, is always accompanied by drawbacks and discomforts."*
Bernard Berenson	*"Consistency requires you to be as ignorant today as you were a year ago."*
Phyllis Bottome	*"Neither situations nor people can be altered by the interference of an outsider. If they are to be altered, that alteration must come from within."*
Anne Bradstreet	*"If we had no winter, the spring would not be so pleasant: if we did not sometimes taste of adversity, prosperity would not be so welcome."*
Francis Hodgson Burnett	*"At first people refuse to believe that a strange new thing can be done, then they begin to hope that it can be done, then they see that it can be done—then it is done and all the world wonders why it was not done centuries ago."*
Leo Buscaglia	*"Change is the end result of all true learning."*
John C. Calhoun	*"The interval between the decay of the old and the formation and establishment of the new constitutes a period of transition which must always necessarily be one of uncertainty, confusion, error, and wild and fierce fanaticism."*
Jimmy Carter	*"We must adjust to changing times and still hold to unchanging principles."*
Chased By Bears	*"When a man does a piece of work which is admired by all we say that it is wonderful; but when we see the changes of day and night, the sun, the moon, and the stars in the sky, and the changing seasons upon the earth, with their ripening fruits, anyone must realize that it is the work of someone more powerful than man."*
Glenda Cloud	*"Change is inevitable, growth is intentional."*
Confucius	*"To be wronged is nothing unless you continue to remember it."*
Ossie Davis	*"Any form of art is a form of power, it has impact, it can affect change—it can not only move us, it makes us move."*
W. Edwards Deming	*"It is not necessary to change. Survival is not mandatory."*
William Drayton	*"Change starts when someone sees the next step."*
Marian Wright Edelman	*"If you don't like the way the world is, you change it. You have an obligation to change it. You just do it one step at a time."*
Dwight David Eisenhower	*"The world moves, and ideas that were once good are not always good."*
Jeff Estep	*"When assuming the throne, great kings are not judged by how many good changes they may make; rather, on how little they change the things which are already good."*
Antoine de Saint Exupery	*"A single event can awaken within us a stranger totally unknown to us. To live is to be slowly born."*
Millard Fillmore	*"It is not strange ... to mistake change for progress."*
Bettina R. Flores	*"Courage is the atom of change."*

Victor Frankl	*"When we are no longer able to change a situation … we are challenged to change ourselves."*
Victor Frankl	*"The last of the human freedoms is to choose one's attitudes."*
John Kenneth Galbraith	*"In the choice between changing one's mind and proving there's no need to do so, most people get busy on the proof."*
Mahatma Gandhi	*"Honest disagreement is often a good sign of progress."*
Mahatma Gandhi	*"Freedom is not worth having if it does not include the freedom to make mistakes."*
Mahatma Gandhi	*"You must be the change you wish to see in the world."*
Shakti Gawain	*"The most powerful thing you can do to change the world is to change your own beliefs about the nature of life, people, and reality to something more positive … and begin to act accordingly."*
German Proverb	*"To change and to change for the better are two different things."*
Kahlil Gibran	*"The lust for comfort murders the passions of the soul."*
Doug Hall	*"Don't make excuses. Make things happen. Make changes. Then make history."*
Frank Herbert	*"Without change, something sleeps inside us, and seldom awakens. The sleeper must awaken."*
Jesse Jackson	*"Both tears and sweat are salty, but they render a different result. Tears will get you sympathy; sweat will get you change."*
Carl G. Jung	*"If there is anything we wish to change in the child, we should first examine it and see whether it is not something that could better be changed in ourselves."*
Carl G. Jung	*"We cannot change anything until we accept it. Condemnation does not liberate, it oppresses."*
John Fitzgerald Kennedy	*"Change is the law of life. And those who look only to the past or present are certain to miss the future."*
Charles F. Kettering	*"People are very open-minded about new things—as long as they're exactly like the old ones."*
Martin Luther King, Jr.	*"Change does not roll in on the wheels of inevitability, but comes through continuous struggle. And so we must straighten our backs and work for our freedom. A man can't ride you unless your back is bent."*
R. D. Laing	*"We live in a moment of history where change is so speeded up that we begin to see the present only when it is disappearing."*
Lao-Tzu	*"If you do not change direction, you may end up where you are heading."*
George B. Leonard	*"To learn is to change. Education is a process that changes the learner."*
Kurt Lewin	*"If you want truly to understand something, try to change it."*

G. C. Lichtenberg	*"I cannot say whether things will get better if we change; what I can say is they must change if they are to get better."*
Abraham Lincoln	*"The dogmas of the quiet past are inadequate to the stormy present. The occasion is piled high with difficulty, and we must rise with the occasion. As our case is new, so we must think anew and act anew."*
Ann Morrow Lindbergh	*"Only in growth, reform, and change, paradoxically enough, is true security to be found."*
John Locke	*"New opinions are always suspected, and usually opposed, without any other reason but because they are not already common."*
Max Lucado	*"You change your life by changing your heart."*
Joan Lunden	*"To be able to look at change as an opportunity to grow—that is the secret to being happy."*
Niccolo Machiavelli	*"It must be remembered that there is nothing more difficult to plan, more doubtful of success nor more dangerous to manage than the creation of a new system. For the initiator has the enmity of all who profit by the preservation of the old institution and merely lukewarm defenders in those who would gain by the new one."*
Niccolo Machiavelli	*"There is nothing more difficult to take in hand, more perilous to conduct or more uncertain in its success than to take the lead in the introduction of a new order of things."*
Shirley MacLaine	*"I realized that if what we call human nature can be changed, then absolutely anything is possible. And from that moment, my life changed."*
Nelson Mandela	*"There is nothing like returning to a place that remains unchanged to find the ways in which you yourself have altered."*
Dr. Phil McGraw	*"Are you doing what you're doing today because you want to do it, or because it's what you were doing yesterday?"*
Margaret Mead	*"Never doubt that a small group of thoughtful, committed citizens can change the world. Indeed, it is the only thing that ever has."*
Gene E. Megiveron	*"To stand still is to lose, to move is to gain, to change is to grow."*
Rickie Moore	*"Tolerate, change, or be grateful."*
John Muir	*"The grand show is eternal. It is always sunrise somewhere; the dew is never dried all at once; a shower is forever falling; vapor is ever rising. Eternal sunrise, eternal dawn and gloaming, on sea and continents and islands, each in its turn, as the round earth rolls."*
Jawharlal Nehru	*"A moment comes, which comes but rarely in history, when we step out from the old to the new; when an age ends; and when the soul of a nation long suppressed finds utterance."*

John Henry Cardinal Newman	*"In a higher world it is otherwise; but here below to live is to change, and to be perfect is to change often."*
Dick Nicolosi	*"Slaying sacred cows makes great steaks."*
Richard M. Nixon	*"Any change is resisted because bureaucrats have a vested interest in the chaos in which they exist."*
Kathleen Norris	*"None of us knows what the next change is going to be, what unexpected opportunity is just around the corner, waiting a few months or a few years to change all the tenor of our lives."*
Herbert Otto	*"Change and growth take place when a person has risked himself and dares to become involved with experimenting with his own life."*
Thomas Paine	*"A long habit of not thinking a thing wrong gives it the superficial appearance of being right, and raises at first a formidable outcry in defense of custom. But the tumult soon subsides. Time makes more converts than reason."*
William Pollard	*"Without change there is no innovation, creativity, or incentive for improvement. Those who initiate change will have a better opportunity to manage the change that is inevitable."*
John Porter	*"People underestimate their capacity for change. There is never a right time to do a difficult thing. A leader's job is to help people have vision of their potential."*
Vince Poscente	*"Judgmentalism assumes that you have the right to change someone else. Well, you don't. You only have the right to choose how you will change and behave. Trust others to make their own choices. Put the accountability for another's actions where it belongs, on the other person's shoulders."*
Lynn Povich	*"Change is often rejuvenating, invigorating, fun ... and necessary."*
Scott Reed	*"This one step—choosing a goal and sticking to it—changes everything."*
Al Rogers	*"In times of profound change, the learners inherit the earth, while the learned find themselves beautifully equipped to deal with a world that no longer exists."*
George Santayana	*"Progress, far from consisting in change, depends on retentiveness. Those who cannot remember the past are condemned to repeat it."*
Gail Sheehy	*"Changes are not only possible and predictable, but to deny them is to be an accomplice to one's own unnecessary vegetation."*
Gail Sheehy	*"If we don't change, we don't grow. If we don't grow, we aren't really living."*
Dave E. Smalley	*"The survival of the fittest is the ageless law of nature, but the fittest are rarely the strong. The fittest are those endowed with the qualifications for adaptation, the ability to accept the inevitable and conform to the unavoidable, to harmonize with existing or changing conditions."*

Elaine St. James	*"Maintaining a complicated life is a great way to avoid changing it."*
Susan Taylor	*"In every crisis there is a message. Crises are nature's way of forcing change, breaking down old structures, shaking loose negative habits so that something new and better can take their place."*
Henry David Thoreau	*"Things do not change; we change."*
L. C. Thurow	*"A competitive world offers two possibilities. You can lose. Or, if you want to win, you can change."*
Leo Tolstoy	*"Everyone thinks of changing the world, but no one thinks of changing himself."*
Mark Twain	*"Loyalty to petrified opinion never yet broke a chain or freed a human soul."*
Mark Twain	*"We are chameleons, and our partialities and prejudices change place with an easy and blessed facility, and we are soon wonted to the change and happy in it."*
Mark Twain	*"Danger lies not in what we don't know, but in what we think we know that just ain't so."*
Andy Warhol	*"They always say time changes things, but you actually have to change them yourself."*
H. G. Wells	*"Adapt or perish, now as ever, is nature's inexorable imperative."*
Colin Wilson	*"The mind has exactly the same power as the hands; not merely to grasp the world, but to change it."*

Declarations and Powerful Statements

Mario Andretti	*"Love what you do. Believe in your instincts. And you'd better be able to pick yourself up and brush yourself off every day."*
Anonymous	*"Expect the people you love to be better. It helps them to become better. But don't get upset when they fail. It helps them keep trying."*
Anonymous	*"'I can't' isn't a reason to give up, it's a reason to try harder."*
Anonymous	*"What I do today is important because I'm exchanging a day of my life for it."*
T. Alan Armstrong	*"If you are not getting better, you are getting left behind."*
Jan Ashford	*"There is no such thing as can't, only won't. If you're qualified, all it takes is a burning desire to accomplish, to make a change. Go forward, go backward. Whatever it takes! But you can't blame other people or society in general. It all comes from your mind. When we do the impossible we realize we are special people."*
Marcus Aurelius	*"People are always blaming their circumstances for what they are. Never esteem anything as of advantage to you that will make you break your word or lose your self-respect."*

Walter Bagehot	*"The greatest pleasure in life is doing what people say you cannot do."*
Jesse Barfield	*"I've always tried to do my best on the ball field. I can't do any more than that. I always try to give one hundred percent; and if my team loses, I come back and give one hundred percent the next day."*
Charles Austin Beard	*"You need only reflect that one of the best ways to get yourself a reputation as a dangerous citizen these days is to go about repeating the very phrases which our founding fathers used in the struggle for independence."*
Warren G. Bennis	*"People who cannot invent and reinvent themselves must be content with borrowed postures, secondhand ideas, fitting in instead of standing out."*
Erma Bombeck	*"When I stand before God at the end of my life, I would hope that I would not have a single bit of talent left, and could say, 'I used everything you gave me.'"*
Bob Briner	*"We do not have to be the best to be effective, but we do have to be at our best."*
Phillip Brooks	*"Be such a man, and live such a life, that if every man were such as you, and every life a life like yours, this earth would be God's Paradise."*
Les Brown	*"Shoot for the moon. Even if you miss it, you will land among the stars."*
Buddha	*"The cause of all pain and suffering is ignorance."*
Dale Carnegie	*"If you believe in what you are doing, then let nothing hold you up in your work. Much of the best work of the world has been done against seeming impossibilities. The thing is to get the work done."*
Queen Christina of Sweden	*"It is necessary to try to pass one's self always; this occupation ought to last as long as life."*
Alistair Cooke	*"A professional is someone who can do his best work when he doesn't feel like it."*
Charles F. Deems	*"That man is blest who does his best and leaves the rest."*
W. Edwards Deming	*"It is not enough to do your best; you must know what to do, and then do your best."*
Charles Dickens	*"Whatever I have tried to do in life, I have tried with all my heart to do it well; whatever I have devoted myself to, I have devoted myself completely; in great aims and in small, I have always thoroughly been in earnest."*
Horotio W. Dresser	*"Do your best every day and your life will gradually expand into satisfying fullness."*
Marie Dressler	*"To know that one has never really tried—that is the only death."*
Marian Wright Edelman	*"You're not obligated to win. You're obligated to keep trying to do the best you can every day."*

Albert Einstein	*"Anyone who has never made a mistake has never tried anything new."*
Albert Einstein	*"Everything that is really great and inspiring is created by the individual who can labour in freedom."*
Albert Einstein	*"Learn from yesterday, live for today, hope for tomorrow. The important thing is not to stop questioning."*
t.s. eliot	*"For us, there is only the trying. The rest is not our business."*
Duke Ellington	*"A problem is a chance for you to do your best."*
Ralph Waldo Emerson	*"Make the most of yourself, for that is all there is of you."*
Ralph Waldo Emerson	*"The reward of a thing well done is to have done it."*
Ralph Waldo Emerson	*"Unless you try to do something beyond what you have already mastered, you will never grow."*
Ralph Waldo Emerson	*"We know better than we do. We do not yet possess ourselves..."*
Harry Emerson Fosdick	*"Rebellion against your handicaps gets you nowhere. Self-pity gets you nowhere. One must have the adventurous daring to accept oneself as a bundle of possibilities and undertake the most interesting game in the world—making the most of one's best."*
Anne Frank	*"Everyone has inside of him a piece of good news. The good news is that you don't know how great you can be! How much you can love! What you can accomplish! And what your potential is!"*
Viktor Frankl	*"Everyone has his own specific vocation or mission in life; everyone must carry out a concrete assignment that demands fulfillment. Therein he cannot be replaced, nor can his life be repeated, thus, everyone's task is unique as his specific opportunity to implement it."*
Benjamin Franklin	*"Well done is better than well said."*
Mahatma Gandhi	*"Men often become what they believe themselves to be. If I believe I cannot do something, it makes me incapable of doing it. But when I believe I can, then I acquire the ability to do it even if I didn't have it in the beginning."*
Mahatma Gandhi	*"Satisfaction lies in the effort, not in the attainment. Full effort is full victory."*
Edward Gibbon	*"The winds and the waves are always on the side of the ablest navigators."*
Kahlil Gibran	*"Yesterday we obeyed kings and bent our necks before emperors. But today we kneel only to truth, follow only beauty, and obey only love."*
Diane Glancy	*"I try. I am trying. I was trying. I will try. I shall in the meantime try. I sometimes have tried. I shall still by that time be trying."*
Johann Wolfgang von Goethe	*"Still this planet's soil for noble deeds grants scope abounding."*

Stephan Grellet	*"I expect to pass through this world but once; any good thing therefore that I can do, or any kindness that I can show to any fellow creature, let me do it now; let me not defer or neglect it, for I shall not pass this way again."*
Tom Hopkins	*"I am not judged by the number of times I fail, but by the number of times I succeed; and the number of times I succeed is in direct proportion to the number of times I can fail and keep on trying."*
Edgar Watson Howe	*"People are always neglecting something they can do in trying to do something they can't do."*
Zora Neale Hurston	*"No matter how far a person can go the horizon is still way beyond you."*
Mick Jagger and Keith Richards	*"You can't always get what you want. But if you try sometimes, you just might find you get what you need."*
William James	*"Act as if what you do makes a difference. It does."*
Thomas Jefferson	*"It is error alone which needs the support of government. Truth can stand by itself."*
Samuel Johnson	*"To strive with difficulties, and to conquer them, is the highest human felicity."*
Lloyd Jones	*"The men who try to do something and fail are infinitely better than those who try to do nothing and succeed."*
Madame Chiang Kai-Shek	*"We become what we do."*
Immanual Kant	*"May you live your life as if the maxim of your actions were to become universal law."*
Helen Keller	*"I long to accomplish a great and noble task, but it is my chief duty to accomplish small tasks as if they were great and noble."*
Helen Keller	*"When we do the best that we can, we never know what miracle is wrought in our life, or in the life of another."*
Kierkegaard	*"People demand freedom of speech as a compensation for the freedom of thought, which they seldom use."*
Martin Luther King, Jr.	*"If a man is called to be a streetsweeper, he should sweep streets even as Michelangelo painted, or Beethoven played music, or Shakespeare wrote poetry. He should sweep streets so well that all the hosts of heaven and earth will pause to say, here lived a great streetsweeper who did his job well."*
Malcolm Kushner	*"People who are resting on their laurels are wearing them on the wrong end."*
David Letterman	*"Sometimes something worth doing is worth overdoing."*
Abraham Lincoln	*"I do the very best I know how—the very best I can; and I mean to keep on doing so until the end."*

Anne Morrow Lindbergh	*"Good communication is as stimulating as black coffee, and just as hard to sleep after."*
Henry Wadsworth Longfellow	*"The talent of success is nothing more than doing what you can do well, and doing well whatever you do without thought of fame. If it comes at all it will come because it is deserved, not because it is sought after."*
Katherine Mansfield	*"I want to be all that I am capable of becoming."*
Ralph Marston	*"Don't lower your expectations to meet your performance. Raise your level of performance to meet your expectations. Expect the best of yourself, and then do what is necessary to make it a reality."*
Moliere	*"It is not only for what we do that we are held responsible, but also for what we do not do."*
Sandra Day O'Conner	*"Do the best you can in every task, no matter how unimportant it may seem at the time. No one learns more about a problem than the person at the bottom."*
Sir William Osler	*"To have striven, to have made the effort, to have been true to certain ideals—this alone is worth the struggle."*
Thomas Paine	*"When it becomes necessary to do a thing, the whole heart and soul should go into the measure, or not attempt it."*
Karen Ravn	*"Only as high as I reach can I grow, only as far as I seek can I go, only as deep as I look can I see, only as much as I dream can I be."*
Betty Reese	*"If you think you're too small to be effective, you have never been in bed with a mosquito."*
Anthony Robbins	*"It is in the moment of your decisions that your destiny is shaped."*
Anthony Robbins	*"It is not what we get. But who we become, what we contribute ... that gives meaning to our lives."*
Wess Roberts	*"Anyone who doesn't make mistakes isn't trying hard enough."*
Jim Rohn	*"The worst thing one can do is not to try, to be aware of what one wants and not give in to it, to spend years in silent hurt wondering if something could have materialized, never knowing."*
Theodore Roosevelt	*"Do what you can with what you have, where you are."*
Theodore Roosevelt	*"Far better it is to dare mighty things, to win glorious triumphs, even though checkered by failure, than to take rank with those poor spirits who neither enjoy nor suffer too much, because they live in the gray twilight that knows not victory nor defeat."*
Theodore I. Rubin	*"Happiness does not come from doing easy work but from the afterglow of satisfaction that comes after the achievement of a difficult task that demanded our best."*
Harold Ruopp	*"Life does not require us to make good; it asks only that we give our best at each level of experience."*

Bill Sands	*"Do more than you're supposed to do and you can have or be or do anything you want."*
Robert H. Schuller	*"What would you attempt to do if you knew you could not fail?"*
Charles M. Schwab	*"Everyone's got it in him, if he'll only make up his mind and stick at it. None of us is born with a stop-valve on his powers or with a set limit to his capacities. There's no limit possible to the expansion of each one of us."*
Seneca	*"The great blessings of mankind are within us, and within our reach; but we shut our eyes and, like people in the dark, fall short of the very thing we search for without finding it."*
Seneca	*"We should every night call ourselves to an account: what infirmity have I mastered today? What passions opposed? What temptation resisted? What virtue acquired? Our vices will abate of themselves if they be brought every day to the shrift."*
Dr. Seuss	*"Unless someone like you cares a whole awful lot, nothing is going to get better. It's not"*
William Shakespeare	*"Our doubts are traitors; and make us lose the good we oft might win, by fearing to attempt."*
George Bernard Shaw	*"I don't believe in circumstances. The people who get on in this world are the people who get up and look for the circumstances they want, and if they can't find them, make them."*
George Bernard Shaw	*"Life isn't about finding yourself. Life is about creating yourself."*
Beverly Sills	*"I've always tried to go a step past wherever people expected me to end up."*
Beverly Sills	*"You may be disappointed if you fail, but you are doomed if you don't try."*
Margaret Chase Smith	*"When people keep telling you that you can't do a thing, you kind of like to try it."*
Sydney Smith	*"It is the greatest of all mistakes to do nothing because you can only do a little. Do what you can."*
Andrea Stier	*"Don't love life, love the people in your life. After all, that's what makes your life."*
W. Clement Stone	*"Try, try, try, and keep on trying is the rule that must be followed to become an expert in anything."*
Meryl Streep	*"Integrate what you believe in every single area of your life. Take your heart to work and ask the most and best of everybody else, too."*
Liz Strehlow	*"Make the best of today, for there is no tomorrow until after today."*
Ed Sullivan	*"If you do a good job for others, you heal yourself at the same time, because a dose of joy is a spiritual cure. It transcends all barriers."*
Publius Syrus	*"No one knows what he can do till he tries."*

Mother Teresa	*"We ourselves feel that what we are doing is just a drop in the ocean. But the ocean would be less because of that missing drop."*
Margaret Thatcher	*"Look at a day when you are supremely satisfied at the end. It's not a day when you lounge around doing nothing; it's when you've had everything to do, and you've done it."*
Lowell Thomas	*"Do a little more each day than you think you possibly can."*
Henry David Thoreau	*"I know of no more encouraging fact than the unquestionable ability of man to elevate his life by conscious endeavor."*
Henry David Thoreau	*"If a man constantly aspires is he not elevated?"*
J.R.R. Tolkien	*"The road must be trod, but it will be very hard. And neither strength nor wisdom will carry us far upon it. This quest may be attempted by the weak with as much hope as the strong. Yet such is oft the course of deeds that move the wheels of the world: small hands do them because they must, while the eyes of the great are elsewhere."*
Henry Truman	*"I studied the lives of great men and famous women, and I found that the men and women who got to the top were those who did the jobs they had in hand, with everything they had of energy and enthusiasm."*
Art Turock	*"There's a difference between interest and commitment. When you're interested in doing something, you do it only when circumstance permit. When you're committed to something, you accept no excuses, only results."*
Mark Twain	*"Keep away from people who try to belittle your ambitions. Small people always do that, but the really great make you feel that you, too, can become great."*
James Ramsey Ullman	*"It is the ultimate wisdom of the mountains that a man is never more a man than when he is striving for what is beyond his grasp."*
Ken Venturi	*"I don't believe you have to be better than everybody else. I believe you have to be better than you ever thought you could be."*
David Viscott	*"To fail is a natural consequence of trying, To succeed takes time and prolonged effort in the face of unfriendly odds. To think it will be any other way, no matter what you do, is to invite yourself to be hurt and to limit your enthusiasm for trying again."*
Voltaire	*"Man is free at the moment he wishes to be."*
William Arthur Ward	*"When we seek to discover the best in others, we somehow bring out the best in ourselves."*
Ruth Westheimer	*"Our way is not soft grass, it's a mountain path with lots of rocks. But it goes upwards, forward, toward the sun."*
Willis Whitney	*"Some men have thousands of reasons why they cannot do what they want to, when all they need is one reason why they can."*

Oprah Winfrey	*"Doing the best at this moment puts you in the best place for the next moment."*
John R. Wooden	*"Don't measure yourself by what you have accomplished, but by what you should have accomplished with your ability."*
Edgar W. Work	*"The real tragedy of life is not in being limited to one talent, but in the failure to use that one talent."*

The Power of Dreams and Aspirations

James Allen	*"Dream lofty dreams, and as you dream, so you shall become. Your vision is the promise of what you shall one day be; your ideal is the prophecy of what you shall at last unveil."*
James Allen	*"You are today where your thoughts have brought you; you will be tomorrow where your thoughts take you."*
Anonymous	*"Don't be pushed by your problems. Be led by your dreams."*
Anonymous	*"Follow your dreams, for as you dream you shall become."*
John A. Appleman	*"I have heard it said that the first ingredient of success—the earliest spark in the dreaming youth—is this; dream a great dream."*
Author Unknown	*"Ships are safe inside their harbor. But, is that what ships are for?"*
Author Unknown	*"No amount of security is worth the suffering of a life chained to a routine that has killed your dreams."*
Author Unknown	*"The main cause for failure and unhappiness is trading what you want most for what you want at the moment."*
Author Unknown	*"We should not let success go to our heads, or our failures go to our hearts."*
Lauren Bacall	*"Imagination is the highest kite one can fly."*
Gaston Bachelard	*"A word is a bud attempting to become a twig. How can one not dream while writing? It is the pen which dreams. The blank page gives the right to dream."*
Toni Cade Bambara	*"The dream is real, my friends. The failure to realize it is the only unreality."*
Gabriel A. Bankes	*"If you know something, it is in your head. When you believe something, it is in your heart."*
Sir James M. Barrie	*"You must have been warned against letting the golden hours slip by. Yes, but some of them are golden only because we let them slip by."*
John Barrymore	*"A man is not old until regrets take the place of dreams."*
Josie Bisset	*"Dreams come in a size too big so that we may grow into them."*
William Blake	*"He who kisses the joy as it flies lives in eternity's sunrise."*

Erma Bombeck	*"There are people who put their dreams in a little box and say, 'Yes, I've got dreams, of course I've got dreams.' Then they put the box away and bring it out once in awhile to look in it, and yep, they're still there. These are great dreams, but they never even get out of the box. It takes an uncommon amount of guts to put your dreams on the line, to hold them up and say, 'How good or how bad am I?' That's where courage comes in."*
Emily Bronte	*"I've dreamt in my life dreams that have stayed with me ever after, and changed my ideas: they've gone through and through me, like wine through water, and altered the color of my mind."*
Phillip Brooks	*"The ideal life is in our blood and never will be still. Sad will be the day for any man when he becomes contented with the thoughts he is thinking and the deeds he is doing—where there is not forever beating at the doors of his soul some great desire to do something larger, which he knows that he was meant and made to do."*
James Broughton	*"The only limits are, as always, those of vision."*
H. Jackson Brown	*"Empower your dreams with deadlines."*
Pearl S. Buck	*"There are many ways of breaking a heart. Stories were full of hearts being broken by love, but what really broke a heart was taking away its dream—whatever that dream might be."*
Edward G. Bulwer-Lytton	*"Dream manfully and nobly, and thy dreams shall be prophets."*
Steven Callahan	*"Dreams, ideas, and plans not only are an escape, they give me purpose, a reason to hang on."*
Ralph Charell	*"Nobody succeeds beyond his or her wildest expectations unless he or she begins with some wild expectations."*
Robert Cooper	*"The way I see it, there are two kinds of dreams. One is a dream that's always going to be just that .... a dream. A vision that you can never really hold in your hand. Then there's a dream that's more than a dream. It's like ... a map. A map that you live by and follow for the rest of your days knowing that someday you're going to stand on top of that mountain holding everything you thought of right there in your hand!"*
Creed	*"What consumes your mind controls your life."*
Russell Crowe	*"You know, when you grow up in the suburbs of Sydney or Auckland or Newcastle, like Ridley or Jamie Bell, well, the suburbs of anywhere, you know, a dream like this seems kind of vaguely ludicrous and completely unattainable. But, this moment is directly connected to those childhood imaginings. And for anybody who's on the down side of advantage and relying purely on courage, it's possible."*
Leonardo da Vinci	*"For once you have tasted flight you will walk the earth with your eyes turned skywards, for there you have been and there you will long to return."*

Charles Darwin	*"Ignorance more frequently begets confidence than does knowledge; it is those who know little, and not those who know much, who so positively assert that this or that problem will never be solved by science."*
Belva Davis	*"Don't be afraid of the space between your dreams and reality. If you can dream it, you can make it so."*
Emily Dickinson	*"Not knowing when the dawn will come, I open every door."*
Walt Disney	*"All our dreams can come true, if we have the courage to pursue them."*
Benjamin Disraeli	*"Nurture your mind with great thoughts, for you will never go any higher than you think."*
Harriet Du Autermont	*"No vision and you perish; no ideal, and you're lost, your heart must ever cherish some faith at any cost. Some hope, some dream to cling to, some rainbow in the sky, some melody to sing to, some service that is high."*
Bernard Edmonds	*"To dream anything that you want to dream, that's the beauty of the human mind. To do anything that you want to do, that is the strength of the human will. To trust yourself to test your limits, that is the courage to succeed."*
Albert Einstein	*"He who can no longer pause to wonder and stand rapt in awe, is as good as dead; his eyes are closed."*
George Eliot	*"It is never too late to be what you might have been."*
Ralph Waldo Emerson	*"What lies behind us and what lies before us are tiny matters compared to what lies within us."*
Douglas Everett	*"There are some people who live in a dream world, and there are some who face reality; and then there are those who turn one into the other."*
Antoine de Saint-Exupery	*"If you want to build a ship, don't drum up people to collect wood and don't assign them tasks and work, but rather teach them to long for the endless immensity of the sea."*
William Faulkner	*"All of us failed to match our dreams of perfection. So I rate us on the basis of our splendid failure to do the impossible."*
William Faulkner	*"Always dream and shoot higher than you know you can do. Don't bother just to be better than your contemporaries or predecessors. Try to be better than yourself."*
Malcolm S. Forbes	*"When you cease to dream you cease to live."*
Anatole France	*"To accomplish great things, we must not only act but also dream. Not only plan but also believe."*
Erich Fromm	*"We all dream. We do not understand our dreams, yet we act as if nothing strange goes on in our sleep minds, strange at least by comparison with the logical, purposeful doings of our minds when we are awake."*

J. G. Gallimore	*"Image creates desire. You will become what you imagine."*
Kahlil Gibran	*"The most pitiful among men is he who turns his dreams into silver and gold."*
Dorothy Gilman	*"People need dreams. There's as much nourishment in 'em as food."*
Dr. Robert H. Goddard	*"It is difficult to say what is impossible, for the dream of yesterday is the reality of tomorrow."*
Johann Wolfgang von Goethe	*"Dream no small dreams for they have no power to move the hearts of men."*
Johann Wolfgang von Goethe	*"Whatever you can do or dream you can, begin it. Boldness has genius, power, and magic in it."*
Oscar Hammerstein II	*"You gotta have a dream. If you don't have a dream, how you gonna make a dream come true?"*
Eric Hoffer	*"It sometimes seems that intense desire creates not only its own opportunities, but its own talents."*
Libby Houston	*"When your dreams tire, they go underground and out of kindness that's where they stay."*
D. B. Hudson	*"Make no little plans. They have no magic to stir men's blood."*
Langston Hughes	*"Hold fast to dreams for if dreams die, life is a broken winged bird that cannot fly. Hold fast to dreams for if dreams go, life is a barren field frozen in snow."*
Aldous Huxley	*"There is only one corner of the universe you can be certain of improving and that is your own self."*
Lee Iacocca	*"The easiest challenges are the ones you dream up for yourself. The tough ones are the ones you don't get to choose."*
Eugene Ionesco	*"Ideologies separate us. Dreams and anguish bring us together."*
Jesse Jackson	*"We've removed the ceiling above our dreams. There are no more impossible dreams."*
Jesse Jackson	*"No one should negotiate their dreams. Dreams must be free to flee and fly high. No government, no legislature, has a right to limit your dreams. You should never agree to surrender your dreams."*
Sarita M. James	*"Remember to always think for yourself and listen to your ideas, even if they sound crazy at first."*
Thomas Jefferson	*"My theory has always been that, if we are to dream, the flatteries of hope are as cheap, and pleasanter, than the gloom of despair."*
Alan Keightley	*"Once in a while it really hits people that they don't have to experience the world in the way they have been told to."*
Helen Keller	*"The best and most beautiful things in the world cannot be seen or even touched. They must be felt with the heart."*
Robert Francis Kennedy	*"There are those who look at things the way they are, and ask why ... I dream of things that never were, and ask why not?"*

Barbara Kingsolver	*"People's dreams are made out of what they do all day. The same way a dog that runs after rabbits will dream of rabbits. It's what you do that makes your soul, not the other way around."*
Michael Korda	*"The more you can dream, the more you can do."*
Stephen Leacock	*"It may be those who do most, dream most."*
Abraham Lincoln	*"Surely God would not have created such a being as man, with an ability to grasp the infinite, to exist only for a day! No, no, man was made for immortality."*
Charles Lindbergh	*"Living in dreams of yesterday, we find ourselves still dreaming of impossible future conquests."*
E. V. Lucas	*"One of the most adventurous things left us is to go to bed. For no one can lay a hand on our dreams."*
Orison Swett Marden	*"All men who have achieved great things have been great dreamers."*
Abraham Maslow	*"We are not in a position in which we have nothing to work with. We already have capacities, talents, direction, missions, callings."*
James Michener	*"The permanent temptation of life is to confuse dreams with reality. The permanent defeat of life comes when dreams are surrendered to reality."*
Natasha Newsome	*"In order to make your dreams come true, you must awaken and take charge."*
Anais Nin	*"The dream was always running ahead of me. To catch up, to live for a moment in unison with it, that was the miracle."*
Anais Nin	*"Throw your dreams into space like a kite, and you do not know what it will bring back, a new life, a new friend, a new love, a new country."*
Norman Vincent Peale	*"Have great hopes and dare to go all out for them. Have great dreams and dare to live them. Have tremendous expectations and believe in them."*
Plato	*"Thinking: the talking of the soul with itself."*
Edgar Allan Poe	*"Those who dream by day are cognizant of many things that escape those who dream only at night."*
Melvin Powers	*"The uncommon man is merely the common man thinking and dreaming of success in larger terms and in more fruitful areas."*
Zadoc Rabinowitz	*"A man's dreams are an index to his greatness."*
Maryanne Radmacher-Herhey	*"Remember your dreams."*
Christopher Reeve	*"So many of our dreams at first seem impossible, then they seem improbable, and then, when we summon the will, they soon become inevitable."*
Eleanor Roosevelt	*"The future belongs to those who believe in the beauty of their dreams."*
Carl Sagan	*"Somewhere, something incredible is waiting to be known."*

Carl Sandburg	*"Nothing happens unless first a dream."*
Diane Sawyer	*"The dream is not the destination but the journey."*
Dr. Laura Schlessinger	*"Self-esteem must be earned! When you dare to dream, dare to follow that dream, dare to suffer through the pain, sacrifice, self-doubts, and friction from the world, you will genuinely impress yourself."*
Robert H. Schuller	*"Commit yourself to a dream .... Nobody who tries to do something great but fails is a total failure. Why? Because he can always rest assured that he succeeded in life's most important battle—he defeated the fear of trying."*
Robert H. Schuller	*"The only place where your dream becomes impossible is in your own thinking."*
Robert H. Schuller	*"Yes, you can be a dreamer and a doer too, if you will remove one word from your vocabulary: impossible."*
Robert H. Schuller	*"You can often measure a person by the size of his dream."*
Arnold Schwarzenegger	*"The mind is the limit. As long as the mind can envision the fact that you can do something, you can do it, as long as you really believe 100 percent."*
George Bernard Shaw	*"You see things; and you say, 'Why?' But I dream things that never were; and I say, 'Why not?'"*
Mary Shelley	*"...my dreams were all my own; I accounted for them to nobody; they were my refuge when annoyed—my dearest pleasure when free."*
Gloria Steinem	*"Without leaps of imagination, or dreaming, we lose the excitement of possibilities. Dreaming, after all, is a form of planning."*
Cat Stevens	*"Take your time, think a lot, think of everything you've got. For you will still be here tomorrow but your dreams may not."*
L.J. Suenens	*"Hope is not a dream but a way of making dreams become reality."*
Susan Taylor	*"We don't have an eternity to realize our dreams, only the time we are here."*
Henry David Thoreau	*"Dreams are the touchstones of our character."*
Henry David Thoreau	*"In the long run, men hit only what they aim at. Therefore, they had better aim at something high."*
Henry David Thoreau	*"If one advances confidently in the direction of his dreams, and endeavors to live the life which he has imagined, he will meet with a success unexpected in common hours."*
Brian Tracy	*"All successful people, men and women, are big dreamers. They imagine what their future could be, ideal in every respect, and then they work every day toward their distant vision, that goal or purpose."*
Dale E. Turner	*"Dreams are renewable. No matter what our age or condition, there are still untapped possibilities within us and new beauty waiting to be born."*

| Mark Twain | "Twenty years from now you will be more disappointed by the things you didn't do than by the ones you did. So throw off the bowlines. Sail away from the safe harbor. Catch the trade winds in your sails. Explore. Dream. Discover." |

| John Updike | "Dreams come true; without that possibility, nature would not incite us to have them." |

| Paul Valery | "The best way to make your dreams come true is to wake up." |

| Vincent Van Gogh | "If one feels the need of something grand, something infinite, something that makes one feel aware of God, one need not go far to find it. I think that I see something deeper, more infinite, more eternal than the ocean in the expression of the eyes of a little baby when it wakes in the morning and coos or laughs because it sees the sun shining on its cradle." |

| Roger Von Oech | "Either you let your life slip away by not doing the things you want to do, or you get up and do them." |

| Robert James Waller | "Life is never easy for those who dream." |

| William Arthur Ward | "If you can imagine it, you can achieve it; if you can dream it, you can become it." |

| Elie Wiesel | "Man walks the moon but his soul remains riveted to earth. Once upon a time, it was the opposite." |

| Woodrow Wilson | "We grow great by dreams. All big men are dreamers. They see things in the soft haze of a spring day or in the red fire of a long winter's evening. Some of us let these dreams die, but others nourish and protect them; nurse them through bad days till they bring them to the sunshine and light which comes always to those who hope that their dreams will come true." |

| Ludwig Wittgenstein | "If people never did silly things nothing intelligent would ever get done." |

| James Womack | "Commitment unlocks the doors of imagination, allows vision, and gives us the 'right stuff' to turn our dreams into reality." |

| W. B. Yeats | "I have spread my dreams under your feet; tread softly because you tread on my dreams." |

Optimism

| Felix Adler | "An optimist is a person who sees only the lights in the picture, whereas a pessimist sees only the shadows. An idealist, however, is one who sees the light and the shadows, but in addition sees something else: the possibility of changing the picture, of making the lights prevail over the shadows." |

James Allen	*"Work joyfully and peacefully, knowing that right thoughts and right efforts inevitably bring about right results."*
Arabic Parable	*"Write the bad things that are done to you in sand, but write the good things that happen to you on a piece of marble."*
Author Unknown	*"A healthy attitude is contagious but don't wait to catch it from others. Be a carrier."*
Author Unknown	*"May you have enough happiness to make you sweet, enough trials to make you strong, enough sorrow to keep you human, and enough hope to bring you joy."*
Author Unknown	*"The happiest of people don't necessarily have the best of everything; they just make the most of everything that comes along their way."*
Author Unknown	*"To achieve the impossible, one must think the absurd; to look where everyone else has looked, but to see what no one else has seen."*
Author Unknown	*"When we stop judging ourselves we stop judging other people. When we start loving ourselves, we start loving other people."*
Lucille Ball	*"One of the things I learned the hard way was that it doesn't pay to get discouraged. Keeping busy and making optimism a way of life can restore your faith in yourself."*
Lucille Ball	*"I don't know anything about luck. I've never banked on it, and I'm afraid of people who do. Luck to me is something else: hard work and realizing what is opportunity and what isn't."*
Bruce Barton	*"Nothing splendid has ever been achieved except by those who dared believe that something inside of them was superior to circumstance."*
Henry Ward Beecher	*"The art of being happy lies in the power of extracting happiness from common things."*
Susan J. Bissonette	*"An optimist is the human personification of spring."*
Dietrich Bonhoeffer	*"The essence of optimism is that it takes no account of the present, but it is a source of inspiration, of vitality and hope where others have resigned; it enables a man to hold his head high, to claim the future for himself and not to abandon it to his enemy."*
George Burns	*"Everyday happiness means getting up in the morning, and you can't wait to finish your breakfast. You can't wait to do your exercises. You can't wait to put on your clothes. You can't wait to get out—and you can't wait to come home because the soup is hot."*
James Branch Caball	*"The optimist proclaims that we live in the best of all possible worlds; and the pessimist fears this is true."*
Pierre Teilhard de Chardin	*"It is our duty as men and women to proceed as though the limits of our abilities do not exist."*
Cherokee Saying	*"When you were born, you cried and the world rejoiced ... Live your life so that when you die, the world cries and you rejoice."*

Chinese Proverb	*"The person who says it cannot be done should not interrupt the person doing it."*
Sir Winston Churchill	*"The pessimist sees difficulty in every opportunity. The optimist sees opportunity in every difficulty."*
Sir Winston Churchill	*"Never, never, never, never give up."*
Confucius	*"Our greatest glory consists not in never falling, but in rising every time we fall."*
Joe Cordare	*"To the question of your life you are the answer, and to the problems of your life you are the solution."*
Duke Ellington	*"Gray skies are just clouds passing over."*
Ralph Waldo Emerson	*"For every minute you are angry you lose sixty seconds of happiness."*
Ralph Waldo Emerson	*"Write it on your heart that every day is the best day in the year."*
Dorothy Fields	*"Grab your coat and get your hat. Leave your worry on the doorstep. Just direct your feet to the sunny side of the street."*
Harrison Ford	*"Being happy is something you have to learn. I often surprise myself by saying 'Wow, this is it. I guess I'm happy. I got a home I love. A career that I love. I'm even feeling more and more at peace with myself.' If there's something else to happiness, let me know. I'm ambitious for that, too."*
Benjamin Franklin	*"Take one thing with another, and the world is a pretty good sort of a world, and it is our duty to make the best of it, and be thankful."*
Benjamin Franklin	*"The constitution only gives people the right to pursue happiness. You have to catch it yourself."*
Fra Giovanni	*"The gloom of the world is but a shadow. Behind it, yet within reach, is joy. There is a radiance and glory in the darkness, could we but see, and to see, we have only to look. I beseech you to look."*
Maxim Gorky	*"Everybody, my friend, everybody lives for something better to come. That's why we want to be considerate of every man—who knows what's in him, why he was born, and what he can do?"*
Paul Harvey	*"I've never seen a monument erected to a pessimist."*
Elbert Hubbard	*"Optimism is a kind of heart stimulant—the digitalis of failure."*
Irish Blessing	*"May the road rise to meet you. May the wind always be at your back. May the sun shine warm upon your face, the rains fall soft upon your fields and, until we meet again, may God hold you in the palm of his hand."*
Jennifer James	*"The accumulation of small, optimistic acts produces quality in our culture and in your life. Our culture resonates in tense times to individual acts of grace."*

Helen Keller	*"Keep your face to the sunshine and you cannot see the shadow."*
Rose Kennedy	*"Birds sing after a storm; why shouldn't people feel as free to delight in whatever sunlight remains to them?"*
Martin Luther King, Jr.	*"Even if I knew that tomorrow the world would go to pieces, I would still plant my apple tree."*
Kyla	*"Happiness comes through doors you didn't know you left open."*
Stanislaw J. Lec	*"He who limps is still walking."*
Art Linkletter	*"Things turn out best for those who make the best of how things turn out."*
Lawrence G. Lovasik	*"Cheerfulness is a very great help in fostering the virtue of charity. Cheerfulness itself is a virtue."*
Lawrence G. Lovasik	*"Genuine love will always feel urged to communicate joy—to be a joy-giver. Mankind needs joy."*
Maurice Maeterlinck	*"An act of goodness is of itself an act of happiness. No reward coming after the event can compare with the sweet reward that went with it."*
Charles Langbridge Morgan	*"The art of living does not consist in preserving and clinging to a particular mood of happiness, but in allowing happiness to change its form without being disappointed by the change; for happiness, like a child, must be allowed to grow up."*
Myth Chaser	*"Life is a gift given to be enjoyed, not a trial meant to be survived."*
Nana (age 103)	*"We don't stop playing because we grow older, we grow older because we stop playing."*
James Oppenheim	*"The foolish man seeks happiness in the distance; the wise grows it under his feet."*
J. Robert Oppenheimer	*"The optimist thinks this is the best of all worlds. The pessimist fears it is true."*
Ovid	*"Chance is always powerful. Let your hook be always cast; in the pool where you least expect it, there will be a fish."*
Grace Paley	*"Rosiness is not a worse windowpane than gloomy gray when viewing the world."*
Colin Powell	*"Perpetual optimism is a force multiplier."*
Agnes Repplier	*"There is an optimism which nobly anticipates the eventual triumph of great moral lows, and there is an optimism which cheerfully tolerates unworthiness."*
James Reston	*"Stick with the optimists. It's going to be tough enough even if they're right."*
Joan Rivers	*"I have become my own version of an optimist. If I can't make it through one door, I'll go through another door—or I'll make a door. Something terrific will come no matter how dark the present."*

Charles M. Schwab	"Don't worry about the world coming to an end today. It's already tomorrow in Australia."
Albert Schweitzer	"An optimist is a person who sees a green light everywhere, while a pessimist sees only the red stoplight ... The truly wise person is color-blind."
Bishop Fulton J. Sheen	"Every man rejoices twice when he has a partner in his joy. He who shares tears with us wipes them away. He divides them in two, and he who laughs with us makes the joy double."
George Shultz	"The minute you start talking about what you're going to do if you lose, you have lost."
Charles R. Swindoll	"When you have vision it affects your attitude. Your attitude is optimistic rather than pessimistic."
Edwin Percy Whipple	"Cheerfulness in most cheerful people is the rich and satisfying result of strenuous discipline."
Paul Wiener	"But few have spoken of the actual pleasure derived from giving to someone, from creating something, from finishing a task, from offering unexpected help almost invisibly and anonymously."
Ziggy	"You can complain that roses have thorns; or rejoice that thorns have roses."

Heroes, Role Models, and Mentors

A. Bronson Alcott	"Strengthen me by sympathizing with my strength, not my weakness."
Arthur Ashe	"True heroism is remarkably sober, very undramatic. It is not the urge to surpass all others at whatever cost, but the urge to serve others at whatever cost."
Author Unknown	"A great mentor is one who aims for others' abilities to surpass his own."
James A. Autry	"I believe it is the nature of people to be heroes, given the chance."
William J. Bennett	"For children to take morality seriously they must be in the presence of adults who take morality seriously. And with their own eyes they must see adults take morality seriously."
Warren G. Bennis	"Every leader needs to have experienced and grown through following —learning to be dedicated, observant, capable of working with and learning from others, never servile, always truthful. Having located these qualities in himself, he can encourage them in others."
Lady Isabel Burton	"An Arabian proverb says there are four sorts of men: He who knows not and knows not he knows not: he is a fool—shun him. He who knows not and knows he knows not: he is simple—teach him. He who knows and knows not he knows: he is asleep—wake him. He who knows and knows he knows: he is wise—follow him."

Hortense Canady	*"If you don't realize there is always someone who knows how to do something better than you, then you don't give proper respect for others' talents."*
Thomas Carruthers	*"A teacher is one who makes himself progressively unnecessary."*
J. M. Charlier	*"The cowards think of what they can lose, the heroes of what they can win."*
Lord Chesterfield	*"Advice is seldom welcome; and those who want it the most always like it the least."*
G. K. Chesterton	*"There is a great man who makes every man feel small. But the real great man is the man who makes every man feel great."*
Chinese Proverb	*"A load of books does not equal one good teacher."*
Chinese Proverb	*"An army of a thousand is easy to find, but, ah, how difficult to find a general."*
Chinese Proverb	*"Tell me, I will forget. Show me, I may remember. Involve me, and I will understand."*
Sir Winston Churchill	*"I am certainly not one of those who need to be prodded. In fact, if anything, I am the prod."*
Sir Winston Churchill	*"I do not resent criticism, even when, for the sake of emphasis, it parts for the time with reality."*
Sir Winston Churchill	*"I was never tired of listening to his wisdom or imparting my own."*
Stephen Covey	*"Nothing is more validating and affirming than feeling understood. And the moment a person begins feeling understood, that person becomes far more open to influence and change."*
Betty Deramus	*"A hero is simply someone who rises above his own human weaknesses, for an hour, a day, a year, to do something stirring."*
Benjamin Disraeli	*"Nurture your minds with great thoughts. To believe in the heroic makes heroes."*
Tryon Edwards	*"If you would thoroughly know anything, teach it to others."*
Dwight David Eisenhower	*"Leadership is the art of getting someone else to do something you want done because he wants to do it."*
Ralph Waldo Emerson	*"A hero is no braver than an ordinary man, but he is braver five minutes longer."*
Anatole France	*"The whole art of teaching is only the art of awakening the natural curiosity of young minds for the purpose of satisfying it afterwards."*
Benjamin Franklin	*"Some people die at twenty-five and aren't buried until they are seventy-five."*
German Proverb	*"Anger hears no counsel."*
German Proverb	*"No one is wise enough to advise himself."*

Arnold H. Glasgow	*"Praise does wonders for our sense of hearing."*
Johann Wolfgang von Goethe	*"Who is the happiest of men? He who values the merits of others, and in their pleasure takes joy, even as though t'were his own."*
Johann Wolfgang von Goethe	*"If I accept you as you are, I will make you worse; however if I treat you as though you are what you are capable of becoming, I help you become that."*
Stedman Graham	*"To pursue success effectively, you must build supportive relationships that will help you work toward your goals. To build those relationships, you need to trust others; and to earn their trust, you in turn must learn to be trustworthy."*
Greek Proverb	*"Without a general an army is lost."*
Bernard Haldane	*"If you want to get the best out of a man, you must look for the best that is in him."*
Alex Haley	*"Find the good—and praise it."*
Robert Half	*"Talent does you no good unless it's recognized by someone else."*
Victor Hugo	*"Man lives more by affirmation than by bread."*
Samuel Johnson	*"He that teaches us anything which we knew not before is undoubtedly to be reverenced as a master."*
Samuel Johnson	*"Example is always more efficacious than precept."*
Joseph Joubert	*"To teach is to learn twice."*
E. M. Kelly	*"The difference between a boss and a leader: a boss says, 'Go!'—a leader says, 'Let's go!'"*
George Kennan	*"Heroism ... is endurance for one moment more."*
Donald A. Laird	*"Abilities wither under faultfinding, blossom with encouragement."*
Blaine Lee	*"The great leaders are like the best conductors—they reach beyond the notes to reach the magic in the players."*
Blaine Lee	*"The leader who exercises power with honor will work from the inside out, starting with himself."*
Blaine Lee	*"We are all capable of change and growth; we just need to know where to begin."*
Thomas Leonard	*"Wisdom is the art of providing a perfect solution simply, instead of trying to give lots of answers or ideas."*
Walter Lippmann	*"The final test of a leader is that he leaves behind him in other men the conviction and the will to carry on."*
Walter Lippmann	*"The genius of a good leader is to leave behind him a situation which common sense, without the grace of genius, can deal with successfully."*
Bernard Malamud	*"Without heroes, we're all plain people and don't know how far we can go."*

André Malraux	*"To command is to serve, nothing more and nothing less."*
Fred A. Manske, Jr.	*"The ultimate leader is one who is willing to develop people to the point that they eventually surpass him or her in knowledge and ability."*
Mary McCarthy	*"We are the hero of our own story."*
Michelangelo	*"The marble not yet carved can hold the form of every thought the greatest artist has."*
Thomas Moore	*"We need not cling anxiously to our own sensitivity, will, and desire; instead we can place our trust in the beings around us who demonstrate many alternative ways to be a contributing, outstanding individual."*
Carol Pearson	*"Heroes take journeys, confront dragons, and discover the treasure of their true selves."*
Philippine Proverb	*"He who seeks advice seldom errs."*
Plautus	*"No man is wise enough by himself."*
Christopher Reeve	*"When the first Superman movie came out I was frequently asked 'What is a hero?' ... My answer was that a hero is someone who commits a courageous action without considering the consequences... Now my definition is completely different. I think a hero is an ordinary individual who finds strength to persevere and endure in spite of overwhelming obstacles."*
Ruth E. Renkel	*"Sometimes the poorest man leaves his children the richest inheritances."*
Dot Richardson	*"A true champion is someone who wants to make a difference, who never gives up, and who gives everything she has no matter what the circumstances are. A true champion works hard and never loses sight of her dreams."*
May Sarton	*"One must think like a hero to behave like a merely decent human being."*
General Norman Schwarzkopf	*"Leadership is a combination of strategy and character. If you must be without one, be without the strategy."*
Seneca	*"There is the need for someone against which our characters can measure themselves. Without a ruler, you won't make the crooked straight."*
Socrates	*"You are not only good yourself, but the cause of goodness in others."*
Socrates	*"I cannot teach anybody anything, I can only make them think."*
King Solomon	*"Where there is no vision, the people perish."*
Paul Shane Spear	*"As one person I cannot change the world, but I can change the world of one person."*

Suard	*"We attract hearts by the qualities we display; we retain them by the qualities we possess."*
Henry David Thoreau	*"How can we remember our ignorance, which our growth requires, when we are using our knowledge all the time?"*
Barbara Tuchman	*"The hero must have some form of higher purpose in life."*
Mark Twain	*"Let us live so that when we come to die even the undertaker will be sorry."*
Thomas J. Watson	*"The great accomplishments of man have resulted from the transmission of ideas and enthusiasm."*
Welsh Proverb	*"The advice of the aged will not mislead you."*
Marianne Williamson	*"Our deepest fear is not that we are inadequate. Our deepest fear is that we are powerful beyond measure. It is our light, not our darkness that most frightens us. We ask ourselves, who am I to be brilliant, gorgeous, talented and fabulous? Actually, who are you not to be? You are a child of God. Your playing small doesn't serve the world. There is nothing enlightened about shrinking so that other people won't feel insecure around you. We were born to make manifest the glory of God that is within us. It's not just in some of us; it's in everyone. And as we let our own light shine, we unconsciously give others permission to do the same. As we are liberated from our own fear, our presence automatically liberates others."*
John R. Wooden	*"It's what you learn after you know it all that counts."*

The Future

Anonymous	*"The future should be something we deserve, not something which is merely reached at the rate of 60 minutes per hour."*
Anonymous	*"The world is so fast that there are days when the person who says it can't be done is interrupted by the person who is doing it."*
Anonymous	*"Every job is a self-portrait of the person who does it. Autograph your work with excellence."*
Anonymous	*"A real leader faces the music, even when he doesn't like the tune."*
Anonymous	*"Though no one can go back and make a brand new start, anyone can start from now and make a brand new ending."*
Aristotle	*"We are what we repeatedly do. Excellence, then, is not an act, but a habit."*
Isaac Asimov	*"It is change, continuing change, inevitable change, that is the dominant factor in society today. No sensible decision can be made any longer without taking into account not only the world as it is, but the world as it will be."*
Norman R. Augustine	*"Motivation will almost always beat mere talent."*

Marcus Aurelius	"Never let the future disturb you. You will meet it, if you have to, with the same weapons of reason which today arm you against the present."
Author Unknown	"You have to expect things of yourself before you can do them."
Author Unknown	"Our background and circumstances may influence who we are, but we are responsible for who we become."
Roger Babson	"Let him who would enjoy a good future waste none of his present."
Byrd Baggett	"Look at life through the windshield, not the rear-view mirror."
J. G. Ballard	"I would sum up my fear about the future in one word: boring. And that's my one fear: that everything has happened; nothing exciting or new or interesting is ever going to happen again ... the future is just going to be a vast, conforming suburb of the soul."
Margaret Fairless Barber	"To look backward for a while is to refresh the eye, to restore it, and to render it more fit for its prime function of looking forward."
Ambrose Bierce	"Future. That period of time in which our affairs prosper, our friends are true and our happiness is assured."
Gary Ryan Blair	"Your future takes precedence over your past. Focus on your future, rather than on the past."
Dietrich Bonhoeffer	"Action springs not from thought, but from a readiness for responsibility."
Edward de Bono	"In the future, instead of striving to be right at a high cost, it will be more appropriate to be flexible and plural at a lower cost. If you cannot accurately predict the future then you must flexibly be prepared to deal with various possible futures."
Edmund Burke	"You can never plan the future by the past."
Albert Camus	"Real generosity towards the future lies in giving all to the present."
Andrew Carnegie	"Do your duty and a little more and the future will take care of itself."
Sir Winston Churchill	"The empires of the future are the empires of the mind."
Michael Cibenko	"One problem with gazing too frequently into the past is that we may turn around to find the future has run out on us."
Hillary Rodham Clinton	"The challenges of change are always hard. It is important that we begin to unpack those challenges that confront this nation and realize that we each have a role that requires us to change and become more responsible for shaping our own future."
Jesse Conrad	"Learn the past, watch the present, and create the future."
Fritz R. S. Dressler	"Predicting the future is easy. It's trying to figure out what's going on now that's hard."
Marian Wright Edelman	"The future which we hold in trust for our own children will be shaped by our fairness to other people's children."

Thomas A. Edison	*"Many of life's failures are people who did not realize how close they were to success when they gave up."*
Ralph Waldo Emerson	*"Do not go where the path may lead, go instead where there is no path and leave a trail."*
Ralph Waldo Emerson	*"Nothing is beneath you if it is in the direction of your life."*
Ralph Waldo Emerson	*"To be yourself in a world that is constantly trying to make you something else is the greatest accomplishment."*
Gloria Estefan	*"The sad truth is that opportunity doesn't knock twice. You can put things off until tomorrow but tomorrow may never come."*
Zelda Fitzgerald	*"By the time a person has achieved years adequate for choosing a direction, the die is cast and the moment has long since passed which determined the future."*
Henry Ford	*"You can't build a reputation on what you are going to do."*
Eugene Forsey	*"I have long considered it one of God's greatest mercies that the future is hidden from us. If it were not, life would surely be unbearable."*
Thomas Fuller	*"He that would have the fruit must climb the tree."*
Kahlil Gibran	*"Progress lies not in enhancing what is, but in advancing toward what will be."*
Kahlil Gibran	*"Time has been transformed, and we have changed; it has advanced and set us in motion; it has unveiled its face, inspiring us with bewilderment and exhilaration."*
Kahlil Gibran	*"We choose our joys and sorrows long before we experience them."*
Johann Wolfgang von Goethe	*"Everybody wants to be somebody; nobody wants to grow."*
Thich Nhat Hahn	*"At any moment, you have a choice that either leads you closer to your spirit or further away from it."*
Hazel Henderson	*"If we can recognize that change and uncertainty are basic principles, we can greet the future and the transformation we are undergoing with the understanding that we do not know enough to be pessimistic."*
Theodore Hesburgh	*"The very essence of leadership is that you have to have a vision."*
Hesiod	*"I see no hope for the future of our people if they are dependent on the frivolous youth of today, for certainly all youth are reckless beyond words. When I was a boy, we were taught to be discrete and respectful of elders, but the present youth are exceedingly wise and impatient of restraint."*
John Heywood	*"Would ye both eat your cake and have your cake?"*
Eric Hoffer	*"The only way to predict the future is to have power to shape the future."*
Robinson Jeffers	*"The future is ever a misted landscape, no man foreknows it, but at cyclical turns there is a change felt in the rhythm of events."*
Alan Kay	*"The best way to predict the future is to invent it."*

John Fitzgerald Kennedy	*"History is a relentless master. It has no present, only the past rushing into the future. To try to hold fast is to be swept aside."*
Charles F. Kettering	*"My interest is in the future because I'm going to spend the rest of my life there."*
George Lamming	*"The architecture of our future is not only unfinished; the scaffolding has hardly gone up."*
Ann Landers	*"Nobody gets to live life backward. Look ahead. That is where your future lies."*
Lao Tzu	*"The journey of a thousand miles must begin with a single step."*
Stanislaw J. Lec	*"Value your words. Each one may be the last."*
Ted Levitt	*"The future belongs to people who see possibilities before they become obvious."*
Abraham Lincoln	*"I do not think much of a man who is not wiser today than he was yesterday."*
Abraham Lincoln	*"Whatever you are, be a good one."*
Henry Wadsworth Longfellow	*"Look not mournfully into the past, it comes not back again. Wisely improve the present, it is thine. Go forth to meet the shadowy future without fear and with a manly heart."*
Norman Mailer	*"There was that law of life, so cruel and so just, that one must grow or else pay more for remaining the same."*
Orison Swett Marden	*"Most of our obstacles would melt away if, instead of cowering before them, we should make up our minds to walk boldly through them."*
Orison Swett Marden	*"Whatever our creed, we feel that no good deed can by any possibility go unrewarded, no evil deed unpunished."*
George Marion, Jr.	*"My future just passed."*
Darius Ogden Mills	*"I was taught very early that I would have to depend entirely upon myself; that my future lay in my own hands."*
Anais Nin	*"When we blindly adopt a religion, a political system, a literary dogma, we become automatons. We cease to grow."*
Andre Norton	*"As for courage and will—we cannot measure how much of each lies within us, we can only trust there will be sufficient to carry through trials which may lie ahead."*
George Orwell	*"He who controls the past commands the future. He who commands the future conquers the past."*
Bob Perelman	*"Learning is what most adults will do for a living in the 21st century."*
Eden Phillpotts	*"The universe is full of magical things, patiently waiting for our wits to grow sharper."*
John Randolph	*"Time is at once the most valuable and most perishable of all our possessions."*

Eric Ransdell	*"The stories that you tell about your past shape your future."*
John M. Richardson, Jr.	*"When it comes to the future, there are three kinds of people: those who let it happen, those who make it happen, and those who wonder what happened."*
Rainer Maria Rilke	*"We see the brightness of a new page where everything yet can happen."*
Franklin Delano Roosevelt	*"The only limit to our realization of tomorrow will be our doubts of today."*
Franklin Delano Roosevelt	*"We cannot always build the future for our youth, but we can build our youth for the future."*
Semisonic	*"Every new beginning comes from some other beginning's end."*
Herbert Spencer	*"The wise man must remember that while he is a descendant of the past, he is a parent of the future."*
Ben Stein	*"Nothing happens by itself... it all will come your way, once you understand that you have to make it come your way, by your own exertions."*
Gloria Steinem	*"The future depends entirely on what each of us does every day."*
Cat Stevens	*"If you want to sing out, sing out, and if you want to be free, be free, 'cause there's a million ways to be, you know that there are ..."*
Sun Tzu	*"Opportunities multiply as they are seized."*
H. G. Wells	*"Every time I see an adult on a bicycle, I no longer despair for the future of the human race."*
Thornton Wilder	*"The future author is one who discovers that language, the exploration and manipulation of the resources of language, will serve him in winning through to his way."*

Taking Small Steps

Eric Allenbaugh	*"Painful as it may be, a significant emotional event can be the catalyst for choosing a direction that serves us and those around us more effectively. Look for the learning."*
Anonymous	*"Discretion is being able to raise your eyebrow instead of your voice."*
Anonymous	*"Every flower must grow through dirt."*
Anonymous	*"We do not remember days; we remember moments."*
Aristotle	*"Pleasure in the job puts perfection in the work."*
Author Unknown	*"Growth requires a temporary surrender of security."*
Author Unknown	*"Obstacles are challenges for winners and excuses for losers."*
Author Unknown	*"Patience and perseverance have a magical effect before which difficulties disappear and obstacles vanish."*

Betty Bender	*"Anything I've ever done that ultimately was worthwhile ... initially scared me to death."*
Arnold Bennett	*"The great advantage of being in a rut is that when one is in a rut, one knows exactly where one is."*
Thomas Arnold Bennett	*"Having once decided to achieve a certain task, achieve it at all costs of tedium and distaste. The gain in self-confidence of having accomplished a tiresome labor is immense."*
Warren G. Bennis	*"Great things are accomplished by talented people who believe they will accomplish them."*
Bible, James 1:2-4	*"When all kinds of trials and temptations crowd into your lives, my brothers, don't resent them as intruders, but welcome them as friends. Realize that they come to test your faith and to produce in you the quality of endurance. But let the process go on until that endurance is fully developed, and you will find you have become men of mature character, men of integrity with no weak spots."*
Napoleon Bonaparte	*"Victory belongs to the most persevering."*
Phillip Brooks	*"Character may be manifested in the great moments, but it is made in the small ones."*
Buddha	*"Do not dwell in the past, do not dream of the future, concentrate the mind on the present moment."*
Jimmy Buffett	*"We got to roll with the punches, play all of our hunches, make the best of whatever comes your way. Forget that blind ambition, learn to trust your intuition—plowing straight ahead, come what may."*
Edmund Burke	*"He that wrestles with us strengthens our nerves and sharpens our skill. Our antagonist is our helper."*
Thomas Carlyle	*"Permanence, perseverance and persistence in spite of all obstacles, discouragements, and impossibilities: It is this, that in all things distinguishes the strong soul from the weak."*
Elizabeth Rundle Charles	*"Great inventors and discoverers seem to have made their discoveries and inventions as it were by the way, in the course of their everyday life."*
Chinese Proverb	*"A journey of a thousand miles begins with a single step."*
Chinese Proverb	*"He who asks is a fool for five minutes, but he who does not ask remains a fool forever."*
Calvin Coolidge	*"I have noticed that nothing I have never said ever did me any harm."*
Liane Cordes	*"Continuous effort—not strength or intelligence—is the key to unlocking our potential."*
Stephen Covey	*"People who exercise their embryonic freedom day after day, little by little, expand that freedom. People who do not will find that it withers until they are literally 'being lived.' They are acting out scripts written by parents, associates and society."*

Fr. Alfred D'Souza	*"For a long time it had seemed to me that life was about to begin—real life. But there was always some obstacle in the way, something to be got through first, some unfinished business, time still to be served, a debt to be paid. Then life would begin. At last it dawned on me that these obstacles were my life."*
Albert Einstein	*"The world is not dangerous because of those who do harm but because of those who look at it without doing anything."*
English Proverb	*"A smooth sea never made a skilled mariner."*
John Erksine	*"In simplest terms, a leader is one who knows where he wants to go, and gets up, and goes."*
Julius Erving	*"Goals determine what you are going to be."*
Ron Jon Finley	*"Fear indecision, for it decides for you."*
F. Scott Fitzgerald	*"Vitality shows in not only the ability to persist but the ability to start over."*
Henry Ford	*"Life is a series of experiences, each one of which makes us bigger, even though it is hard to realize this. For the world was built to develop character, and we must learn that the setbacks and griefs which we endure help us in our marching onward."*
Mahatma Gandhi	*"Whatever you do will be insignificant, but it is most important that you do it."*
Billy Graham	*"Comfort and prosperity have never enriched the world as much as adversity has. Out of pain and problems have come the sweetest songs, and the most gripping stories."*
Thich Nhat Hahn	*"Sometimes your joy is the source of your smile, but sometimes your smile can be the source of your joy."*
Josh Hinds	*"In each of our lives, for whatever reason, there are times that we are faced with things that just don't make sense to us. And the more we struggle to understand our hardships, the less any of it makes sense. I have found that in every challenge and obstacle that we are faced with there can be good that can come from it! While it's almost never easy to identify, I assure you that it is there lying dormant just waiting for us to release it! I urge everyone to spend your days looking for positives in your life."*
Chamique Holdsclaw	*"When you struggle, that's when you realize what you're made of, and that's when you realize what the people around you can do. You learn who you'd want to take with you to a war, and who you'd only want to take to lunch."*
Lena Horne	*"It's not the load that breaks you down, it's the way you carry it."*
Kin Hubbard	*"Don't knock the weather; nine-tenths of the people couldn't start a conversation if it didn't change once in a while."*

Aldous Huxley	*"Perhaps the most valuable result of all education is the ability to make yourself do the thing you have to do, when it ought to be done, whether you like it or not."*
Thomas Henry Huxley	*"The rung of a ladder was never meant to rest upon, but only to hold a man's foot long enough to enable him to put the other somewhat higher."*
I Ching	*"When flowing water ... meets with obstacles on its path, a blockage in its journey, it pauses. It increases in volume and strength, filling up in front of the obstacle and eventually spilling past i t... Do not turn and run, for there is nowhere worthwhile for you to go. Do not attempt to push ahead into the danger ... emulate the example of the water: Pause and build up your strength until the obstacle no longer represents a blockage."*
Irish Proverb	*"You've got to do your own growing, no matter how tall your grandfather was."*
Akbarali H. Jetha	*"Quite often we change jobs, friends and spouses instead of ourselves."*
Samuel Johnson	*"He knows not his own strength who hath not met adversity."*
Samuel Johnson	*"Life affords no higher pleasure than that of surmounting difficulties, passing from one step of success to another, forming new wishes, and seeing them gratified. He that labors in any great or laudable undertaking has his fatigues first supported by hope, and afterwards rewarded by joy...To strive with difficulties, and to conquer them, is the highest human felicity."*
Robert Kall	*"We encounter the grinding wheels that sharpen our mental blades many places in life. Adversity, school, parents, spiritual guides, books, experience are all sharpening teachers. As we grow older, to stay sharp we must find new grindstones to whet and sharpen our potential and keep us at our brightest, most penetrating best."*
Helen Keller	*"Avoiding danger is no safer in the long run than outright exposure. Life is either a daring adventure or nothing at all."*
Fredrick Koeing	*"We tend to forget that happiness doesn't come as a result of getting something we don't have, but rather of recognizing and appreciating what we do have."*
Elisabeth Kubler-Ross	*"Should you shield the valleys from the windstorms, you would never see the beauty of their canyons."*
Maya Lin	*"To fly, we have to have resistance."*
Abraham Lincoln	*"Better to remain silent and be thought a fool than to speak out and remove all doubt."*
Vince Lombardi	*"It's not whether you get knocked down, it's whether you get back up."*

Orison Swett Marden	"*Obstacles are like wild animals. They are cowards but they will bluff you if they can. If they see you are afraid of them ... they are liable to spring upon you; but if you look them squarely in the eye, they will slink out of sight.*"
Peter Marshall	"*Small deeds done are better than great deeds planned.*"
John Stuart Mill	"*He who knows only his own side of the case, knows little of that.*"
John Stuart Mill	"*We can never be sure that the opinion we are endeavoring to stifle is a false opinion; and if we were sure, stifling it would be an evil still.*"
Reinhold Niebuhr	"*God grant me the serenity to accept the things I cannot change, the courage to change the things I can, and the wisdom to know the difference.*"
Ancient Oriental Teaching	"*Problems are sent to us as gifts.*"
Norman Vincent Peale	"*Cushion the painful effects of hard blows by keeping the enthusiasm going strong, even if doing so requires struggle.*"
Norman Vincent Peale	"*Enthusiasm releases the drive to carry you over obstacles and adds significance to all you do.*"
Norman Vincent Peale	"*Stand up to your obstacles and do something about them. You will find that they haven't half the strength you think they have.*"
Norman Vincent Peale	"*Understanding can overcome any situation, however mysterious or insurmountable it may appear to be.*"
M. Scott Peck	"*Life is a series of problems. Do we want to moan about them or solve them?*"
M. Scott Peck	"*Life is difficult. This is a great truth, one of the greatest truths. It is a great truth because once we truly see this truth, we transcend it. Once we truly know that life is difficult, once we truly understand and accept it, then life is no longer difficult. Because once it is accepted, the fact that life is difficult no longer matters.*"
Plautus	"'*He means well' is useless unless he does well.*"
Franklin Delano Roosevelt	"*There are many ways of going forward, but only one way of standing still.*"
Leslie Jeanne Sahler	"*It is best to learn as we go, not go as we have learned.*"
General Norman Schwarzkopf	"*The truth of the matter is that you always know the right thing to do. Thehard part is doing it.*"
Seneca	"*If one does not know to which port one is sailing, no wind is favorable.*"
Seneca	"*The pressure of adversity does not affect the mind of the brave man ... It is more powerful than external circumstances.*"

Barbara Sher	*" 'Now' is the operative word. Everything you put in your way is just a method of putting off the hour when you could actually be doing your dream. You don't need endless time and perfect conditions. Do it now. Do it today. Do it for twenty minutes and watch your heart start beating."*
Barbara Sher	*"Imaginary obstacles are insurmountable. Real ones aren't. But you can't tell the difference when you have no real information. Fear can create even more imaginary obstacles than ignorance can. That's why the smallest step away from speculation and into reality can be an amazing relief ... The Reality Solution means: Do it before you're ready."*
Barbara Sher	*"Real obstacles don't take you in circles. They can be overcome. Invented ones are like a maze."*
Marsha Sinetar	*"Life's up and downs provide windows of opportunity to determine ... [your] values and goals ... think of using all obstacles as stepping stones to build the life you want."*
Marsha Sinetar	*"Rather than denying problems, focus inventively, intentionally on what solutions might look or feel like ... our mind is meant to generate ideas that help us escape circumstantial traps—if we trust it to do so. Naturally, not all hunches are useful. But then you only need a single good idea to solve a problem."*
B. F. Skinner	*"Education is what survives when what has been learned has been forgotten."*
James Stephens	*"Curiosity will conquer fear even more than bravery will."*
Fran Tarkenton	*"Success, in my view, is the willingness to strive for something you really want. The person not reaching the top is no less a success than the one who achieved it, if they both sweated blood, sweat and tears and overcame obstacles and fears. The failure to be perfect does not mean you're not a success."*
Mother Teresa	*"Kind words can be short and easy to speak, but their echoes are truly endless."*
Booker T. Washington	*"I have learnt that success is to be measured not so much by the position that one has reached in life as by the obstacles which he has overcome while trying to succeed."*
Woodrow Wilson	*"The man who is swimming against the stream knows the strength of it."*
Wesley Woo	*"To succeed, you must improve, to practice, you must learn, to learn, you must fail."*
John R. Wooden	*"Success is peace of mind which is a direct result of self-satisfaction in knowing you did your best to become the best you are capable of becoming."*

Understanding the Nature of Support

George Matthew Adams	*"There are high spots in all of our lives and most of them have come about through encouragement from someone else. I don't care how great, how famous or successful a man or woman may be, each hungers for applause."*
Scott Adams	*"I'm slowly becoming a convert to the principle that you can't motivate people to do things, you can only demotivate them. The primary job of the manager is not to empower but to remove obstacles."*
Aesop	*"No act of kindness, no matter how small, is ever wasted."*
John Akers	*"Set your expectations high; find men and women whose integrity and values you respect; get their agreement on a course of action; and give them your ultimate trust."*
Anonymous	*"It is impossible to defeat an ignorant man in an argument."*
Anonymous	*"If you think that praise is due, now's the time to show it, 'cause a man can't read his tombstone when he's dead."*
Anonymous	*"Remember, people will judge you by your actions, not your intentions. You may have a heart of gold—but so does a hard-boiled egg."*
Anonymous	*"Success stems from motivation, effort, and a commitment to excellence."*
Anonymous	*"Silence is one great art of conversation."*
Author Unknown	*"A candle loses nothing by lighting another candle."*
Author Unknown	*"It's not as hard to die for a friend as it is to find a friend to die for."*
James Matthew Barrie	*"Those who bring sunshine into the lives of others cannot keep it from themselves."*
Warren G. Bennis	*"Good leaders make people feel that they're at the very heart of things, not at the periphery. Everyone feels that he or she makes a difference to the success of the organization. When that happens people feel centered and that gives their work meaning."*
Bible, Matthew 7:12	*"Do to others what you would have them do to you."*
Paul Boese	*"Forgiveness does not change the past, but it does enlarge the future."*
Edward G. Bulwer-Lytton	*"The best teacher is the one who suggests rather than dogmatizes, and inspires his listener with the wish to teach himself."*
Edward G. Bulwer-Lytton	*"The true spirit of conversation consists in building on another man's observation, not overturning it."*
Eileen Caddy	*"Set your sights high, the higher the better. Expect the most wonderful things to happen, not in the future but right now. Realize that nothing is too good. Allow absolutely nothing to hamper you or hold you up in any way."*

G. K. Chesterton	*"If I can put one touch of rosy sunset into the life of any man or woman, I shall feel that I have worked with God."*
Chinese Proverb	*"If you are patient in one moment of anger, you will escape a hundred days of sorrow."*
Calvin Coolidge	*"It takes a great man to be a good listener."*
Margaret Cousins	*"Appreciation can make a day—even change a life. Your willingness to put it into words is all that is necessary."*
Peter Davies	*"Motivation is like food for the brain. You cannot get enough in one sitting. It needs continual and regular top-offs."*
Sue Atchley Ebaugh	*"The greatest gift we can give one another is rapt attention to one another's existence."*
William Ellery	*"Great minds are to make others great. Their superiority is to be used, not to break the multitude to intellectual vassalage, not to establish over them a spiritual tyranny, but to rouse them from lethargy, and to aid them to judge for themselves."*
Robert Frost	*"You are educated when you have the ability to listen to almost anything without losing your temper or self-confidence."*
Sister Gervase	*"That's what's wrong with the world—people don't compliment other people enough. They would change the world if they did."*
Loretta Girzartis	*"If someone listens, or stretches out a hand, or whispers a word of encouragement, or attempts to understand a lonely person, extraordinary things begin to happen."*
Johann Wolfgang von Goethe	*"Correction does much, but encouragement does more."*
Francesco Guicciardini	*"As it is our nature to be more moved by hope than fear, the example of one we see abundantly rewarded cheers and encourages us far more than the slights of many who have not been well treated disquiets us."*
Robert Half	*"There is something that is much more scarce, something rarer than ability. It is the ability to recognize ability."*
Alexander Hamilton	*"The desire of reward is one of the strongest incentives of human conduct; ... the best security for the fidelity of mankind is to make their interest coincide with their duty."*
David R. Hawkins	*"The more we give love, the greater our capacity to do so."*
Ernest Hemingway	*"When people talk, listen completely. Most people never listen."*
Eric Hoffer	*"No matter what our achievements might be, we think well of ourselves only in rare moments. We need people to bear witness against our inner judge, who keeps book on our shortcomings and transgressions. We need people to convince us that we are not as bad as we think we are."*

Celeste Holm	*"We live by encouragement and die without it—slowly, sadly, angrily."*
Elbert Hubbard	*"Often we can help each other most by leaving each other alone; at other times we need the hand-grasp and the word of cheer."*
Obi-Wan Kenobi	*"Trust your feelings, Luke."*
Lao-Tzu	*"When you are content to be simply yourself and don't compare or compete, everybody will respect you."*
Abraham Lincoln	*"Die when I may, I want it said of me that I plucked a weed and planted a flower wherever I thought a flower would grow."*
Abraham Lincoln	*"Tact is the ability to describe others as they see themselves."*
St. Maximus the Confessor	*"In all our actions, God considers the intention: whether we act for Him or for some other motive."*
John Maxwell	*"Leaders must be close enough to relate to others, but far enough ahead to motivate them."*
Gen. George Patton	*"If you tell people where to go, but not how to get there, you'll be amazed at the results."*
Maria de Lourdes Pintasilgo	*"I feel that what we must say to one another is based on encouraging each of us to be true to herself. 'Now that we are equal, let us dare to be different!'"*
Vince Poscente	*"Walking your talk is a great way to motivate yourself. No one likes to live a lie. Be honest with yourself, and you will find the motivation to do what you advise others to do."*
Ambrose Redmoon	*"Courage is not the absence of fear, but rather the judgment that something else is more important than fear."*
Virginia Satir	*"Feelings of worth can flourish only in an atmosphere where individual differences are appreciated, mistakes are tolerated, communication is open, and rules are flexible the kind of atmosphere that is found in a nurturing family."*
Albert Schweitzer	*"Sometimes our light goes out but is blown into flame by another human being. Each of us owes deepest thanks to those who have rekindled this light."*
George Bernard Shaw	*"To withhold deserved praise lest it should make its object conceited is as dishonest as to withhold payment of a just debt lest your creditor should spend the money badly."*
Jim Stovall	*"You need to be aware of what others are doing, applaud their efforts, acknowledge their successes, and encourage them in their pursuits. When we all help one another, everybody wins."*
Madame Swetchine	*"We deceive ourselves when we fancy that only weakness needs support. Strength needs it far more."*

Mother Teresa	*"Let no one come to you without leaving better and happier."*
William Arthur Ward	*"Flatter me, and I may not believe you. Criticize me, and I may not like you. Ignore me, and I may not forgive you. Encourage me, and I will not forget you. Love me and I may be forced to love you."*
Booker T. Washington	*"I believe that any man's life will be filled with constant and unexpected encouragement, if he makes up his mind to do his level best each day, and as nearly as possible reaching the high water mark of pure and useful living."*
Simone Weil	*"Difficult as it is really to listen to someone in affliction, it is just as difficult for him to know that compassion is listening to him."*
Len Wein	*"A true friend is one who is there for you when he'd rather be anywhere else."*

Miscellaneous

Author Unknown	*"Sometimes the majority only means that all the fools are on the same side."*
Author Unknown	*"To worry is like rocking in a rocking chair. It gives you something to do, but gets you nowhere."*
Author Unknown	*"Worry does not empty tomorrow of its sorrow; it empties today of its strength."*
Author Unknown	*"You wouldn't worry so much about what people really thought of you if you knew just how seldom they actually do."*
Henry Ford	*"Chop your own wood, and it will warm you twice."*
John Herschel	*"Self-respect is the cornerstone of all virtue."*
Indian Proverb	*"I had no shoes and complained, until I met a man who had no feet."*
Martin Luther King, Jr.	*"In the end we'll remember not the words of our enemies, but the silence of our friends."*
Martin Luther King, Jr.	*"The ultimate measure of a man is not where he stands in moments of comfort and convenience, but where he stands at times of challenge and controversy."*
Jude D. McCoy	*"Perception is reality to the perceiver."*
James D. Miles	*"You can easily judge the character of a man by how he treats those who can do nothing for him."*
Earl Nightingale	*"When you judge others, you do not define them, you define yourself."*

CHAPTER 10
EXERCISES FOR ESSENTIAL SKILLS

*I*n Chapter 4, six categories of essential skills that can be taught and reinforced were discussed:

- Problem-solving skills
- Decision-making skills
- Information-gathering and synthesizing skills
- Imagery and memory skills
- Critical thinking and reasoning skills
- Self-control and self-regulation skills

However, two of these skill areas—problem solving and critical thinking and reasoning—are best thought of as involving two subcomponents. In all, then, there are eight types of essential skills that you might teach and reinforce as part of the Pathfinder Project. These are:

- Problem solving (general) } **Problem Solving**
- Solving academic problems }
- Decision making
- Information gathering and synthesizing
- Imagery and memory
- Analyzing errors } **Critical Thinking and Reasoning**
- Analyzing deductive conclusions }
- Self-control and self-regulation

Chapter 4 describes instructional activities you can use to develop each of these eight skill areas. This chapter provides reproducible worksheets you can use with all areas above, except for information gathering and synthesizing and for imagery and memory (which simply do not lend themselves to a worksheet format). Before using these worksheets, it is important to read the corresponding section in Chapter 4. General directions and answers are provided for each set of worksheets.

Problem Solving (General)

General Directions and Answers

This set of worksheets helps reinforce some of the steps to the expanded version of problem solving presented in Chapter 4. Prior to using these worksheets, present the steps to the expanded version of problem solving, describing and exemplifying each as concretely as possible. Then use selected worksheets from this set to address those steps that need added reinforcement.

Answers to Worksheet 1

Student responses will vary but should provide a clear description of how the problem was addressed.

Answers to Worksheet 2

Student responses will vary but should provide a rationale for why something is or is not considered a problem.

Answers to Worksheet 3

Student responses will vary but should provide a rationale for why the situation was not considered to be a problem.

Answers to Worksheet 4

Student responses will vary but should provide a description of negative comments students make to themselves.

Answers to Worksheet 5

Student responses will vary but should clearly identify what is missing or the obstacle in each situation.

Answer to Worksheet 6

Student responses will vary but should identify multiple possible solutions.

Answers to Worksheet 7

Student responses will vary but should clearly articulate what is missing, or the obstacles and possible solutions.

Answers to Worksheet 8

Student responses will vary but should clearly differentiate between solutions that are likely versus unlikely to succeed.

Answers to Worksheet 9

Student responses will vary but should provide a clear rationale for why a specific solution was selected.

Answers to Worksheet 10

Student responses will vary but should clearly describe alternative goals.

Answers to Worksheet 11

Student responses will vary but should clearly describe how the student's attitude changed.

Worksheet 1

Directions:

Each day we are faced with many problems to solve—some large, some small. Describe two problems that you faced recently. For each problem, describe how you solved it. Then describe the results—what happened after you solved the problem?

Describe the problem:

How I solved the problem:

Results:

Describe the problem:

How I solved the problem:

Results:

Directions:

Sometimes we choose to walk away from situations that could be perceived as problems. For example, if you wanted to make a salad and discovered there was no lettuce, you might have a problem. To make your salad, you would somehow have to get lettuce. However, you could simply decide not to have a salad made out of lettuce (for example, opt for a pasta salad instead). Then there would be no problem. We can sometimes choose whether we consider a situation to be a problem. For each of the situations described below:

1. Determine whether the situation would be a problem for you.

2. Explain why it would or wouldn't be a problem for you.

3. Describe what you would do.

Example 1:

You have a project due in art class. However, you left home in such a hurry that you forgot to bring the project with you.

1. Is this a problem?

2. Why is it or isn't it a problem?

3. What would you do?

Example 2:

You are standing in line to see a museum exhibit in which you are very interested. You get to the ticket counter and realize you have no money. You have no friends with you from whom you can borrow the money.

1. Is this a problem?

2. Why is it or isn't it a problem?

3. What would you do?

Example 3:

You have bought a special present for your sister's birthday. On her birthday, you realize that you have left the present over at a friend's house, where you had wrapped it.

1. Is this a problem?

2. Why is it or isn't it a problem?

3. What would you do?

Directions:

Describe a situation that could have been a problem for you but wasn't because you chose to ignore it. Explain why you chose not to make the situation a problem.

A situation I chose not to make a problem:

Why I chose not to make the situation a problem:

Directions:

Sometimes, when faced with a very difficult problem, we say things to ourselves that make it harder to solve the problem. For example, you might say to yourself, "This is impossible" or, "No one is around to help me." When you start saying these things to yourself, you may set yourself up to fail. It's better to say more positive things. For example, you could say to yourself, "I know I can figure this out" or, "I'm sure I can find help if I really look." Talking to yourself this way helps you become a better problem solver. In the spaces below, write some things you could say to yourself to be a better problem solver. Then draw a symbol or a picture that represents you as a good problem solver.

Things I could say to myself to make me a better problem solver:

A symbol or picture of myself as a good problem solver:

Directions:

Many times a situation becomes a problem when something is missing or an obstacle presents itself. For example, if you want to make a cheese sandwich and there is no bread, the situation is a problem because "bread" is missing. The way you describe what is missing sets up how you go about solving the problem. For example, if you say that "bread" is not the thing missing but something to put the cheese on is, then you try to solve the problem differently. For example, you might find crackers to put the cheese on.

Read the situations below that contain problems you might encounter. For each situation, identify at least two ways of describing what is missing or identifying the real obstacle.

1. You work hard, but you continue to receive poor grades in science class.
   What is missing/what obstacles exist?

2. You cannot afford to buy the new bicycle you have wanted for a long while.
   What is missing/what obstacles exist?

3. You missed the bus to school this morning.
   What is missing/what obstacles exist?

4. Your watch stops running.
   What is missing/what obstacles exist?

5. You are ready to go to a dance and you find out that your favorite outfit is still in the hamper.
   What is missing/what obstacles exist?

6. You cannot find your portable CD player.
   What is missing/what obstacles exist?

7. The air conditioner breaks down in the middle of summer.
   What is missing/what obstacles exist?

8. You lose your student ID card.
   What is missing/what obstacles exist?

9. You find you cannot go to summer camp this year.
   What is missing/what obstacles exist?

10. You move to a new town where you do not know anyone.
    What is missing/what obstacles exist?

Directions:

Once you have identified what you consider to be missing or what obstacles exist in a given problem, you start looking for ways to provide what is missing or to overcome the obstacle. For example, once you decide that you are missing bread for your cheese sandwich, then you start to identify ways to get bread. Usually, the more ways you can think of to fill in what is missing or to overcome the obstacle, the easier it is to solve the problem. Read the situation described below. Then do the following:

1) Describe the problem in your own words.
2) Describe what is missing/what obstacles exist.
3) Identify a number of possible ways to fill in what is missing and overcome the obstacles.

Situation: Friday morning, Joe went to the bus stop to go to work. While he was walking, he began reading the morning paper and discovered that the bus drivers were on strike. No buses would be running that day.

Describe the problem situation:

What is missing/what obstacles exist?

What are some possible ways of filling in what is missing or overcoming the obstacles?

Worksheet 7

Directions:

1) Identify a problem you see around school.

2) Identify what is missing and what obstacles exist.

3) Describe at least two ways of filling in what is missing and overcoming the obstacle.

4) Describe the alternative you would select first and explain why you would select that alternative.

What is the problem?

What is missing/what obstacles exist?

What are some ways to fill in what is missing?

Describe the alternative you would select and why you would select it:

Directions:

Sometimes there are a number of possible solutions to a problem, but not every solution will bring success. It's important to consider how likely success is with each possible solution and to pick a solution that inspires you (makes you feel comfortable and seems likely) to succeed.

For each example below:

1) Identify a solution you consider likely to succeed.
2) Identify a solution you do not consider likely to succeed.
3) Identify the solution you would select and explain why.

Example 1:   Your car has a flat tire and you can't drive to school.

Successful solution:

Unsuccessful solution:

Solution you would select. Explain why:

Example 2:   Band practice is today, but you forgot your instrument at home.

Successful solution:

Unsuccessful solution:

Solution you would select. Explain why:

Example 3:   You discover that you will have a surprise math test tomorrow for which you are not well-prepared.

Successful solution:

Unsuccessful solution:

Solution you would select. Explain why:

Example 4:   You're on the varsity basketball team, and you develop the flu with a high fever the night before the big basketball game.

Successful solution:

Unsuccessful solution:

Solution you would select. Explain why:

Directions:

Identify a problem you once faced for which there were a range of solutions you could have selected. Describe the problem, the solutions, and the feasibility of each solution. Then describe the solution you selected and explain why you selected it. Try several options.

Problem situation:

Solutions available:

Solution I selected and why I selected it:

Directions:

What happens when you keep trying to solve a problem and nothing works? What do you do when you realize that you can't possibly accomplish your goal? For example, you try to solve he problem of making the swim team even though you are not a very strong swimmer. You train as hard as you can and give it everything you've got, but when the team is picked, you don't make it. At times like this, it is useful to find another goal that you can accomplish—one that is fairly close to your original goal. For example, although you didn't make the school swim team, you could join a competitive swimming club in town.

For each situation below, identify alternative goals you can accomplish even though you can't accomplish the initial one.

1. You try out for a part in the school play, but you don't make the cast.

   Alternative goals:

2. You organize a fund-raiser for an important cause, but the event makes little or no money.

   Alternative goals:

3. You campaign for the office of class president, but your opponent gets more votes.

   Alternative goals:

Directions:

Identify a time when you tried to accomplish a goal and failed, but were able to identify another goal that you did accomplish.

Problem situation at which I failed:

Alternative goal I reached:

How I accomplished my alternative goal:

How I felt after accomplishing alternative goal:

How my attitude toward the original goal changed:

Academic Problems

As described in Chapter 4, the process for solving academic problems is somewhat different from the process for general problem solving. Worksheets for four types of academic problems are provided in this section.

- Problems of unusual thinking
- Quantitative problems
- Spatial problems
- Analogy problems

Although the process for solving academic problems described in Chapter 4 applies to all four types, you might want to modify it slightly by adding or changing some steps to address the specific requirements of a given problem type.

Problems of Unusual Thinking

General Directions and Answers

This set of worksheets involves problems of unusual thinking because, to solve them, students must think in ways that are different from their normal approach to problems. Prior to presenting problems of unusual thinking, go over the general steps for solving academic problems. Then, emphasize the importance of thinking in different ways about problems. You might also give students an advanced understanding of this type of problem by presenting the following exercise:

Connect the nine X s using four straight lines and without lifting your pencil off the paper:

X   X   X

X   X   X

X   X   X

The normal approach to this problem assumes that you must stay within the perimeter of the nine X s when drawing the four lines. However, the problem is impossible to solve within the context of this assumption. Once you realize that you can draw your lines outside of the perimeter

of the nine X s, the problem is easily solved even without lifting your pencil off the paper:

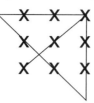

First, let students try to solve the problem under the erroneous assumption. When they have become convinced that the problem can't be solved, discuss the nature of "assumptions" and point out how the assumptions they are making about this problem prevents them from seeing the answer. Impress the importance of examining assumptions when a problem seems difficult or impossible to solve. Then explain that all of the problems of this type have hidden assumptions that must be identified before they can be solved.

Answer for Worksheet 1

Assumption: *Squares must be touching on their sides.*

Answer:

Answer for Worksheet 2

Assumption: *Each time the words "a squirrel" are used they refer to different squirrels.*

Answer: *Three squirrels.*

Answer for Worksheet 3

Assumptions: *You have to weigh all the marbles in a sack. You must weigh marbles from different sacks separately.*

Answer: *Take one marble from bag 1, two marbles from bag 2, three marbles from bag 3, and so on. You will have a total of 61 marbles. If each marble weighed 10 grams, the total weight of the 61 marbles would be 610 grams. If the first bag had the defective marbles, the total weight would be 611 grams. If the second bag contains the defective marbles, the total weight would be 612 grams, and so on.*

Answer for Worksheet 4

Assumption: *The length from which the half-length is calculated is 75 yards.*

Answer: *150 yards. If the playground is 75 yards plus half its own length, then 75 yards must be the other half. Algebraically, the formula for the length of the playground is:*

$$Length = 75 + \frac{length}{2}$$

Answer for Worksheet 5

Assumption: *The triangle must be divided using straight lines that go all the way through it.*

Answer:

Answer for Worksheet 6

Assumption: *The ancestors for each person living are different.*

Answer: *As you go back each generation, ancestors begin to overlap. Therefore, if you go back far enough, you can show that everyone living is related to the same set of people.*

Answer for Worksheet 7

Assumption: *The only statements to consider are the five equations.*

Answer: *Problems 4 and 5 are incorrect equalities. So, of the five equalities, only two are false. This makes the statement at the top of the problem: "There are three false statements here" false also. Therefore, this statement is the third false statement in the problem.*

Answer for Worksheet 8

Assumption: *When you mix the two stacks, you keep the same total value of the items if they were considered independently.*

Answer: *When you begin, you have 30 CDs worth 50 cents each (the ones sold at two for $1) and 30 CDs worth 33 $\frac{1}{3}$ cents each (the ones sold at three for $9). The value of the*

stack of 30 for 50 cents is $15. The value of the stack of 30 for 33 $\frac{1}{3}$ cents is $10. The value of the total inventory is $25. When you mix the stacks, you sell 12 sets altogether and each CD was worth 40 cents which adds up to $24.*

Answer for Worksheet 9

Assumption: *You must consider both types of animals simultaneously when calculating their respective number.*

Answer: *Six llamas, four ostriches. Since there were 20 eyes, there must have been 10 animals. If all animals were ostriches, there would have been only 20 legs showing, but there were 32 legs. So, six of the animals must have had four legs each. Therefore, six were llamas. That leaves four left to be ostriches.*

Answer for Worksheet 10

Assumption: *William must give the manager one new link each day that is separate from the other links.*

Answer: *If William cuts the third link, he will have three units that he can trade back and forth each day: 1) a single link, 2) a chunk with two links, and 3) a chunk with four links. The first day, he gives the manager the single link. The second day, he takes the single link back and gives him the two-link chunk. The third day he gives him the single link plus the two-link chunk, and so on.*

Answer for Worksheet 11

Assumption: *The distance between the comets when they begin affects how far apart they will be three seconds before they crash.*

Answer: *255 miles apart. The distance between the comets at the beginning is irrelevant information. The only thing important is how quickly they are approaching each other. Since comet A is traveling at 50 miles per second and comet B at 35 miles per second, they are approaching each other at a speed of 85 miles per second. Three seconds before they collide, they will be 255 miles (3 x 85) apart.*

Answer for Worksheet 12

Assumption: *You have to know how full the container is at each stage of the cell's reproduction.*

Answer: *6:00 a.m. If each cell produced two other cells just like it over an hour's period of time, then each hour the container always holds 1/3 the volume it will hold one hour later. Since it takes a cell one hour to produce two cells just like it, the container must have been 1/3-full one hour before it was completely full.*

Answer for Worksheet 13

Assumption: *The square must be formed by the long sides of the sticks.*

Answer: *Form the square using the small end of the sticks.*

Answer for Worksheet 14

Assumption: *During the intervals of time when no train is at the station, both trains have an equal probability of arriving at the station.*

Answer: *Because the northbound train runs one minute after the southbound train, there are only four minutes each hour that Sarah could arrive at the station and catch a northbound train.*

For example:

> *1:00 to 1:01*
>
> *1:15 to 1:16*
>
> *1:30 to 1:31*
>
> *1:45 to 1:46*

If Sarah arrives during the other 56 minutes in the hour, the first train that comes into the station will be a southbound train.

Answer for Worksheet 15

Assumption: *Tom's walking at different rates negates his covering the same distance in the same interval of time.*

Answer: *If you cover the same distance within the same interval of time coming and going, you must reach a spot at precisely the same time coming and going regardless of the differing paces during ascent and descent. To illustrate this, imagine that Tom had a double who started down the mountain at precisely the same time that Tom started up the mountain. Even if one of the Toms walked at steady pace and the other walked at differing paces, they would invariably meet one another at some point on the trail.*

Directions:

For the problem below:

1) Identify some assumptions you are making.

2) Identify alternatives to your assumptions.

3) Identify the correct answer.

Problem:

Below are 12 sticks arranged so that they make four squares. Moving only three sticks, form three squares of the same size.

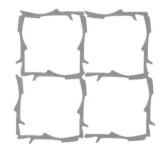

Assumptions:

Alternatives:

Answer:

Directions:

For the problem below:

1) Identify some assumptions you are making.

2) Identify alternatives to your assumptions.

3) Identify the correct answer.

Problem:

Joan went for a walk and saw two squirrels in front of a squirrel, two squirrels in back of a squirrel, and a squirrel in the middle position. What's the smallest number of squirrels Joan could have seen?

Assumptions:

Alternatives:

Answer:

Directions:

For the problem below:

1) Identify some assumptions you are making.

2) Identify alternatives to your assumptions.

3) Identify the correct answer.

Problem:

You have 10 bags of marbles. Each bag contains 100 marbles and each marble should weigh 10 grams. However, the manufacturer has made an error and sent you one bag with marbles weighing 11 grams each. Using a scale only once, identify which bag has the overweight marbles.

Assumptions:

Alternatives:

Answer:

Directions:

For the problem below:

1) Identify some assumptions you are making.

2) Identify alternatives to your assumptions.

3) Identify the correct answer.

Problem:

If a playground is 75 yards plus half its own length, how long is it?

Assumptions:

Alternatives:

Answer:

Directions:

For the problem below:

1) Identify some assumptions you are making.

2) Identify alternatives to your assumptions.

3) Identify the correct answer.

Problem:

Divide the figure below into three equal parts.

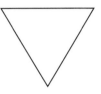

Assumptions:

Alternatives:

Answer:

Directions:

For the problem below:

1) Identify some assumptions you are making.

2) Identify alternatives to your assumptions.

3) Identify the correct answer.

Problem:

Richard has heard that the population of Earth is growing so fast that it will soon be overcrowded. But then he runs into Dr. Jones, who says that the Earth's population is getting smaller. He explains it this way: every person living now has a mother and a father—two parents. Each of those two parents had two parents—that makes four ancestors for every one on Earth. Each of those four ancestors had two parents—that makes eight ancestors. Dr. Jones says, "See, each generation you go back doubles the number of ancestors you have. If you go back 20 generations, each person has 1,048,576 ancestors. So the earth's population is actually getting smaller!" Richard knows that Dr. Jones must be wrong. Describe the fallacy in Dr. Jones' reasoning.

Assumptions:

Alternatives:

Answer:

Directions:

For the problem below:

1) Identify some assumptions you are making.

2) Identify alternatives to your assumptions.

3) Identify the correct answer.

Problem:

There are three false statements here. Identify them:

1. $3 \times 5 = 15$
2. $14 - 6 = 8$
3. $(4 \times 8) - 7 = 25$
4. $25 \div 5 = 3$
5. $12 + 11 = 33$

Assumptions:

Alternatives:

Answer:

Directions:

For the problem below:

1) Identify some assumptions you are making.

2) Identify alternatives to your assumptions.

3) Identify the correct answer.

Problem:

Camille owns a used-CD store. She decides to have a sale. She puts 30 copies of CD A on sale at two for $1; she puts 30 copies of CD B on sale at three for $1. When the CDs are all sold, the two for $1 CDs have brought in $15. The three for $1 CDs have brought in $10. She made $25 on the sale. The next day she takes out 30 more copies of CD A and 30 more copies of CD B. But instead of selling them separately, she decides to mix them. She says, "If I sold two for $1 and three for $1, why not mix the piles and sell five for $2?" After the sale, she adds up her money. She has made one dollar less than the day before. She sold 12 sets of CDs for $2 a set. She made $24 today and $25 the day before. What happened to the dollar?

Assumptions:

Alternatives:

Answer:

Directions:

For the problem below:

1) Identify some assumptions you are making.

2) Identify alternatives to your assumptions.

3) Identify the correct answer.

Problem:

Walking through the zoo, George and Marsha passed an area that contained llamas and ostriches. After they left the zoo, Marsha said to George, "Did you count the llamas and ostriches?" "No," said George, "how many were there?" Marsha replied, "Altogether there were 20 eyes and 32 legs." How many llamas and how many ostriches were in the pen?

Assumptions:

Alternatives:

Answer:

Directions:

For the problem below:

1) Identify some assumptions you are making.

2) Identify alternatives to your assumptions.

3) Identify the correct answer.

Problem:

William has a gold chain with seven links (see figure below). He wants to stay at a hotel but he has very little money. He and the manager agree that William will give the manager one link for every day he stays at the hotel. William has seven links, so he can stay seven days. But he still has a problem. The jeweler will charge him money each time a link is cut. William has enough money to have only one link cut from his chain of seven links. How can he give the manager one link for each of the seven days he stays and still only cut one link from the chain?

Assumptions:

Alternatives:

Answer:

Directions:

For the problem below:

1) Identify some assumptions you are making.

2) Identify alternatives to your assumptions.

3) Identify the correct answer.

Problem:
Two comets are on a crash course in space. They start out 1,000 miles apart. Comet A is traveling at a speed of 50 miles per second. Comet B is traveling at a speed of 35 miles per second. How far apart will they be three seconds before they crash?

Assumptions:

Alternatives:

Answer:

Directions:

For the problem below:

1) Identify some assumptions you are making.

2) Identify alternatives to your assumptions.

3) Identify the correct answer.

Problem:

Dr. Smith has invented a new type of cellular organism that reproduces itself. Within an hour, each cell creates two other cells just like it. Dr. Smith puts one cell of her new organism in a huge container at 12:00 a.m. At 7:00 a.m., the container is completely filled with the organism. At what time was the container 1/3 full?

Assumptions:

Alternatives:

Answer:

Directions:

For the problem below:

1) Identify some assumptions you are making.

2) Identify alternatives to your assumptions.

3) Identify the correct answer.

Problem:

How can you make a square by moving only one of the four sticks below that are arranged in the form of a cross?

Assumptions:

Alternatives:

Answer:

Directions:

For the problem below:

1) Identify some assumptions you are making.

2) Identify alternatives to your assumptions.

3) Identify the correct answer.

Problem:

Sarah has a boyfriend in each of two neighborhoods. One lives directly north of where she lives; the other lives directly south. She can never decide which boyfriend to visit so she lets probability do it for her. Each day, she goes to the subway station at a different time and takes the first train that comes in. The trains run at 15-minute intervals and the northbound trains leave one minute after the southbound trains.

Northbound	Southbound
1:00	1:01
1:15	1:16
1:30	1:31

After a few months, Sarah realizes that she has been seeing her northern boyfriend most of the time, but seeing her southern boyfriend only once in a while.
Explain why this is so.

Assumptions:

Alternatives:

Answer:

Directions:

For the problem below:

1) Identify some assumptions you are making.

2) Identify alternatives to your assumptions.

3) Identify the correct answer.

Problem:

Tom starts up the mountain trail at 7:00 a.m. on Monday. He keeps walking at a steady pace and arrives at the top at 3:00 p.m. that day. He camps on the top for the night and starts back down the next morning. He leaves at 7:00 a.m. on the second day. This time he walks down the same trail at different rates, sometimes walking very quickly, other times very slowly and still other times he stops to see the scenery. He arrives back where he started at 3:00 p.m. on the second day. That night, Tom runs into Betty who tells him, "You know, Tom, coming down the mountain you passed a spot at exactly the same time you passed it going up the mountain." Tom says, "No way! Coming down the mountain I walked at different speeds." But Betty was right. Explain why.

Assumptions:

Alternatives:

Answer:

Quantitative Problems

General Directions and Answers

As their name implies, quantitative problems involve mathematic concepts. A step in the process for solving quantitaative academic problems that is almost always useful is to draw a diagram or a picture of the problem. Another is to restate the problem in your own words. There are four worksheets in this section, each with a number of examples of a specific type of problem. By the time each worksheet is completed, students should have a good understanding of that particular type of problem. To facilitate understanding of a particular problem type, it is helpful to involve students in a discussion of the similarities they noticed among the problems in a worksheet.

Answers for Worksheet 1

1. *48 miles*
2. *15 miles west, 7 miles south*
3. *42*
4. *54*
5. *4*

Answers for Worksheet 2

1. *6*
2. *21*
3.

People at meeting	Number of handshakes
1	0
2	1
3	3
4	6
5	10
6	15
7	21
8	28
9	36
10	45

4. *The difference in the number of handshakes required increases by one each time you add a new person to the meeting.*

People at meeting	Number of handshakes	Difference in number of handshakes
1	0	0
2	1	1
3	3	2
4	6	3
5	10	4
6	15	5
7	21	6
8	28	7
9	36	8
10	45	9

5. Important point: *Draw students' attention to the fact that the difference between the number of handshakes increases by one each time the number of people involved increases by one, as depicted in the chart below by the > sign.*

Number of people	Number of handshakes	Number of people	Number of handshakes
			> 13
1	0	14	91
	> 1		> 14
2	1	15	105
	> 2		> 15
3	3	16	120
	> 3		> 16
4	6	17	136
	> 4		> 17
5	10	18	153
	> 5		> 18
6	15	19	171
	> 6		> 19
7	21	20	190
	> 7		> 20
8	28	21	210
	> 8		> 21
9	36	22	231
	> 9		> 22
10	45	23	253
	> 10		> 23
11	55	24	276
	> 11		> 24
12	66	25	300
	> 12		
13	78		

Answers for Worksheet 3

1. *15*
2. *633*
3. *10*

Answers for Worksheet 4

1. *3*
2. *4*
3.

Number of different colors	Maximum number of draws required to obtain two marbles of the same color
2	3
3	4
4	5
5	6
6	7
7	8
8	9
9	10
10	11

Rule: *The maximum number of draws is one greater than the number of different colors.*

4. *5*

5.

Number of marbles of same color (two different colors in container)	Maximum number of draws
2	5
3	7
4	9
5	11
6	13
7	15
8	17
9	19
10	21

Rule: *The maximum number of draws is one greater than two times the number of marbles required of the same color.*

6. *Let m = the number of marbles of the same color; let c = the number of different colors.*

Number of marbles of same color

Number of different colors	2	3	4	5	6	7	8	9	10
2	3	5	7	9	11	13	15	17	19
3	4	7	10	13	16	19	22	25	28
4	5	9	13	17	21	25	29	33	37
5	6	11	16	21	26	31	36	41	46
6	7	13	19	25	31	37	43	49	55
7	8	15	22	29	36	43	50	57	64
8	9	17	25	33	41	49	57	65	73
9	10	19	28	37	46	55	64	73	82
10	11	21	31	41	51	61	71	81	91
	$1c + 1 = ((m\text{-}1) \times c) + 1$	$2c + 1 = ((m\text{-}1) \times c) + 1$	$3c + 1 = ((m\text{-}1) \times c) + 1$	$4c + 1 = ((m\text{-}1) \times c) + 1$	$5c + 1 = ((m\text{-}1) \times c) + 1$	$6c + 1 = ((m\text{-}1) \times c) + 1$	$7c + 1 = ((m\text{-}1) \times c) + 1$	$8c + 1 = ((m\text{-}1) \times c) + 1$	$9c + 1 = ((m\text{-}1) \times c) + 1$

Rule: *The maximum number of draws equals one less than the number of marbles required of the same color times the number of colors. One is then added to that quantity.* $[(m\text{-}1) \times c] + 1$

Worksheet 1a

Directions:

The problems in this worksheet involve mathematical thinking. That's why they are referred to as "quantitative problems." Two very important steps in solving them are: 1) to restate the problem in your own words, and 2) to draw a picture or a diagram of the problem. Each of the problems below includes a diagram to help you better understand it. There is also space to write your own description of the problem. Before you write your description of a problem, think through different ways to describe it.

Problem 1:

Starting at her house, Susan runs three miles north, 12 miles east, five miles north, four miles east, eight miles south, and 16 miles west back to her house. How far did Susan run?

Diagram:

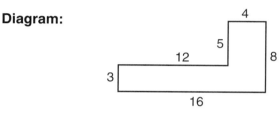

Problem description:

Answer:

Problem 2:

Starting at school, John ran east 20 blocks, then north 18 blocks. Then he ran west five blocks, then south 11 blocks. Next he ran west and finally south until he returned to the school. How far did John go on the last two legs of his run?

Diagram:

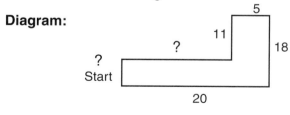

Problem description:

Answer:

Problem 3:

Find the perimeter (the total length of the outside edge) of the figure below.

Diagram:

Problem description:

Answer:

Problem 4:

If a rectangle that is 4" x 10" is placed next to one that is 5" x 12", what is the perimeter of the combined figure?

Diagram:

Problem description:

Answer:

Problem 5:

If you have a figure like the one below, what is the fewest number of sides you must know to accurately calculate the perimeter? Explain your answer.

Diagram:

Problem description:

Answer:

Directions:

All but one of the problems below include diagrams to help you better understand them. For the other problem, you will have to create your own diagram. There is also space to write your own description of the problem. Before you write your description of the problem, think through different ways to do so.

Problem 1:

Four people were at a meeting during which each person shook hands exactly once with every other person. How many handshakes were there?

Diagram:

	1	2	3	4
1		X	X	X
2			X	X
3				X
4				

Problem description:

Answer:

Problem 2:

If there had been seven people at the meeting, how many handshakes would there have been?

Diagram:

	1	2	3	4	5	6	7
1							
2							
3							
4							
5							
6							
7							

Problem description:

Answer:

Problem 3:

Identify the number of handshakes that would take place if one to ten people were at the meeting.

Diagram:

	1	2	3	4	5	6	7	8	9	10
1										
2										
3										
4										
5										
6										
7										
8										
9										
10										

Problem description:

Answer:

People at meeting	Number of handshakes
1	
2	
3	
4	
5	
6	
7	
8	
9	
10	

Worksheet 2c

Problem 4:

Describe the relationship between the increase in the number of people at the meeting and the increase in the number of handshakes. *(Hint: Look at the differences between the number of handshakes as you add more people to the party.)*

Diagram:

People at meeting	Number of handshakes	Difference in number of handshakes
1		
2		
3		
4		
5		
6		
7		
8		
9		
10		

Number of handshakes required for two people minus the number of handshakes required for one person

Problem description:

Answer:

Problem 5:

Use the rule you discovered in Problem 4 to determine how many handshakes there would be if there were 25 people at the meeting.

Create your own diagram:

Problem description:

Answer:

Directions:

All but one of the problems below include diagrams to help you better understand them. For the other problem, you will have to create your own diagram. There is also space to write your own description of the problem. Before you write your description of the problem, think through different ways to do so.

Problem 1:

In an animal shelter, there were 10 dogs and 20 cats. Half of the dogs were short-haired and half of the cats were short-haired. How many short-haired dogs and short-haired cats were there?

Diagram:

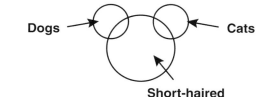

Dogs →   ← Cats

Short-haired

Problem description:

Answer:

Problem 2:

The school principal wanted to send announcements to all seniors and all honor students in the school. There were 428 seniors, 386 honor students, and 181 seniors who were honor students. How many announcements did the principal send out?

Diagram:

Honors   Seniors

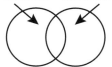

Problem description:

Answer:

Problem 3:

At a family reunion, every nephew was a cousin. Half of all uncles were cousins. Half of all cousins were nephews. There were 40 uncles and 30 nephews. How many cousins were neither uncles nor nephews?

Diagram:

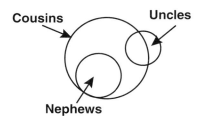

Problem description:

Answer:

Worksheet 4a

Directions:

For each problem below: 1) Describe the problem in your own words. 2) Create a diagram to represent the problem (if one is not provided for you). 3) Identify an answer you believe is correct. 4) Be ready to explain how you arrived at your answer.

Problem 1:

A jar has an equal number of clear marbles and white marbles. If you reach in with your eyes closed and take out a marble, what is the greatest number of times you will have to reach in to take out two marbles of the same color?

Diagram:

Problem description:

Answer:

Problem 2:

Now suppose that the jar has an equal number of clear, white, and red marbles. What is the greatest number of times you will have to reach in to take out two marbles of the same color?

Diagram:

Problem description:

Answer:

Problem 3:
Make a chart of the maximum number of draws required to obtain two marbles of the same color when the container has from two to ten different colored marbles of equal numbers. Then write a rule that describes the relationship between the number of different colors and the maximum number of draws.

Diagram:

Problem description:

Answer:

Number of different colors	Maximum number of draws required to obtain two marbles of the same color
2	
3	
4	
5	
6	
7	
8	
9	
10	

Rule:

Problem 4:

If you have two different colors of marbles in the jar, what is the maximum number of draws that will be required to obtain three marbles of the same color?

Diagram:

	Number of different colors	
Number of marbles of the same color	1	2
1	X	X
2	X	X
3	X	

Problem description:

Answer:

Rule:

Problem 5:

Make a chart of the maximum number of draws required to draw two to ten marbles of the same color when there are two different colors of marbles in the jar. Then write a rule that describes the relationship between the maximum number of draws required and the number of marbles of the same color when there are only two different colors of marbles.

Diagram:

Problem description:

Answer:

Number of marbles of same color (two different colors in container)	Maximum number of draws
2	
3	
4	
5	
6	
7	
8	
9	
10	

Rule:

Problem 6:

You now have a rule for the maximum number of draws required when:

1. You want two marbles of the same color and you have two to ten different colors.
2. You want two to ten marbles of the same color and you have two different colors.

Now see if you can put these rules together. Create a table that represents the maximum number of draws required when: 1) the number of marbles required of the same color increases from two to ten, and 2) the number of different types of colors increases from two through ten. Finally, write a rule that describes the relationship between the maximum number of draws required and the number of marbles required of the same color and the number of different colors as both increase. *(Hint: Write rules that describe the pattern of numbers for each column. Let m = the number of marbles required of the same color; let c = the number of colors.)*

Diagram:

Problem description:

Answer:

Number of marbles of same color

	2	3	4	5	6	7	8	9	10
2									
3									
4									
5									
6									
7									
8									
9									
10									

Number of different colors

Rule:

Spatial Problems

General Directions and Answers

This set of worksheets involves spatial problems, which are frequently found on cognitive ability tests. Prior to presenting spatial problems to students, go over the general steps for solving academic problems as articulated in Chapter 4. One of the keys to solving spatial problems is to identify the pattern of changes in the figures. This is best addressed in Step 3 of the academic problem solving process, in which students are asked to state the problem in their own words.

Answers for Worksheet 1

1. b
2. b
3. b
4. c
5. c

Answers for Worksheet 2

1. c
2. c
3. c
4. a
5. c

Answers for Worksheet 3

1. b   6. a
2. a   7. b
3. c   8. b
4. c   9. c
5. c

Answers for Worksheet 4

1. a   6. a
2. b   7. b
3. b   8. c
4. b   9. a
5. b

Answer for Worksheet 5

1. b
2. c
3. b
4. b
5. a

Answers for Worksheet 6

1. a   5. c
2. a   6. a
3. b   7. b
4. c   8. a

Answers for Worksheet 7

Student responses will vary.

Answers for Worksheet 8

Student responses will vary.

Answers for Worksheet 9

1.   4.
2.   5.
3.   6.

Answers for Worksheet 10

1.   5.
2.   6.
3.   7.
4.   8.

Answers for Worksheet 11

1. c
2. c
3. a
4. a
5. c

Worksheet 1

Directions:

In each problem below, identify the figure that would most likely come next. Pay attention to the change you see occurring in the first two figures and then ask yourself, "What would be the next change that follows the same pattern?"

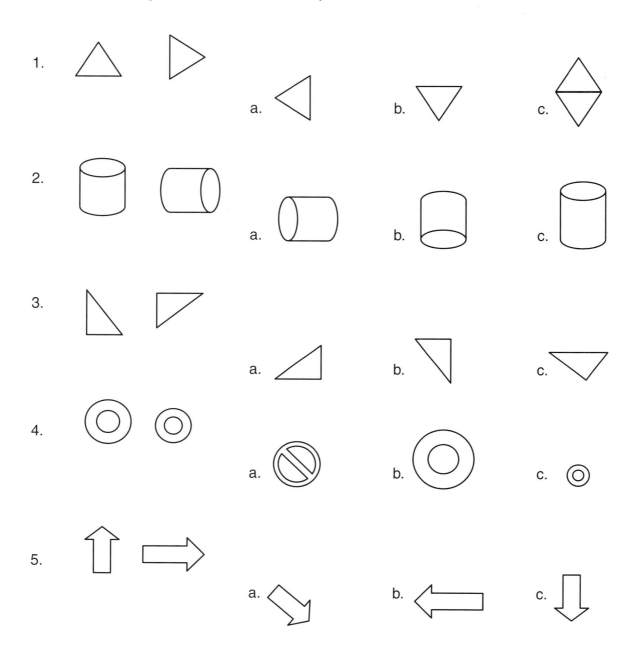

Directions:
This worksheet follows the same pattern Worksheet 1. Determine the figure that would come next given the changes you see in the first two figures.

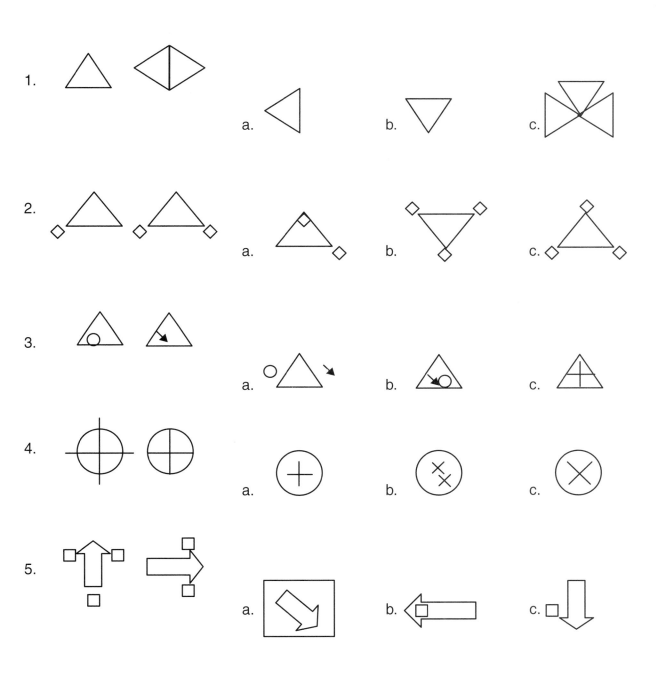

Worksheet 3a

Directions:

You might be given a test in which you have to figure out the pattern made by a group of figures. For example, if you were given the following figures you could probably determine that the  figure comes next:

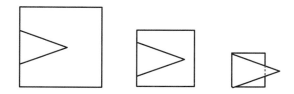

To determine the answers to problems like this, it is useful to know the changes you can expect in the parts of the figures. Below are nine changes that you will commonly find in tests that use figures:

1. **Size Change.** One part becomes larger or smaller.

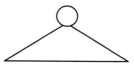

2. **Rotation.** A part is turned around in some way.

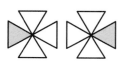

3. **Shading Change.** The shading is either partially or totally removed or added.

4. **Shape Change.** One part of a figure alters its shape.

5. **Position Switch.** Some parts move to the positions of other parts.

6. **Key Part Vanishes or Appears.** An element is removed from one figure or added to another figure.

7. **Position Change.** A part moves to another position.

8. **Break-up.** A piece of the figure is split.

9. **Multiplier Change.** A part of the figure is repeated one or more times.

Now, see if you can recognize these nine different types of changes. For each series of shapes below, identify the next figure in the pattern. Describe the changes you see from figure to figure, using one of the nine change types described.

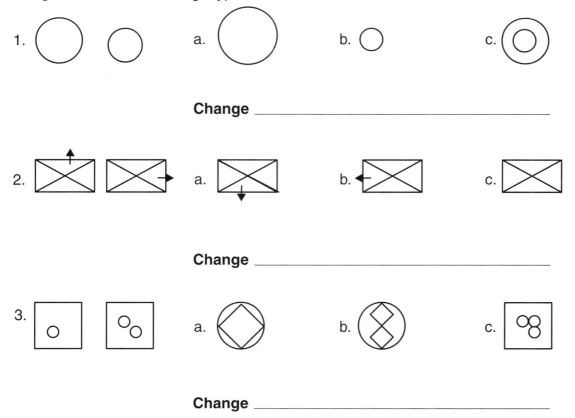

1.   a.   b.   c.

Change _____

2.   a.   b.   c.

Change _____

3.   a.   b.   c.

Change _____

Worksheet 3c

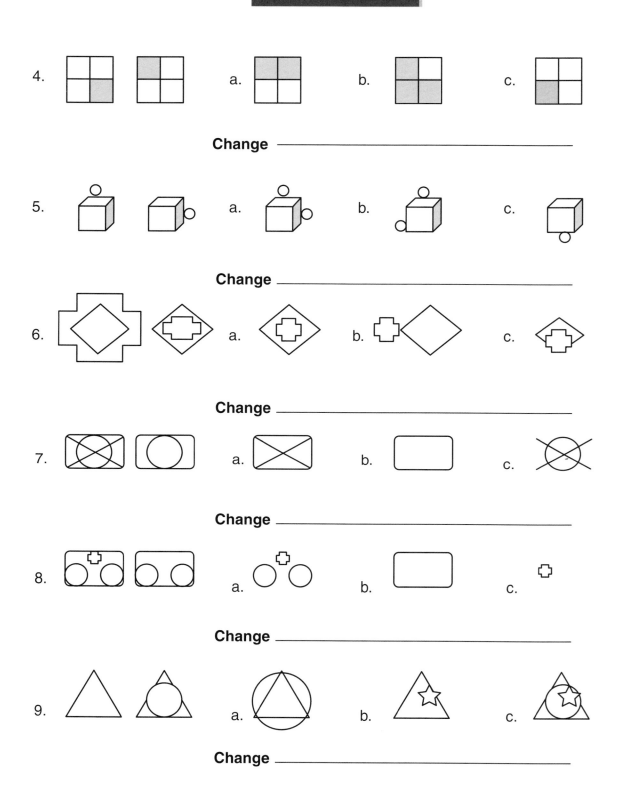

4.   a.   b.   c.

Change _____

5.   a.   b.   c.

Change _____

6.   a.   b.   c.

Change _____

7.   a.   b.   c.

Change _____

8.   a.   b.   c.

Change _____

9.   a.   b.   c.

Change _____

Directions:

Some of the problems in this worksheet are in the form of an analogy, and some are in the form of a series of figures. For each one, identify the figure that would come next. Explain the type of change that indicated the right answer.

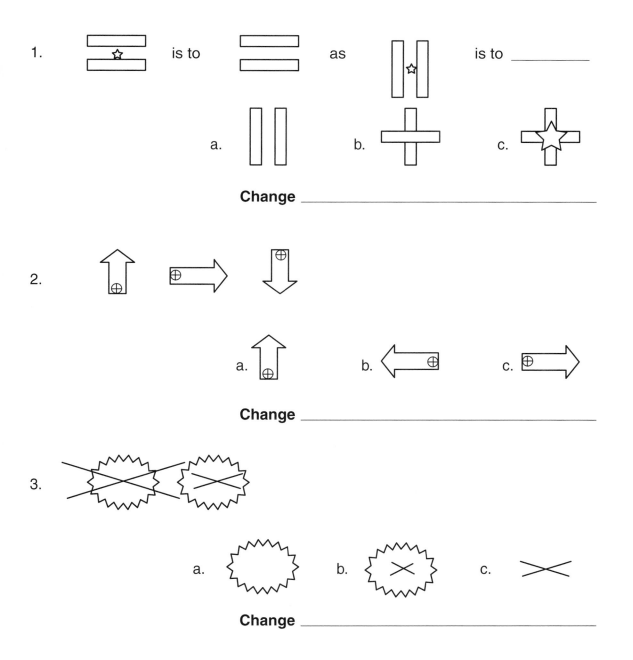

1. ☐☆☐ is to ☐☐ as ‖☆ is to _____

    a. ‖   b. ⊟   c. ✚

    Change _____

2. ⬆⊕   ⊕⮕   ⊕⬇

    a. ⬆⊕   b. ⬅⊕   c. ⊕➡

    Change _____

3.

    a.   b. ⊗   c. ✕

    Change _____

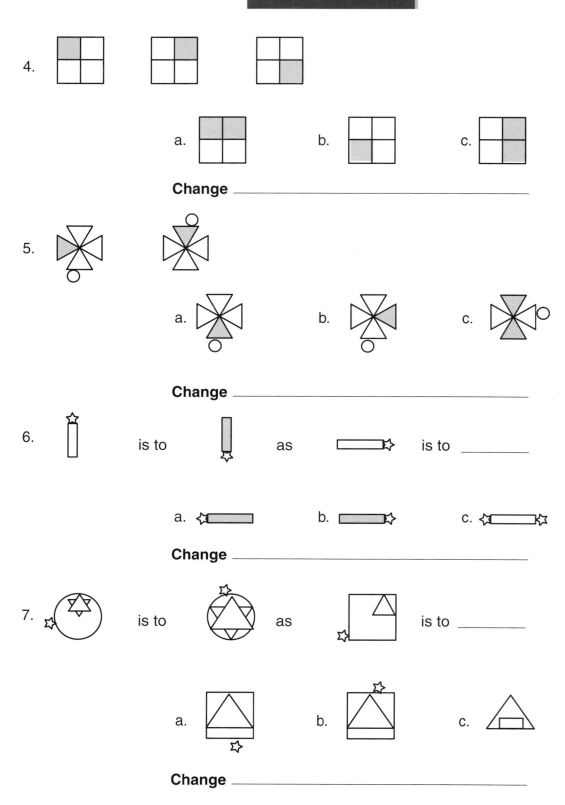

4.

a.   b.   c.

Change _____

5.

a.   b.   c.

Change _____

6.   is to   as   is to _____

a.   b.   c.

Change _____

7.   is to   as   is to _____

a.   b.   c.

Change _____

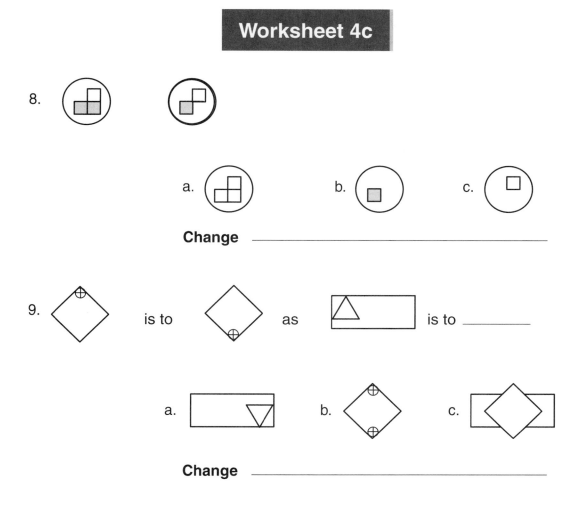

8.

a.

b.

c.

Change _____

9.

is to   as   is to _____

a.

b.

c.

Change _____

Worksheet 5a

Directions:
Complete each figural analogy, and describe the change you noticed.

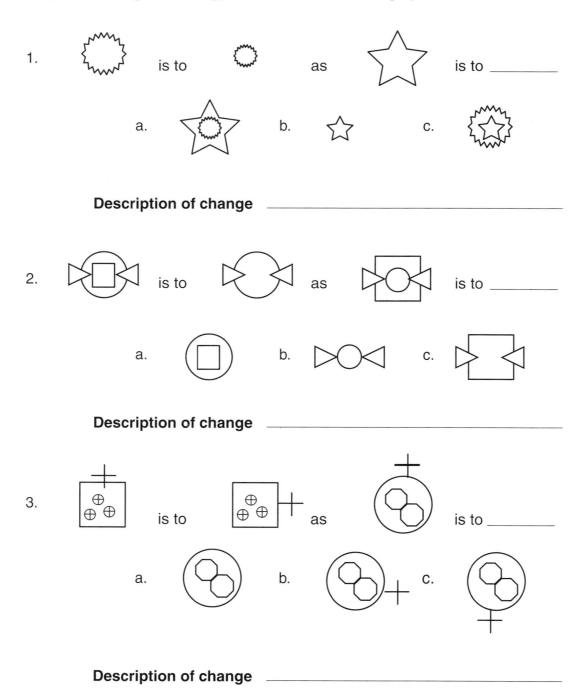

1.   is to   as   is to _____

    a.   b.   c.

    Description of change _____

2.   is to   as   is to _____

    a.   b.   c.

    Description of change _____

3.   is to   as   is to _____

    a.   b.   c.

    Description of change _____

4.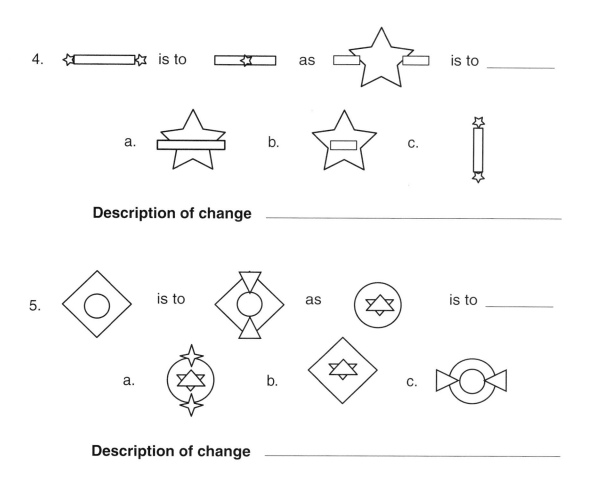

Description of change _____

5.

Description of change _____

Directions:
Complete each figural analogy and describe the change you noticed.

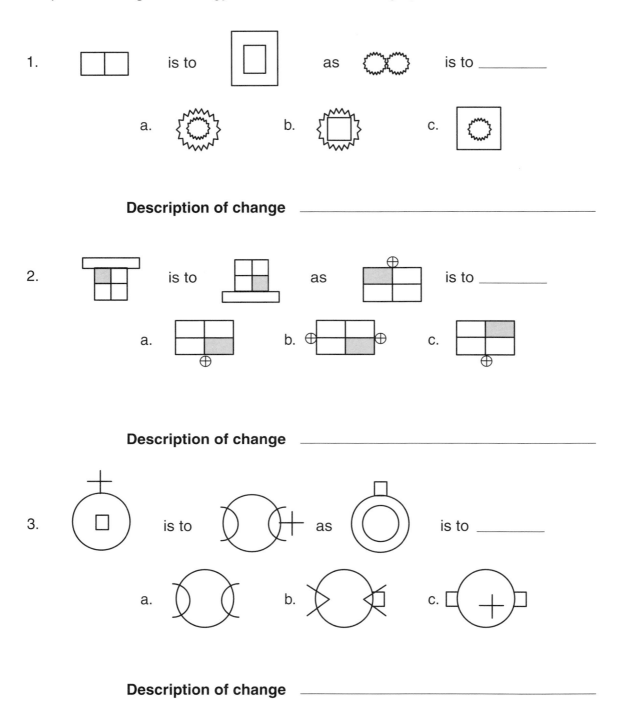

1. [ ][ ] is to [□] as [✸✸] is to _____

   a. [✸]   b. [✸▢]   c. [▢✸]

   Description of change _____

2. is to as _____

   a.   b.   c.

   Description of change _____

3. is to as _____

   a.   b.   c.

   Description of change _____

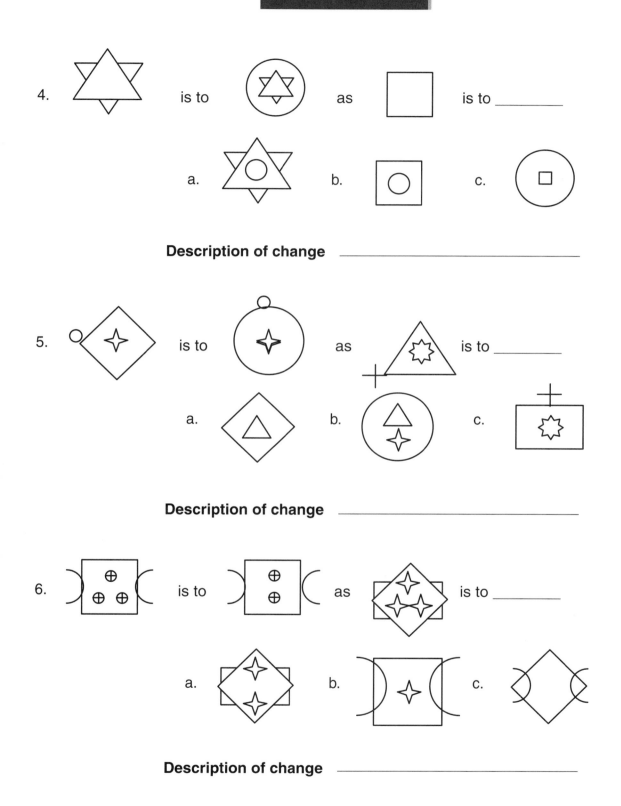

4.   is to   as   is to _____

    a.   b.   c.

Description of change _____

5.   is to   as   is to _____

    a.   b.   c.

Description of change _____

6.   is to   as   is to _____

    a.   b.   c.

Description of change _____

Worksheet 6c

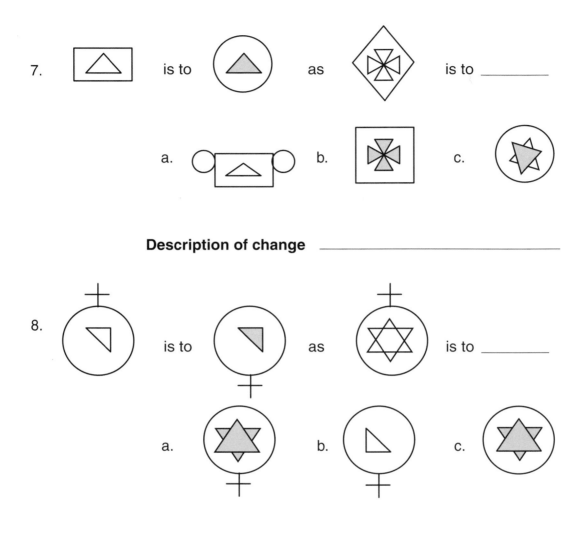

7. ▭ is to ◯ as ◇ is to _____

a. b. c.

Description of change _____

8. is to as is to _____

a. b. c.

Description of change _____

Directions:
Now make your own figural analogies. Below are the beginning parts of figural analogies.
Complete the analogies and describe the change you have made to create them.

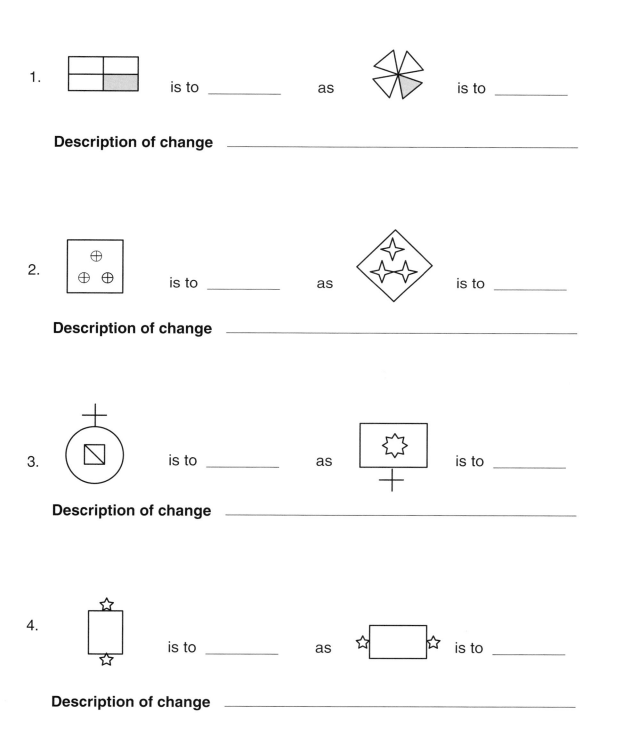

1.
   is to _____ as   is to _____

   Description of change _____

2.
   is to _____ as   is to _____

   Description of change _____

3.
   is to _____ as   is to _____

   Description of change _____

4.
   is to _____ as   is to _____

   Description of change _____

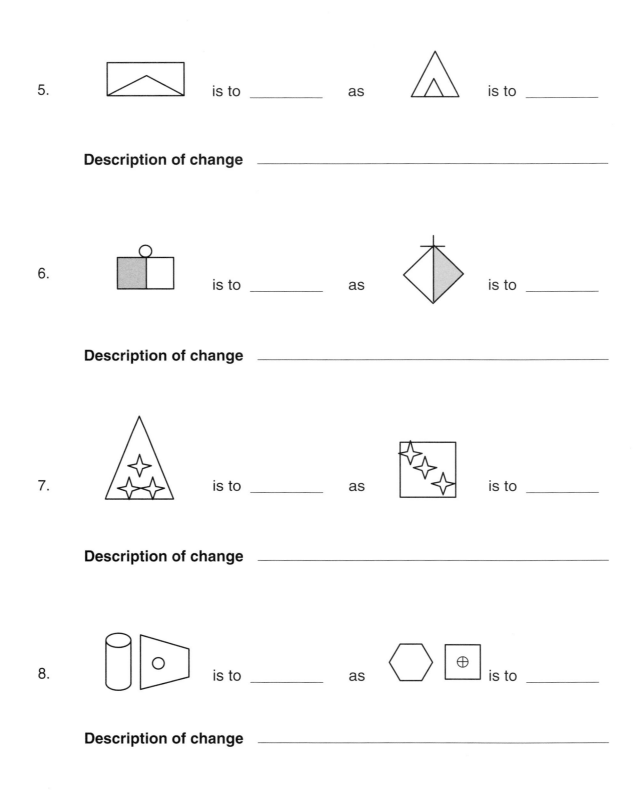

5. ____ is to _____ as ____ is to _____

Description of change _____

6. ____ is to _____ as ____ is to _____

Description of change _____

7. ____ is to _____ as ____ is to _____

Description of change _____

8. ____ is to _____ as ____ is to _____

Description of change _____

Directions:
Complete each figural analogy and describe the change you used.

1. is to _____ as is to _____

Description of change _____

2. is to _____ as is to _____

Description of change _____

3. is to _____ as is to _____

Description of change _____

4. is to _____ as is to _____

Description of change _____

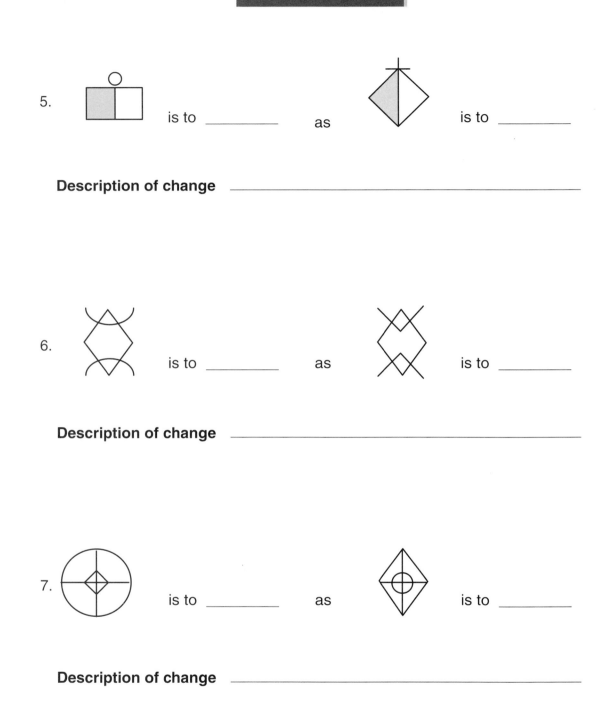

5. _____ is to _____ as _____ is to _____

Description of change _____

6. _____ is to _____ as _____ is to _____

Description of change _____

7. _____ is to _____ as _____ is to _____

Description of change _____

8. 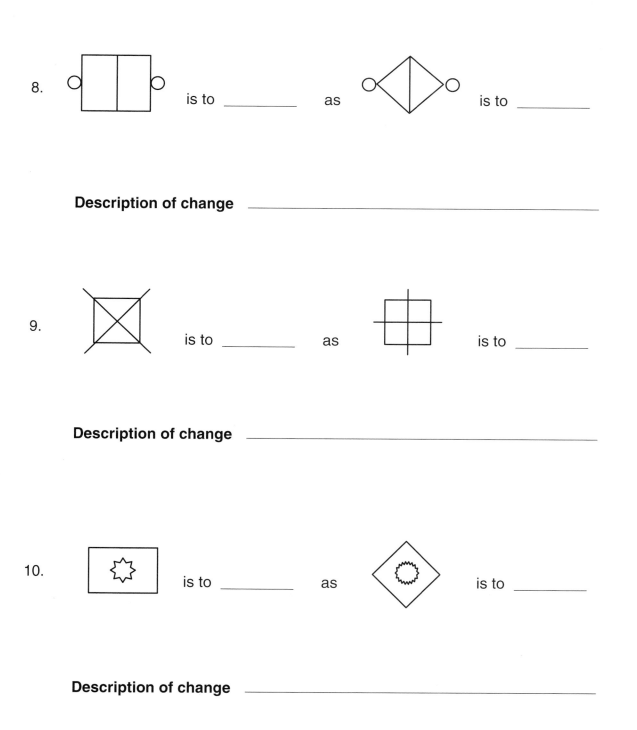 is to _____ as is to _____

Description of change _____

9. is to _____ as is to _____

Description of change _____

10. is to _____ as is to _____

Description of change _____

Directions:

Fill in the missing figure for each problem below. Describe the pattern of changes you found.

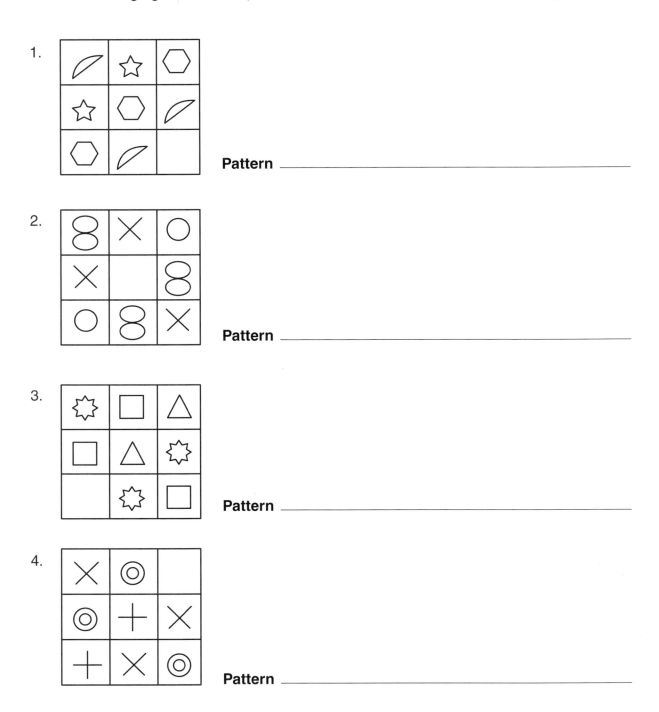

1.

Pattern _____

2.

Pattern _____

3.

Pattern _____

4.

Pattern _____

5. 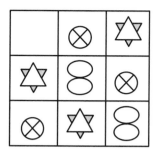 **Pattern** _____

6. 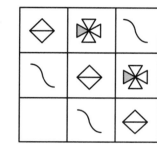 **Pattern** _____

Directions:

Fill in the missing figure for each problem below. Describe the pattern of changes you found.

1.

Pattern _____

2.

Pattern _____

3.

Pattern _____

4.

Pattern _____

5.

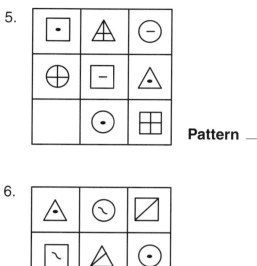

Pattern _____

6.

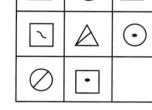

Pattern _____

7.

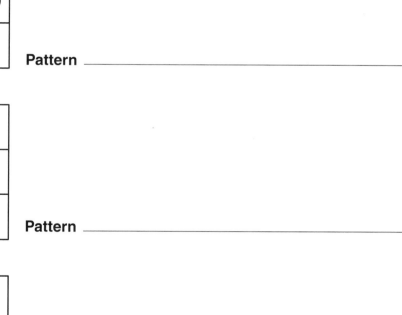

Pattern _____

8.

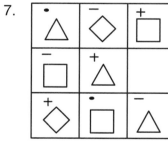

Pattern _____

Directions:
Complete the figural problems below and describe the patterns you observe.

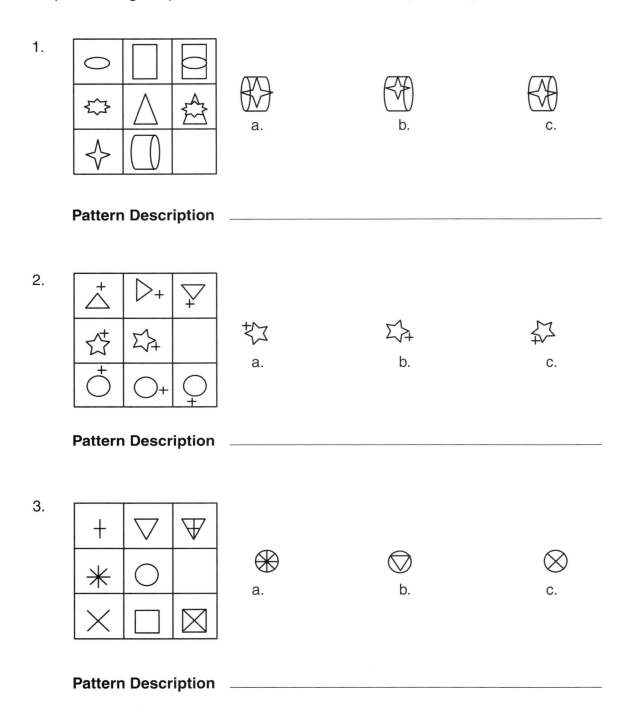

1.

Pattern Description _____

2.

Pattern Description _____

3.

Pattern Description _____

4.

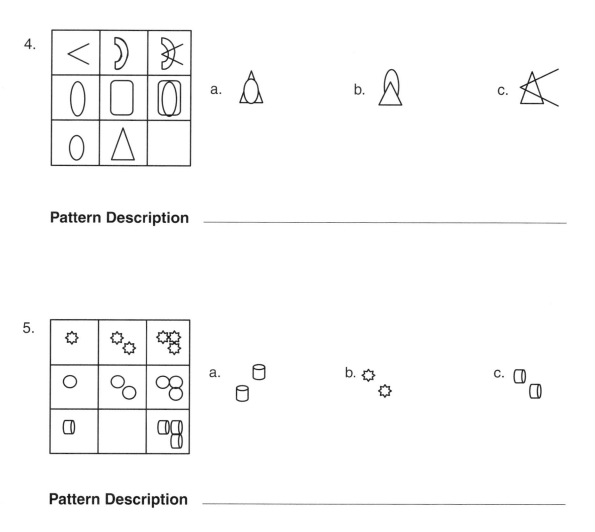

Pattern Description _____

5.

Pattern Description _____

Analogical Reasoning Problems

General Directions and Answers

Analogical reasoning problems have a common format which might be stated as A is to B as C is to D. With these types of problems, it is important that students focus on the relationship between concepts. This is best addressed in Step 3 of the academic problem-solving process during which students are asked to describe the problem in their own words. There are nine worksheets in this section involving analogical reasoning problems. Worksheet 4 addresses nine types of relationships commonly found in analogical problems. If students are familiar with these relationships, they will be better prepared to solve analogical problems commonly found on cognitive ability tests.

Answers for Worksheet 1

1. *a*	6. *b*
2. *c*	7. *a*
3. *b*	8. *b*
4. *b*	9. *b*
5. *a*	10. *a*

Answers for Worksheet 2

1. *b*	6. *b*	11. *b*
2. *a*	7. *c*	12. *a*
3. *a*	8. *c*	13. *a*
4. *a*	9. *c*	14. *c*
5. *b*	10. *b*	15. *c*

Answers for Worksheet 3

1. *c*	6. *a*
2. *b*	7. *b*
3. *a*	8. *a*
4. *a*	9. *c*
5. *c*	10. *b*

Answers for Worksheet 4

1. *opposite*
2. *same class or category*
3. *time or sequence*
4. *part of*
5. *similar meanings*
6. *size or amount*
7. *category/member*
8. *does something to or for*
9. *part of*
10. *time or sequence*
11. *opposite*
12. *turns into or causes*
13. *part of*
14. *size or amount*
15. *similar meanings*
16. *size or amount*
17. *does something to or for*
18. *similar meaning*
19. *same class or category*
20. *similar meaning*

Answers for Worksheet 5

Student responses will vary.

Answers for Worksheet 6

Student responses will vary.

Answers for Worksheet 7

1. *b*	8. *c*	15. *c*
2. *c*	9. *c*	16. *a*
3. *c*	10. *a*	17. *c*
4. *b*	11. *a*	18. *c*
5. *b*	12. *b*	19. *a*
6. *c*	13. *c*	20. *a*
7. *a*	14. *b*	

Answers for Worksheet 8:

Student responses will vary.

Answers for Worksheet 9:

Student responses will vary.

Directions:

The problems in this exercise are referred to as analogies. Analogy problems include two sets of concepts. The concepts in the first set are related to each other in some way.

Example: bird : cage

The relationship between these two concepts is that a bird is kept in a cage.

You are then given one of the concepts in the second set, and you choose the second concept that forms the same relationship as the concepts in the first set.

Example: First Set   **Second Set**
        bird : cage   ::   dog : _____

The way to read an analogy is: "Bird is to cage as dog is to what?" The colon (:) means "is to" and the double colon (::) means "as." The concepts you can choose from to solve this problem are:

     a. leash
     b. kennel
     c. collar

The answer for this analogy is b., "kennel." "Dog" is related to "collar" and "leash" but not in the same way that "bird" is related to "cage." Therefore, they don't fit this particular analogy. "Kennel" fits because dogs are kept in kennels just like birds are kept in cages.

Solve the analogy problems below by identifying the relationship between the first two concepts and writing it in the space provided. Then identify the correct answer.

    First Set   **Second Set**

1. shirt : garment   ::   sandwich : _____

    (Relationship:_____)
    a. food
    b. nourishment
    c. calories

2. food : restaurant   ::   knowledge : _____

    (Relationship:_____)
    a. book
    b. geography
    c. school

3. asphalt : road   ::   cover :_____

    (Relationship:_____)
    a. photograph
    b. book
    c. camera

First Set		Second Set

4. tricycle : motorcycle   ::   glider : _____

(Relationship:_____)
a. helicopter
b. airplane
c. kite

5. mosquito : larva   ::   moth : _____

(Relationship:_____)
a. pupa
b. ant
c. butterfly

6. electricity : fan   ::   hammer : _____

(Relationship:_____)
a. builder
b. nail
c. sawdust

7. winter : spring   ::   kindergarten :_____

(Relationship:_____)

a. first grade
b. graduation
c. high school

8. Dallas : Boston   ::   Texas : _____

(Relationship:_____)
a. Oklahoma
b. Massachusetts
c. Chicago

9. child : adult   ::   tadpole :_____

(Relationship:_____)

a. amphibian
b. frog
c. fish

10. engine : automobile   ::   pedals : _____

(Relationship:_____)

a. bicycle
b. feet
c. sewing machine

Directions:

Solve the analogy problems below. Be prepared to describe the relationship between the concepts in the first set and explain why the relationship in the second set is similar.

First Set		**Second Set**

1. governor : state   ::   councilman : _____

   a. state
   b. city
   c. nation

2. vehicle : scooter   ::   book : _____

   a. encyclopedia
   b. newspaper
   c. stationery

3. grow : fertilize   ::   learn : _____

   a. study
   b. read
   c. graduate

4. tire : wheel   ::   sole : _____

   a. shoe
   b. foot
   c. bottom

5. liquid : solid   ::   water : _____

   a. steam
   b. ice
   c. vapor

6. menu : restaurant   ::   card catalog : _____

   a. classroom
   b. library
   c. book

7. flour : bread   ::   trees : _____

   a. desert
   b. forest
   c. paper

Worksheet 2b

First Set		**Second Set**

8. ship : rudder   ::   airplane : _____
   a. wing
   b. pilot
   c. rudder

9. room : house   ::   page : _____
   a. tree
   b. fiber
   c. book

10. yellow : banana   ::   purple : _____
    a. Barney
    b. grape
    c. scarf

11. seal : shark   ::   leaf : _____
    a. tree
    b. caterpillar
    c. moth

12. skeleton : body   ::   frame : _____
    a. house
    b. floor
    c. room

13. hill : mountain   ::   pond : _____
    a. ocean
    b. pool
    c. river

14. Jupiter : planet   ::   water : _____
    a. element
    b. organism
    c. liquid

15. yes : no   ::   accept : _____
    a. choose
    b. choice
    c. decline

Directions:

Solve the analogy problems below. Be prepared to describe the relationship between the concepts in the first set then explain why the relationship in the second set is similar.

First Set		**Second Set**

1. movie stars : Tom Hanks   ::   superheroes : _____

   a. Mickey Mouse
   b. President Clinton
   c. Spiderman

2. Mia Hamm : Tiger Woods   ::   Emily Dickinson : _____

   a. Marie Curie
   b. William Shakespeare
   c. Charles Schulz

3. plumber : pipes   ::   carpenter : _____

   a. wood
   b. shop
   c. bookshelf

4. popcorn : salt   ::   rice : _____

   a. soy sauce
   b. water
   c. chow mein noodles

5. peel : potato   ::   scale : _____

   a. piano
   b. tree
   c. fish

6. broth : soup   ::   lettuce : _____

   a. salad
   b. dressing
   c. croutons

First Set   **Second Set**

7. exercise : sweat   ::   eating peanut butter : _____

   a. empty mouth
   b. sticky mouth
   c. sleep

8. lantern : light bulb   ::   tailor : _____

   a. seamstress
   b. manager
   c. teacher

9. rose : flower   ::   kidney : _____
   a. heart
   b. pump
   c. organ

10. meteorologist : forecast ::   cologne : _____

   a. vaporizer
   b. scent
   c. perfume

Directions:

Generally, the most difficult part of solving analogy problems is identifying the relationship between the words in the first set. Nine types of relationships are listed below. If you become familiar with these, you will improve your skills in solving analogy problems.

1. Synonyms, or words with **SIMILAR MEANINGS**
   sofa : couch
   rapid : quick

2. Antonyms, or words with **OPPOSITE MEANINGS**
   smart : dumb
   short : tall

3. Words within the **SAME CLASS OR CATEGORY**
   mini van : truck
   blue jeans : blouse

4. One word is a class or category and the other word is a member of that class or category (**CATEGORY/MEMBER**)
   steak : sirloin
   vehicle : Jeep

5. One word **TURNS INTO OR CAUSES** another
   caterpillar : butterfly
   haste : waste

6. One words **DOES SOMETHING TO OR FOR** another
   shark : prey
   clerk : customer

7. One word has a **TIME OR SEQUENCE** relationship to another
   New Year's Day : St. Patrick's Day
   spring : summer

8. One word has a **SIZE OR AMOUNT** relationship with another
   lake : sea
   shoe : boot

9. One word is **PART OF** another
   lead : pencil
   desk : office

Below are 20 pairs of words that could be the first set of an analogy problem. Decide how the two words are related, and label them with one of the nine types of relationships from Worksheet 4a.

Examples of First Sets   **Type of Relationship**

1. defense : prosecution   _____

2. thistle : crabgrass   _____

3. election: inauguration   _____

4. allergies : watery eyes   _____

5. monitor : watch   _____

6. yard : park   _____

7. money : dollar   _____

8. plumber : pipes   _____

9. branch : tree   _____

10. first : second   _____

11. white : black   _____

12. plum : prune   _____

13. street : map   _____

14. chair : throne   _____

15. automobile : car   _____

16. city library : Library of Congress   _____

17. accountant : taxes   _____

18. couch : sofa   _____

19. tennis shoes : boots   _____

20. jacket : coat   _____

Directions:
The first column below contains one concept that could be in the first set of an analogy problem. The second column indicates the type of relationship that should be created. Fill in the blank with a word that will create this relationship.

Examples of First Sets	**Type of Relationship**
1. team :_____	category/member
2. January : _____	time or sequence
3. button : _____	part of
4. secretary : _____	does something to or for
5. raise : _____	opposite
6. modern : _____	similar meanings
7. far : _____	same class or category
8. charcoal : _____	turns into or causes
9. kernel : _____	size or amount
10. rectangle : _____	same class or category
11. pessimistic : _____	opposite
12. Chihuahua : _____	category/member
13. Alps: _____	size or amount
14. harvest : _____	similar meanings
15. hurricane : _____	turns into or causes
16. glossary : _____	part of
17. gloves :_____	does something to or for
18. birth : _____	time or sequence

Directions:

In this exercise, you are to make up your own pairs of words that could be used as first sets in analogy problems. Create two examples for each of the nine common types of relationships. Be creative by using concepts from school, movies, books, friends, food, etc.

1. similar meanings

   _____ : _____

   _____ : _____

2. opposite words

   _____ : _____

   _____ : _____

3. same class or category

   _____ : _____

   _____ : _____

4. category/member

   _____ : _____

   _____ : _____

5. turns into or causes

   _____ : _____

   _____ : _____

6. does something to or for

   _____ : _____

   _____ : _____

7. time or sequence

   _____ : _____

   _____ : _____

8. size or amount

   _____ : _____

   _____ : _____

9. part of

   _____ : _____

   _____ : _____

Worksheet 7a

Directions:
Solve the following analogy problems, which are based on the nine common relationships you have been studying. Remember that these are not the only relationships you might find in analogy problems, but they are some common ones.

1. operator : telephone :: stoplights : _____
   a. green
   b. vehicles
   c. roads

2. zinc : mineral :: Florida : _____
   a. nation
   b. capitol
   c. state

3. U2 : *NSYNC :: William J. Clinton : _____
   a. George Washington
   b. Franklin Delano Roosevelt
   c. George W. Bush

4. fact : fiction :: elastic : _____
   a. yielding
   b. brittle
   c. rubber

5. friend : pal :: adolescent : _____
   a. adult
   b. teenager
   c. rubber

6. room : house :: word : _____
   a. noun
   b. preposition
   c. paragraph

7. flour : grain :: diamond : _____
   a. charcoal
   b. gold
   c. pearl

8. dollar : peso   ::   wool : _____

   a. sweater
   b. sheep
   c. cotton

9. watch : Big Ben   ::   rose bush : _____

   a. tree
   b. forest
   c. redwood

10. cool : scalding   ::   filthy : _____

   a. immaculate
   b. mud
   c. hot

11. wind : sailboat   ::   gasoline : _____

   a. car
   b. motor
   c. gas

12. elbow : joint   ::   piano : _____

   a. jazz
   b. instrument
   c. rock

13. essay : report   ::   conclusion : _____

   a. experiment
   b. attempt
   c. result

14. up : down   ::   coarse:_____

   a. rough
   b. smooth
   c. sandpaper

15. penny : dollar   ::   raft : _____

   a. kayak
   b. cruise
   c. ship

16. monitor : computer   ::   bulb : _____
    a. chandelier
    b. tulip
    c. filament

17. dog : collar   ::   horse : _____
    a. barn
    b. stirrup
    c. saddle

18. pencil : chalk   ::   St. Louis : _____
    a. Missouri
    b. Midwest
    c. Atlanta

19. China : Cuba   ::   cow : _____
    a. horse
    b. milk
    c. pasture

20. apartment : dwelling   ::   poodle : _____
    a. canine
    b. feline
    c. pit bull

Directions:
Looking at the different relationships that exist among things in the world can sometimes help us to see things differently. Fill in the blanks in the problems below with words that you think complete the analogies. Be prepared to explain your answers.

1. water : trees   ::   _____ : kitten

2. water : lake   ::   _____ : house

3. tailor : suit   ::   _____ : portrait

4. fan : breeze   ::   _____ : _____

5. laces : hiking boots   ::   _____ : books

6. _____ : catcher   ::   _____ : quarterback

7. _____ : Des Moines ::   _____ : Denver

8. chores : ranch   ::   _____ : pickup truck

9. _____ : newspaper   ::   _____ : magazine

10. candle : light   ::   producer   : _____

11. hydrogen: water   ::   _____ : _____

12. _____ : gas   ::   _____ : liquid

13. caviar : corn dog   ::   _____ : _____

14. _____ : puzzles   ::   _____ : sweepstakes

15. president : king   ::   _____ : _____

Directions:

Try to form your own analogies using concepts from different content areas (for example, English and mathematics).

1. In Column 1, write five concepts you have been studying in your classes at school.
2. In Column 2, identify a related concept and its relation to the concept on the left.
3. Then identify two other concepts, from a different content area, that have relationships similar to those in the first two columns. For example:

Concept	Related concept and relationship	Two concepts with a similar relationship
conjunction :	grammar	addition : arithmetic

Column 1	Column 2	Column 3	Column 4
1. _____	_____	_____	_____
2. _____	_____	_____	_____
3. _____	_____	_____	_____
4. _____	_____	_____	_____
5. _____	_____	_____	_____

Decision-Making Exercises

General Directions and Answers

This set of worksheets reinforces some of the expanded decision-making steps described in Chapter 4. Prior to using these worksheets, present the steps to the expanded version of decision making, describing and exemplifying each as concretely as possible. Then use selected worksheets from this set to address those steps that need added reinforcement.

Answers to Worksheet 1

Student responses will vary but should identify the steps taken to make a decision.

Answers to Worksheet 2

Student responses will vary but should identify the criteria and the reasons for each criterion.

Answers to Worksheet 3

Student responses will vary but should identify and justify a value score for each criterion.

Answers to Worksheet 4

Student responses will vary but should identify and justify a value score for each criterion.

Answers to Worksheet 5

Student responses will vary but should identify and justify a value score for each criterion.

Answer to Worksheet 6

Student responses will vary but should identify the difference between difficult and easy decisions.

Answers to Worksheet 7

Student responses will vary but should identify and address the value scores for the criteria and the alternatives.

Answers to Worksheet 8

Student responses will vary but should clearly identify a best "mathematical" choice.

Answers to Worksheet 9

Student responses will vary but should contain clear descriptions and evaluations of the decisions made.

Worksheet 1

Directions:

We have to make decisions every day—what to wear, what to eat for dinner. Some decisions that we make are very important and impact our lives greatly. For example, deciding what college to attend is an important decision. What are some things you do when you have to make an important decision? Identify an important decision that you made recently. Then write down the things you did that helped you make the decision.

A decision I made recently was:

The things I did to help me make the decision were:

Directions:

One part of making an important decision is to identify the possible alternatives. For example, if you are trying to choose a college, several colleges that appeal to you may come to mind. Based on these alternatives, you might start to think about the criteria you want the college to have. You might want it to be located close to home, or you might want it to offer a specific degree program. Practice identifying criteria by pretending that you are trying to choose a college. Determine the criteria you would want in a college and explain why you have chosen each criterion.

Alternatives:

1.

2.

3.

4.

5.

Criteria I would like my college to have:	Why I think these criteria are important:
1.	1.
2.	2.
3.	3.
4.	4.
5.	5.
6.	6.
7.	7.
8.	8.
9.	9.

Directions:

Once you have identified important criteria, it is useful to assign values to those criteria based on which are most important to you. When you assign values to criteria, you use numbers or scores to indicate how important they are. If you assign a score of 3 to a criterion, it is very important. If you assign a score of 2, it is less important than a score of 3. If you assign a 1, the criterion is the least important. Try assigning values to the criteria you identified on Worksheet 2 in the space below. Then explain your answer.

Criteria	Value of Importance	Explanation
1.		
2.		
3.		
4.		
5.		
6.		
7.		
8.		
9.		

Directions:

Below are some criteria you might consider if you were buying a car. For each one, assign an importance score. 3 means it is very important, 2 means it is less important and 1 means it is the least important. When you are finished, explain why you assigned the value scores that you did.

Criteria	Value of Importance	Explanation
1. Color of vehicle		
2. Gas mileage vehicle gets in city/highway		
3. Number of people the vehicle holds		
4. Price of vehicle		
5. Manufacturer of vehicle		
6. Cost of insurance for vehicle		
7. Vehicle's features (e.g., 4-wheel drive, CD player, towing capacity, etc.)		

Directions:

Assigning values to the criteria you've identified is a significatnt step. Using scores of 3 to 1 (3 = very important, 1 = not very important), evaluate how important you think each of the following criteria would be if you were choosing a career. When you are done, explain why you assigned the value scores you did.

Criteria:

_____1. How difficult it is to find a job in your chosen career.

_____2. How much money you would make.

_____3. How you would be contributing to society.

_____4. How well-respected the career is.

_____5. Where you would have to live if you worked in that career.

_____6. How your family feels about the career.

Explanation:

Directions:

Some decisions are very easy, but others are difficult. Describe a time when you made a very easy decision. Then describe a time when you made a very difficult decision. Compare and contrast the two decision-making processes. Describe what makes a decision easy for you and what makes a decision hard for you.

A time when I made an easy decision:

A time when I made a difficult decision:

The differences between the two processes:

Those things that make decisions easy for me are:

Those things that make decisions difficult for me are:

Worksheet 7

Directions:

Think carefully about careers you might want to pursue when you finish school. Identify three possible alternatives. Fill them in on the top line of the grid (Alternatives A, B, and C) Then list five criteria that are important to your career choice along the side of the grid. Assign values to each criterion. If a criterion is very important to you, assign it a 3. If it's less important, assign a 2, and assign a value of 1 if it is even less important. Place the values in the parentheses next to the criteria. Next, identify the extent to which each alternative possesses each criterion. If it doesn't possess the criterion at all, put a 0 in the brackets. If it possesses the criterion totally, put a 3 in the brackets.

ALTERNATIVES

CRITERIA (value)   A _____   B _____   C _____

1. _____ ( ) [ ]_____ [ ]_____ [ ]_____

2. _____ ( ) [ ]_____ [ ]_____ [ ]_____

3. _____ ( ) [ ]_____ [ ]_____ [ ]_____

4. _____ ( ) [ ] _____ [ ]_____ [ ]_____

5. _____ ( ) [ ]_____ [ ]_____ [ ]_____

Directions:

Using the grid you developed on Worksheet 7, compute the totals for each alternative by multiplying the value of the criteria (found in parentheses) with the value of each alternative (found in the brackets). Fill in the grid below with the resulting values, and then add up the totals. Evaluate your reactions.

ALTERNATIVES

CRITERIA (value) A. _____ B. _____ C. _____

1. _____ ( ) [ ] x ( ) = ____ [ ] x ( ) = ____ [ ] x ( ) = ____

2. _____ ( ) [ ] x ( ) = ____ [ ] x ( ) = ____ [ ] x ( ) = ____

3. _____ ( ) [ ] x ( ) = ____ [ ] x ( ) = ____ [ ] x ( ) = ____

4. _____ ( ) [ ] x ( ) = ____ [ ] x ( ) = ____ [ ] x ( ) = ____

5. _____ ( ) [ ] x ( ) = ____ [ ] x ( ) = ____ [ ] x ( ) = ____

TOTALS: _____   _____   _____

Evaluation:

How do you feel about the "best" choice? Explain:

Directions:

Think about all the decisions you must make each day. For one entire day, keep a journal of all the decisions that you made. (You should have at least three.) For each decision, describe the alternatives you considered and explain why you made the choice you did based on the criteria involved in each decision.

1. Decision:

Alternatives being considered:

Why I made my decision:

2. Decision:

Alternatives considered:

Why I made my decision:

3. Decision:

Alternatives considered:

Why I made my decision:

Errors in Thinking

General Directions and Answers

As described in Chapter 4, there are four general categories of errors in thinking. They are: (1) faulty logic, (2) attacks, (3) weak reference, and (4) misinformation. In this section, one worksheet is devoted to each category of errors. Before you give any of these worksheets to students, make sure that you have gone over the types of errors exemplified in some depth. For each error, present a clear explanation and as many concrete examples as possible. It is also useful to have students construct their own examples. One important note of caution: The answers to these exercises are not as clear cut as the answers for other types of exercises. Therefore, it is important for students to explain the rationale for their answers. You might find that, even though students' answers are not the same as those provided here, they make good sense. When you go over the answers to these exercises with students, allow for and accept different possibilities as long as they are logical.

Answers for Worksheet 1

1. *false cause*
2. *begging the question*
3. *accident*
4. *contradiction*
5. *arguing from ignorance*
6. *false cause*
7. *division*
8. *evading the issue*
9. *composition*
10. *contradiction*

Answers for Worksheet 2

1. *arguing against the person*
2. *appealing to force*
3. *poisoning the well*
4. *arguing against the person*
5. *appealing to force*

Answers for Worksheet 3

1. *bias*
2. *bias*
3. *appealing to authority*
4. *appealing to the people*
5. *appealing to emotion*
6. *appealing to emotion*
7. *bias*
8. *appealing to the people*
9. *lack of credibility*

Answers for Worksheet 4

1. *confusing the facts*
2. *misapplying a concept*
3. *confusing the facts*
4. *misapplying a concept*
5. *misapplying a concept*
6. *confusing the facts*

Worksheet 1a

Directions:

In this exercise you are asked to identify errors referred to as "faulty logic." There are seven types of faulty logic errors:

- Contradiction
- Accident
- False cause
- Begging the question
- Evading the issue
- Arguing from ignorance
- Composition and division

Worksheets 1a and 1b present 10 examples of faulty logic. For each one, identify the type of faulty logic illustrated, and be prepared to explain your answer.

1. Following the corporate scandal at Enron, the U.S. economy experienced an economic slump and Mary was laid off from her job. Mary says Enron caused her to lose her job.

   This is an example of: _____

2. Joe argues that Santa is real because Santa exists.

   This is an example of: _____

3. After observing an ambulance with its siren blaring speed through a red light, William concludes it is okay to drive through red lights.

   This is an example of: _____

4. Susan tells her friends in the school cafeteria that she hates broccoli. That same evening at dinner, Susan thanks her mom for making broccoli because it's one of her favorite foods.

   This is an example of: _____

5. Miss Jones argues that there is no cure for cancer because scientists have not discovered one yet.

   This is an example of: _____

6. President Lincoln was assassinated as the American Civil War came to an end. Mark concludes that the Civil War's end caused President Lincoln's assassination.

   This is an example of: _____

7. Since Colorado has a Republican governor, Julie concludes that all residents of Colorado are Republicans.

   This is an example of: _____

8. When Walter's teacher asks him where his book report is, Walter tells his teacher that he admires the sweater she's wearing.

   This is an example of: _____

9. Because water is wet, Rick concludes that the elements that make water—hydrogen and oxygen—must also be wet.

   This is an example of: _____
   Ann tells her parents that she never drives over the speed limit in the family car.

10. On her way to school, Ann drives 50 mph in a 40 mph zone because she's late for school.

    This is an example of: _____

Worksheet 2

Directions:

In this exercise you are asked to identify a number of errors that are referred to as "attacks." There are three types of attacks:

- Poisoning the well
- Arguing against the person
- Appealing to force

Five examples of attacks follow. For each one, identify the type of attack illustrated, and be prepared to explain your answer.

1. Michael is an expert in world religions and is a practicing Muslim. When he makes a statement about Christianity, Sally argues, "How would you know? You're a Muslim."

   This is an example of _____

2. Carrie tells George that if he doesn't vote for her in the class elections, she won't go with him to the homecoming dance.

   This is an example of: _____

3. Ben believes mail-in ballots are the only way to cast a vote. When Meg asks Ben what happens if a candidate dies after a mail-in vote is cast for that candidate, Ben argues that those instances are too rare to make him change his mind. When Steve tells Ben he prefers to cast ballots at the poll, Ben says Steve is living in the past and needs to modernize his voting methods. Any time somebody tries to present an argument against mail-in balloting, Ben explains away those arguments.

   This is an example of:_____

4. Doug lives on the north side of town. Francis lives on the south side of town. Doug tells his friends that they shouldn't believe anything Francis says because of the neighborhood she lives in.

   This is an example of: _____

5. The leader of a large nation, Empira, tells the leader of a smaller nation, Teenyra, that if Teenyra doesn't allow Empira to use Teenyra's sea ports, Empira's army will invade Teenyra.

   This is an example of:_____.

Directions:

In this exercise you are asked to identify a number of errors that are referred to as "weak reference." There are five types of weak reference:

- References that show bias
- Using sources that lack credibility
- Appealing to authority
- Appealing to the people
- Appealing to emotion

Nine examples of weak reference follow. For each one, identify the type of weak reference illustrated, and be prepared to explain your answer.

1. Harold believes that all red meat is bad for a person's health. When a commercial appeared on TV that encouraged people to eat beef, he turned the channel.

   This is an example of _____

2. Gail's parents and relatives were ardent supporters of President John F. Kennedy. Now, Gail always votes for a Kennedy when one runs for political office.

   This is an example of: _____

3. Kathy asks Larry why he believes that democracy is the best form of government. Larry replies, "Because the President of the United States says it is."

   This is an example of: _____

4. Mack wants to get a tattoo but his parents object. In response, Mack says, "But all the guys in my class have tattoos."

   This is an example of: _____

5. Ingrid tells the teacher that she deserves an A in class because she has had a lot of bad things happen to her this semester.

   This is an example of: _____

6. A person sitting on a street corner holds up a sign that says, "Need money. Lost legs in bus accident. Have no job, no prospects. Please help."

   This is an example of: _____

7. Nan's family never listens to jazz music. When Nan's friend suggests they listen to a jazz tape in the car, Nan says that jazz is an inferior type of music.

   This is an example of: _____

8. Oliver refused to wear a hat during the cold weather. When his mother insisted that he wear a hat, Oliver responded, "None of the kids at school wear hats. It's too geeky."

   This is an example of: _____

9. The president of a major corporation speaks to a local city council, encouraging them to reduce the taxes that corporations pay. He argues that the tax cuts are good for the economy.

   This is an example of: _____

Worksheet 4

Directions:

In this exercise you are asked to identify errors referred to as "misinformation." There are two types of misinformation:

- Confusing the facts
- Misapplying generalizations

Below are four examples of misinformation. For each one, identify the type of misinformation error illustrated and be prepared to explain your answer.

1. While talking on the cell phone to tell her friend Randy that she saw his dog on the street, Patty drove her dad's car into the ditch. When her dad asked her how the car ended up in the ditch, Patty said that Randy's dog ran out in front of her and she swerved to miss it.

   This is an example of: _____

2. Skip was infuriated after reading a newspaper editorial that criticized the mayor. Skip called the editor and said the editorial was a criminal offense.

   This is an example of: _____

3. Terry spent the night cleaning his room and watching TV. He didn't study for his geometry test. When Terry did poorly on his test, he said it was because he spent too much time cleaning his room.

   This is an example of: _____

4. Valerie doesn't think parents should spank their children. In an essay on the topic, Valerie writes that capital punishment is wrong.

   This is an example of: _____

5. Cassie says she thinks it is wrong when men are married to more than one woman at a time. She tells her friend Jerry that misogyny should be outlawed.

   This is an example of: _____

6. Last winter, Lorraine washed her hair and went outside with wet hair. At the time, the flu was going around school. When Lorraine contracted the flu, her mother told her not to go out in the cold with wet hair or she would get the flu again.

   This is an example of: _____

Analyzing Deductive Conclusions

General Directions and Answers

There are six worksheets that deal with categorical syllogisms as a tool for analyzing deductive conclusions. The first two address categorical syllogisms expressed in symbolic form using letters (e.g., **A**, **B**, and **C**). Use of symbols allows students to practice syllogistic reasoning in a content-free environment. As you go through Worksheets 1 and 2, be sure students use the circle diagrams as described in Chapter 4 to help them identify valid conclusions.

Worksheets 3 and 4 involve the same type of syllogisms as Worksheets 1 and 2, but instead of using letters they employ real sentences. Again, use of the circle diagrams should help students identify valid conclusions.

Worksheets 5a–d introduce the concept of the *truth* of a conclusion as opposed to the *validity* of a conclusion. It is useful to spend some time explaining this concept to students and providing multiple examples. Some students might find it hard to understand how a conclusion can be both valid and untrue at the same time.

Worksheet 6 provides practice translating statements that include the word "because" into syllogisms, and then examining the truth and validity of their conclusions. Prior to presenting this worksheet to students, you might have to spend some time explaining and exemplifying the process of translating statements into their underlying syllogisms.

Answers for Worksheet 1

1. *All A are C.*
2. *Some A are C. Some C are A.*
3. *Some C are not A.*
4. *Some C are not A.*
5. *No A are C. No C are A.*
6. *Some A are not C.*
7. *Some A are C. Some C are A.*
8. *Some A are C. Some C are A.*
9. *Some C are not A.*
10. *Some A are C. Some C are A.*
11. *Some C are not A.*
12. *Some A are not C.*
13. *All C are A.*

Answers for Worksheet 2

1. *Some A are not C.*
2. *No C are A. No A are C.*
3. *Some C are A. Some A are C.*
4. *No A are C. No C are A.*
5. *Some A are not C.*
6. *Some C are not A.*
7. *No C are A. No A are C.*
8. *Some A are not C.*
9. *Some C are not A.*
10. *Some C are not A.*
11. *Some A are not C.*
12. *Some A are not C.*

Answers for Worksheet 3

1. *All salmon are vertebrates.*
2. *Some rock stars are musicians. Some musicians are rock stars.*
3. *Some people who live in the United States are not foreigners.*
4. *Some Hondas are not cars.*
5. *No felines are dogs. No dogs are felines.*
6. *Some clouds are not cirrus.*
7. *Some starches are tubers. Some tubers are starches.*
8. *Some pets are canines. Some canines are pets.*
9. *Some parents are not fathers.*
10. *Some citrus fruits are Sunkist. Some Sunkist are citrus fruits.*
11. *Some adults are not sisters.*
12. *Some trees are not maples.*
13. *All bus drivers are invited to the picnic.*

Answers for Worksheet 4

1. *Some waterfowl are not geese.*

2. *No poodles are birds. No birds are poodles.*

3. *Some rock stars are musicians. Some musicians are rock stars.*

4. *No triangles are squares. No squares are triangles.*

5. *Some movies are not mysteries.*

6. *Some Senators are not Democrats.*

7. *No gases are beverages. No beverages are gases.*

8. *Some New Yorkers are not millionaires.*

9. *Some Americans are not Coloradoans.*

10. *Some pets are not fish.*

11. *Some scavengers are not tigers.*

12. *Some pies are not entrees.*

Answers for Worksheet 5

Note: Students' answers may vary slightly from the explanations provided here.

1. *Conclusion is false. Premise #2 is untrue. There are people in Seattle who don't like the rain.*

2. *Conclusion is false. Premise #2 is untrue. Backaches are caused by more than just bad mattresses.*

3. *Conclusion is true.*

4. *Conclusion is true.*

5. *Conclusion is false. Premise #1 is untrue, not all cars are made by Toyota.*

6. *Conclusion is false. Premise #1 is untrue, not all dog owners hate cat owners.*

7. *Conclusion is true.*

8. *Conclusion is false. Premise #1 is untrue, not everyone who loves popcorn goes to the movies every week.*

9. *Conclusion is false. Premise #2 is untrue. There are people in Denver who make at least $250,000 per year.*

10. *Conclusion is false. Premise #1 is untrue. Some cowboys may live in New York.*

11. *Conclusion is true.*

12. *Conclusion is false. Premise #1 and #2 are untrue. Some musicians make more than $100,000 each year and some celebrities make less than $100,000 each year.*

13. *Conclusion is false. Premise #1 is untrue. Not all forms of exercise require great physical endurance.*

14. *Conclusion is true.*

15. *Conclusion is false. Premise #1 is untrue. Some lawyers are politicians.*

Answers for Worksheet 6

Note: Students' answers may vary slightly from the explanations provided here.

1. *1ˢᵗ premise:* All people who lift weights every day are strong.

   2ⁿᵈ premise: Mark lifts weights every day.

   Conclusion: Mark is strong.

   This conclusion is true because lifting weights every day will make a person strong.

2. *1ˢᵗ premise:* All police officers ride around in squad cars.

   2ⁿᵈ premise: Edward is a police officer.

   Conclusion: Edward rides around in a squad car.

   This conclusion is false because not all police officers ride around in squad cars.

3. *1ˢᵗ premise:* All people who are crying are very sad.

   2ⁿᵈ premise: Sam is crying.

   Conclusion: Sam is very sad.

   This conclusion is false because some people cry when they are happy.

4. *1ˢᵗ premise:* All people who own computers know a lot about computers.

   2ⁿᵈ premise: Joyce owns a computer.

   Conclusion: Joyce knows a lot about computers.

   This conclusion is false because not all people who own computers know a lot about computers.

5. *1st premise:* All sons and daughters have the same hair color as their father.

2nd premise: Ricky's father has red hair.

Conclusion: Ricky has red hair.

This conclusion is false because some sons and daughters don't have the same hair color as their fathers.

6. *1st premise:* Everyone in Switzerland loves to ski.

2nd premise: Terry lives in Switzerland.

Conclusion: Terry loves to ski.

This conclusion is false because not everyone in Switzerland loves to ski.

7. *1st premise:* People who take care of their teeth and see the dentist regularly have healthy teeth.

2nd premise: Elizabeth takes care of her teeth and sees the dentist regularly.*

Conclusion: Elizabeth has healthy teeth.

This conclusion is true because proper dental care leads to healthy teeth.

8. *1st premise:* People who smoke will eventually die of cancer.

2nd premise: Violet smokes.

Conclusion: Violet will eventually die of cancer.

This conclusion is false because not everyone who smokes dies of cancer.

9. *1st premise:* People who grew up in places where there are no lakes or rivers can't swim well.

2nd premise: Bill grew up in a place where there are no lakes or rivers.

Conclusion: Bill can't swim well.

This conclusion is false because people who grew up in places where there are no lakes or rivers might have learned how to swim in a swimming pool.

10. *1st premise:* All dinosaurs are extinct.

2nd premise: Stegosaurus are dinosaurs.

Conclusion: Stegosaurus are extinct.

This conclusion is true.

11. *1st premise:* Cats who play in the street will soon die.

2nd premise: Bucky is a cat who plays in the street.

Conclusion: Bucky the cat will soon die.

This conclusion is true.

12. *1st premise:* People who shave their chin every day do not grow long beards.

2nd premise: Craig shaves his chin every day.

Conclusion: Craig won't grow a long beard.

This conclusion is true.

13. *1st premise:* No people who work at airports were born in non-U.S. countries.

2nd premise: Donna was born in Ireland.

Conclusion: Donna doesn't work at the airport.

This conclusion is false because some people who work in airports may not have been born in the United States.

14. *1st premise:* People who eat too much candy are people who won't sleep well.

2nd premise: Fritz ate too much candy.

Conclusion: Fritz won't sleep well.

This conclusion is false because eating candy doesn't cause everyone to sleep poorly.

15. *1st premise:* People who smoke while they eat are not allowed to eat in restaurants.

2nd premise: Gabrielle likes to smoke when she eats.

Conclusion: Gabrielle is not allowed to eat in restaurants.

This conclusion is false because some restaurants have smoking sections where people can eat and smoke at the same time.

Directions:

The problems in this worksheet, called categorical syllogisms, will give you practice forming logical conclusions. For each problem you are given two premises and asked to fill in a valid conclusion. For example:

1st premise: All A are C
2nd premise: All C are B
Valid conclusion: _____

There is a way to represent these premises using circles. For the first premise you will have a circle for A and a circle for C. The A circle will be inside the C circle as shown:

The next premise introduces a third circle for B. This circle will go all of the way around the A and C circles as shown:

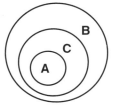

Based on the positions of the circles, we can see that a valid conclusion is that all A are B. Use the circle diagramming technique for each of the syllogisms below to identify valid conclusions (there may be more than one for each problem).

1. *1st premise:* All A are B.
   2nd premise: All B are C.
   Valid conclusion: _____

2. *1st premise:* Some A are B.
   2nd premise: All B are C.
   Valid conclusion: _____

3. *1st premise:* No A are B.
   2nd premise: All B are C.
   Valid conclusion: _____

4. *1st premise:* No A are B.
   2nd premise: Some B are C.
   Valid conclusion: _____

5. *1st premise:* All A are B.
   2nd premise: No B are C.
   Valid conclusion: _____

6. *1st premise:* Some A are B.
   2nd premise: No B are C.
   Valid conclusion: _____

7. *1st premise:* All B are A.
   2nd premise: All B are C.
   Valid conclusion: _____

8. *1st premise:* Some B are A.
   2nd premise: All B are C.
   Valid conclusions: _____

9. *1st premise:* No B are A.
   2nd premise: All B are C.
   Valid conclusion: _____

10. *1st premise:* All B are A.
    2nd premise: Some B are C.
    Valid conclusions: _____

11. *1st premise:* No B are A.
    2nd premise: Some B are C.
    Valid conclusion: _____

12. *1st premise:* All B are A.
    2nd premise: No B are C.
    Valid conclusion: _____

13. *1st premise:* All B are A.
    2nd premise: All C are B.
    Valid conclusion: _____

Directions:

This set of syllogisms is like the previous, but some require a little more thinking than you had to do before. Remember to use circle diagrams to help you figure out the answers.

1. *1st premise:* Some B are A.
   2nd premise: No B are C.
   Valid conclusion: _____

2. *1st premise:* No B are A.
   2nd premise: All C are B.
   Valid conclusions: _____

3. *1st premise:* All B are A.
   2nd premise: Some C are B.
   Valid conclusions: _____

4. *1st premise:* No A are B.
   2nd premise: All C are B.
   Valid conclusions: _____

5. *1st premise:* Some A are not B.
   2nd premise: All C are B.
   Valid conclusion: _____

6. *1st premise:* No A are B.
   2nd premise: Some C are B.
   Valid conclusion: _____

7. *1st premise:* All A are B.
   2nd premise: No C are B.
   Valid conclusion: _____

8. *1st premise:* Some A are B.
   2nd premise: No C are B.
   Valid conclusion: _____

9. *1st premise:* All A are B.
   2nd premise: Some C are not B.
   Valid conclusion: _____

10. *1st premise:* No B are A.
    2nd premise: Some C are B.
    Valid conclusion: _____

11. *1st premise:* All B are A.
    2nd premise: No C are B.
    Valid conclusion: _____

12. *1st premise:* Some B are A.
    2nd premise: No C are B.
    Valid conclusion: _____

Directions:

This set of syllogisms uses premises with real people and real situations as opposed to letters. You are given two premises and asked to form a valid conclusion. Consider the example below:

1st premise: All major league baseball players make at least $250,000 per year.
2nd premise: Bill is a major league baseball player.
*Valid conclusion:*_____

Again, you will find it beneficial to use circle diagrams to help you identify a valid conclusion. The first premise can be diagrammed in the following way:

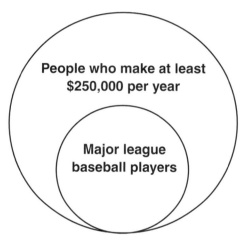

The second premise adds a circle for Bill inside the circle for "Major league baseball players."

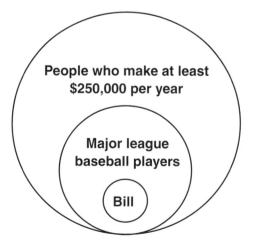

A valid conclusion is that Bill makes at least $250,000 per year, as shown in the circle diagram.

Use the circle diagramming technique for each of the following syllogisms to identify valid conclusions (there may be more than one per problem).

1. *1st premise:* All salmon are fish.
   2nd premise: All fish are vertebrates.
   Valid conclusion: _____

2. *1st premise:* Some rock stars are guitar players.
   2nd premise: All guitar players are musicians.
   Valid conclusion: _____

3. *1st premise:* No foreigners are senators.
   2nd premise: All senators live in the United States.
   Valid conclusion: _____

4. *1st premise:* No cars are motorcycles.
   2nd premise: Some motorcycles are Hondas.
   Valid conclusion: _____

5. *1st premise:* All felines are cats.
   2nd premise: No cats are dogs.
   Valid conclusion: _____

6. *1st premise:* Some clouds are cumulonimbus.
   2nd premise: No cumulonimbus clouds are cirrus.
   Valid conclusion: _____

7. *1st premise:* All potatoes are starches.
   2nd premise: All potatoes are tubers.
   Valid conclusions: _____

8. *1st premise:* Some dogs are pets.
   2nd premise: All dogs are canines.
   Valid conclusions: _____

9. *1st premise:* No mothers are fathers.
   2nd premise: All mothers are parents.
   Valid conclusion: _____

10. *1st premise:* All oranges are citrus fruits.
    2nd premise: Some oranges are Sunkist.
    Valid conclusions: _____

11. *1st premise:* No brothers are sisters.
    2nd premise: Some brothers are adults.
    Valid conclusion: _____

12. *1st premise:* All firs are trees.
    2nd premise: No firs are maples.
    Valid conclusion: _____

13. *1st premise:* All union members are invited to the picnic.
    2nd premise: All bus drivers are union members.
    Valid conclusion: _____

Directions:

This set of categorical syllogism follows the same pattern as the previous one. Use circle diagrams to help you identify valid conclusions.

1. *1st premise:* Some ducks are waterfowl.
   2nd premise: No ducks are geese.
   Valid conclusion: _____

2. *1st premise:* No dogs are birds.
   2nd premise: All poodles are dogs.
   Valid conclusion: _____

3. *1st premise:* All guitar players are musicians.
   2nd premise: Some rock stars are guitar players.
   Valid conclusions: _____

4. *1st premise:* No triangles are rectangles.
   2nd premise: All squares are rectangles.
   Valid conclusions: _____

5. *1st premise:* Some movies are not dramas.
   2nd premise: All mysteries are dramas.
   Valid conclusion: _____

6. *1st premise:* No Democrats are Republicans.
   2nd premise: Some senators are Republicans.
   Valid conclusion: _____

7. *1st premise:* All beverages are liquids.
   2nd premise: No gases are liquids.
   Valid conclusion: _____

8. *1st premise:* Some New Yorkers are taxi drivers.
   2nd premise: No millionaires are taxi drivers.
   Valid conclusion: _____

9. *1st premise:* All Coloradoans are Westerners.
   2nd premise: Some Americans are not Westerners.
   Valid conclusion: _____

10. *1st premise:* No parrots are fish.
    2nd premise: Some pets are parrots.
    Valid conclusion: _____

11. *1st premise:* All vultures are scavengers.
    2nd premise: No tigers are vultures.
    Valid conclusion: _____

12. *1st premise:* Some desserts are pies.
    2nd premise: No entrees are desserts.
    Valid conclusion: _____

Directions:

Up to this point you have been determining whether the conclusions in a syllogism are logical or not—whether the conclusions are valid. Next, we examine another aspect of conclusions—their truth. A conclusion can be valid, but not true. Consider the following syllogism:

1st premise: Bill is very tall.
2nd premise: All tall people are good at basketball.
Valid conclusion: Bill is good at basketball.

Using circle diagrams, we see the conclusion, "Bill is a good basketball player" is valid.

However, there is something wrong with this conclusion—it's not true. There are people who are tall but who aren't good at basketball. In fact, there are people who are tall and are terrible at basketball. How can a conclusion be valid but not true? It all depends on the truth of premises on which a conclusion is based. Look back at the second premise above, and you'll see that it is causing the problem in this example. It is not true that "all tall people are good at basketball." When you examine this type of thinking, it is very important to consider not only whether the conclusion is valid, but also whether it is true.

The problems that follow all contain valid conclusions. But some are true and some are not. Determine whether each conclusion is true or not. For conclusions that are not true, identify the untrue premise that creates the untrue but valid conclusion.

1. *1st premise:* Mike lives in Seattle.
   2nd premise: People who live in Seattle like the rain.
   Valid conclusion: Mike likes the rain.

   Is this conclusion true or false? _____
   If it is false, which premise or premises create the false conclusion? Explain what is wrong with the premise. _____

2. *1st premise:* Joan has a backache.
   2nd premise: Backaches are caused by bad mattresses.
   Valid conclusion: Joan has a bad mattress.

   Is this conclusion true or false? _____
   If it is false, which premise or premises create the false conclusion? Explain what is wrong with the premise. _____

3. *1st premise:* Maurice lives in the capital of Missouri.
   2nd premise: The capitol of Missouri is a city named Columbia.
   Valid conclusion: Maurice lives in a city named Columbia.

   Is this conclusion true or false? _____
   If it is false, which premise or premises create the false conclusion? Explain what is wrong with the premise. _____

4. *1st premise:* Stanley works for XYZ Corporation.
   2nd premise: All employees of XYZ Corporation have college degrees.
   Valid conclusion: Stanley has a college degree.

   Is this conclusion true or false? _____
   If it is false, which premise or premises create the false conclusion? Explain what is wrong with the premise. _____

5. *1st premise:* All cars are made by Toyota.
   2nd premise: Mary drives a car to work.
   Valid conclusion: Mary drives a car made by Toyota.

   Is this conclusion true or false? _____
   If it is false, which premise or premises create the false conclusion? Explain what is wrong with the premise. _____

6. *1st premise:* Dog owners hate cat owners.
   2nd premise: Ralph owns a dog.
   Valid conclusion: Ralph hates cat owners.

   Is this conclusion true or false? _____
   If it is false, which premise or premises create the false conclusion? Explain what is wrong with the premise. _____

7. *1st premise:* Betty is a good cook.
   2nd premise: Good cooks know how to make delicious food.
   Valid conclusion: Betty knows how to make delicious food.

   Is this conclusion true or false? _____
   If it is false, which premise or premises create the false conclusion? Explain what is wrong with the premise. _____

8. *1st premise:* People who love popcorn go to the movies every week.
   2nd premise: Sylvester loves popcorn.
   Valid conclusion: Sylvester goes to the movies every week.

   Is this conclusion true or false? _____
   If it is false, which premise or premises create the false conclusion? Explain what is wrong with the premise. _____

9. *1st premise:* All professional football players make at least $250,000 per year.
   2nd premise: No people who live in Denver make at least $250,000 per year.
   Valid conclusion: No professional football players live in Denver.

   Is this conclusion true or false? _____
   If it is false, which premise or premises create the untrue conclusion? Explain what is wrong with the premise. _____

10. *1st premise:* No cowboys live in New York.
    2nd premise: Doug lives in New York.
    Valid conclusion: Doug is not a cowboy.

    Is this conclusion true or false? _____
    If it is false, which premise or premises create the false conclusion? Explain what is wrong with the premise. _____

11. *1st premise:* All circles are round.
    2nd premise: No squares are round.
    Valid conclusion: No squares are circles and no circles are squares.

    Is this conclusion true or false? _____
    If it is false, which premise or premises create the false conclusion? Explain what is wrong with the premise. _____

12. *1st premise:* All musicians make less than $100,000 per year.
    2nd premise: No celebrities make less than $100,000 per year.
    Valid conclusion: No celebrities are musicians and no musicians are celebrities.

    Is this conclusion true or false? _____
    If it is false, which premise or premises create the false conclusion? Explain what is wrong with the premise. _____

13. *1st premise:* All forms of exercise require great physical endurance.
    2nd premise: Bowling does not require great physical endurance.
    Valid conclusion: Bowling is not a form of exercise.

    Is this conclusion true or false? _____
    If it is false, which premise or premises create the false conclusion? Explain what is wrong with the premise. _____

14. *1st premise:* All grapes are fruits.
    2nd premise: No meat products are fruits.
    Valid conclusion: No meat products are grapes and no grapes are meat products.

    Is this conclusion true or false? _____
    If it is false, which premise or premises create the false conclusion? Explain what is wrong with the premise. _____

15. *1st premise:* No lawyers are politicians.
    2nd premise: All politicians run for office.
    Valid conclusion: No lawyers run for office and no one who runs for office is a lawyer.

    Is this conclusion true or false? _____
    If it is false, which premise or premises create the false conclusion? Explain what is wrong with the premise. _____

Directions:

By now you should have a good sense of how to evaluate syllogisms in terms of the validity or logic of their conclusions, and the truth of those conclusions. This exercise will help you use your knowledge of syllogisms to analyze the things you hear people say or things you read that people have said. This is because many statements people make have a hidden syllogism underlying them. For example, suppose you hear someone say, "Sally is good at mathematics because her family has a lot of money." If you pull this statement apart, you find the following syllogism:

1st premise: All people who come from families with a lot of money are smart.
2nd premise: Sally comes from a family with a lot of money.
Conclusion: Sally is smart.

Circle diagrams that show the conclusion, "Sally is smart" is a valid one:

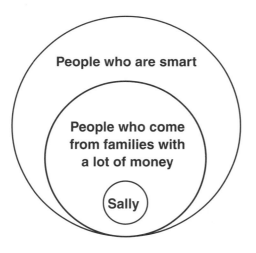

But we also know that even if a conclusion is valid, it is untrue if it is based on one or more premises that are not true. In the example about Sally, the conclusion is valid but it is not true. This is because the premise that "all people who come from families with a lot of money are smart" is false. Therefore, the conclusion is false.

This exercise includes statements like the one about Sally. They are all based on syllogisms with valid conclusions, but some of these conclusions are false and some are true. Pull each statement apart and write down the underlying premises and conclusion. Then explain why the conclusion is true or false.

1. Mark is strong because he lifts weights everyday.

   1st premise: _____

   2nd premise: _____

   Conclusion: _____

   This conclusion is (true/false) _____ because _____

2. Edward must ride around in a squad car because he is a police officer.

   1st premise: _____

   2nd premise: _____

   Conclusion: _____

   This conclusion is (true/false) _____ because _____

3. Sam must be very sad because he is crying.

   1st premise: _____

   2nd premise: _____

   Conclusion: _____

   This conclusion is (true/false) _____ because _____

4. Joyce must know a lot about computers because she owns a computer.

   1st premise: _____

   2nd premise: _____

   Conclusion: _____

   This conclusion is (true/false) _____ because _____

5. Ricky must have red hair because his dad has red hair.

   1st premise: _____

   2nd premise: _____

   Conclusion: _____

   This conclusion is (true/false) _____ because _____

6. Terry loves to ski because she lives in Switzerland.

   1st premise: —————————————————————————————

   2nd premise: —————————————————————————————

   Conclusion: —————————————————————————————

   This conclusion is (true/false) ——— because —————————————————

7. Elizabeth must have healthy teeth because she takes care of them and goes
   to the dentist regularly.

   1st premise: —————————————————————————————

   2nd premise: —————————————————————————————

   Conclusion: —————————————————————————————

   This conclusion is (true/false) ——— because —————————————————

8. Violet will eventually die of cancer because she smokes.

   1st premise: —————————————————————————————

   2nd premise: —————————————————————————————

   Conclusion: —————————————————————————————

   This conclusion is (true/false) ——— because —————————————————

9. Bill can't swim well because he grew up in a place where there are no lakes or rivers.

   1st premise: —————————————————————————————

   2nd premise: —————————————————————————————

   Conclusion: —————————————————————————————

   This conclusion is (true/false) ——— because —————————————————

10. Stegosaurus don't exist today because all dinosaurs are extinct.

    1st premise: —————————————————————————————

    2nd premise: —————————————————————————————

    Conclusion: —————————————————————————————

    This conclusion is (true/false) ——— because —————————————————

11. Bucky the cat will soon die because he likes to play in the street.

    1st premise: _____

    2nd premise: _____

    Conclusion: _____

    This conclusion is (true/false) _____ because _____

12. Craig can't grow a long beard because he keeps shaving his chin every day.

    1st premise: _____

    2nd premise: _____

    Conclusion: _____

    This conclusion is (true/false) _____ because _____

13. Donna doesn't work at an airport because she was born in Ireland.

    1st premise: _____

    2nd premise: _____

    Conclusion: _____

    This conclusion is (true/false) _____ because _____

14. Fritz won't be able to get to sleep because he ate too much candy.

    1st premise: _____

    2nd premise: _____

    Conclusion: _____

    This conclusion is (true/false) _____ because _____

15. Gabrielle will not be allowed to eat in restaurants because she likes to smoke when she eats.

    1st premise: _____

    2nd premise: _____

    Conclusion: _____

    This conclusion is (true/false) _____ because _____

CHAPTER 11
BLACKLINE MASTERS

This chapter contains reproducible blackline masters that may be used to teach and reinforce skills and various aspects of the personal project. Possible uses of these blackline masters are described in Chapters 2 through 6 of this Manual.

THE PATHFINDER PROJECT

Inspirational Stories and Quotes

- Literal comprehension skills
- Inferential comprehension skills
- Self-Analysis Skills

Personal Project

- Phase 1: Identifying a personal goal to pursue
- Phase 2: Eliciting support
- Phase 3: Gathering information about the goal
- Phase 4: Discerning discrepancies between current and future self
- Phase 5: Creating a plan
- Phase 6: Moving into action
- Phase 7: Evaluating the effectiveness of your actions

Life Skills

- Information-gathering and synthesizing skills
- Problem-solving skills
- Decision-making skills
- Imagery and memory skills
- Critical thinking and reasoning skills
- Skills of self-control and self-regulation

Finding the General Pattern

Todd's Story	General Pattern
1.	1. An individual is inspired to make a decision about pursuing a personal goal.
2.	2. The individual receives guidance, support, and encouragement for pursuing this goal.
3.	3. The individual identifies the knowledge, skills, and resources necessary to obtain this goal.
4.	4. The individual must overcome obstacles and barriers to meeting the goal.
5.	5. Planning, determination, and hard work make it possible for the individual to overcome the obstacles.
6.	6. The individual reaches or even exceeds his or her goal.

Applying the General Pattern

General Pattern	New Story or Example
1. An individual is inspired to make a decision about pursuing a personal goal.	1.
2. The individual receives guidance, support, and encouragement for pursuing this goal.	2.
3. The individual identifies the knowledge, skills, and resources necessary to obtain this goal.	3.
4. The individual must overcome obstacles and barriers to meeting the goal.	4.
5. Planning, determination, and hard work make it possible for the individual to overcome the obstacles.	5.
6. The individual reaches or even exceeds his or her goal.	6.

A Comprehension Strategy

In school, you are frequently asked questions after you have read something. This simple process will enhance your ability to answer those questions.

1 Do you know the answer?

2 If you don't, go to where it might be in the story.

3 If you still can't find it, scan the whole story.

4 If you still can't find it, look for clues to the answers and make your best guess.

Solving Academic Problems

Step One	Read over or look over the entire problem and get a sense of what you are being asked to do.
Step Two	Listen to your self-talk. If your self talk is negative, replace it with statements like: • *"These problems might be tricky but once you know how to do them, they are easy."* • *"I can figure this out if I work at it and give myself time."* • *"It's okay if I have to ask for help and there is plenty of help available to me."* • *"Putting energy into those problems that will pay off later for me."*
Step Three	State the problem in your own words.
Step Four	Try representing the problem in some way by drawing a picture of it or making a model of it.
Step Five	Try out different ways to solve the problem. If one solution doesn't work, move on to another.
Step Six	When you have come up with an answer, ask yourself, "Does this answer make sense?"
Step Seven	When you've completed the problem or problems, answer the questions: • *What did I do that worked well?* • *What did I do that did not work well?* • *What have I learned about myself as a problem solver?*

The Problem-Solving Process

Step One	State the intended goal.
Step Two	List the obstacles to the goal.
Step Three	Create a list of options for overcoming the obstacles.
Step Four	Determine which option is best and try it out.
Step Five	If your first option doesn't work, try another option.

The Problem-Solving Process

Step One	Determine whether you really have a problem. Is the goal truly important to you or is it something you can ignore?
Step Two	If you determine that you really do have a problem, take a moment to affirm the following beliefs: • *There are probably a number of ways to solve the problem and I will surely find one of them.* • *Help is probably available if I look for it.* • *I am perfectly capable of solving this problem.*
Step Three	Start talking to yourself about the problem. Verbalize the thoughts you are having.
Step Four	Start looking for the obstacles in your way—what's missing? Identify possible solutions for replacing what is missing or for overcoming the obstacle.
Step Five	For each of the possible solutions you have identified, determine how likely it is to succeed. Consider the resources each solution requires and how accessible they are to you. Here is where you might have to look for help.
Step Six	Try out the solution you believe has the greatest chance of success and fits your comfort level for risk.
Step Seven	If your solution doesn't work, clear your mind, go back to another solution you have identified, and try it out.
Step Eight	If no solution can be found that works, "revalue" what you are trying to accomplish. Look for a more basic goal that can be accomplished.

The Decision-Making Process

Step One	Clearly state the decision you are faced with.
Step Two	State the options or alternatives available to you.
Step Three	Consider the criteria or attributes a good decision will meet.
Step Four	Identify the alternative that best meets the defined attributes.

The Decision-Making Process

Step One	Identify the alternatives you are considering.
Step Two	Identify the attributes or criteria that your ideal decision will meet.
Step Three	For each attribute, assign an importance score (very important = 3, moderately important = 2, not terribly important = 1).
Step Four	For each alternative, assign a score indicating the extent to which it possesses each attribute (possesses the attribute to a great extent = 3, possesses the attribute moderately = 2, possesses the attribute to a small degree = 1, doesn't possess the attribute = 0).
Step Five	Multiply the importance score for each attribute by the score predicting the extent to which each alternative possesses the attribute.
Step Six	For each alternative, add up the product scores. The alternative with the highest total score is the most logical choice.
Step Seven	Based on your reaction to the selected alternative, determine if you want to change the importance scores for attributes or even add or delete attributes.
Step Eight	If you have changed something, go back and re-compute the scores.

Rhyming Pegword

1 is a	bun
2 is a	shoe
3 is a	tree
4 is a	door
5 is a	hive
6 is a	stack of sticks
7 is	heaven
8 is a	gate
9 is a	line
10 is a	hen

Familiar Place Framework

My first place is	
My second place is	
My third place is	
My fourth place is	
My fifth place is	
My sixth place is	
My seventh place is	
My eighth place is	
My ninth place is	
My tenth place is	
My eleventh place is	
My twelfth place is	

Process For Analyzing Errors

Step One	Determine whether the information presented to you is intended to influence your thinking or your actions.
Step Two	If the information is intended to influence you, identify things that seem wrong— statements that are unusual or go against what you know to be true.
Step Three	Look for errors in the thinking that underlies the statements you have identified.
Step Four	If you find errors, ask for clarification.

Errors in Thinking: Faulty Logic

Contradiction	**Presenting conflicting information.** If a politician runs on a platform supporting term limits, then votes against an amendment would set term limits, that politician has committed an error of contradiction.
Accident	**Failing to recognize that an argument is based on an exception to a rule.** For example, if a student concludes that the principal always goes to dinner at a fancy restaurant on Fridays because she sees him once on a given Friday which just happens to be his birthday, that student has committed the error of accident.
False cause	**Confusing a temporal (time) order of events with causality or oversimplifying the reasons behind some event or occurrence.** For example, if a person concludes that the war in Vietnam ended because of the protests, he is guilty of ascribing a false cause. The anti-war protests might have something to do with the cessation of the war, but there were also many other interesting causes.
Begging the question	**Making a claim and then arguing for the claim by using statements that are simply the equivalent of the original claim.** For example, if a person says that product **x** is the best detergent on the market and then backs up this statement by saying that it is superior to any other detergent, he is begging the question.
Evading the issue	**Changing the topic to avoid addressing the issue.** For example, a person is evading the issue if he begins talking about the evils of the news media when he is asked by a reporter about his alleged involvement in fraudulent banking procedures.
Arguing from ignorance	**Arguing that a claim in justified simply because its opposite has not been proven true.** For example, if a person argues that there is no life on other planets because there has been no proof of such existence, he is arguing from ignorance.
Composition/ division	**Asserting something about a whole that is really only true of its parts is** *composition*; **on the flip side,** *division* **is asserting about all of the parts something that is generally, but not always, true of the whole.** For example, if a person asserts that Republicans generally but not always are corrupt because one Republican is found to be corrupt, she is committing the error of composition. If a person states that a particular Democrat supports big government simply because Democrats are generally known for supporting government programs, he is committing the error of division.

Errors in Thinking: Weak References

Bias	**Consistently accepting information that supports what we already believe to be true, or consistently rejecting information that goes against what we believe to be true.** For example, a person is guilty of bias if he believes that a person has committed a crime and will not even consider DNA evidence indicating that the individual is innocent.
Lack of credibility	**Using a source that is not reputable for a given topic.** Determining credibility can be subjective but there are some characteristics that most people agree damage credibility, such as when a source is known to be biased or has little knowledge of the topic. A person is guilty of using a source that lacks credibility when he backs up his belief that the government has a conspiracy to ruin the atmosphere by citing a tabloid journal known for sensational stories that are fabricated.
Appealing to authority	**Invoking authority as the last word on an issue.** If a person says, "Socialism is evil" and supports this claim by saying that the governor said so, she is appealing to authority.
Appealing to the people	**Attempting to justify a claim based on its popularity.** For example, if a girl tells her parents she should have a pierced belly button because everyone else has one, she is appealing to the people.
Appealing to emotion	**Using a "sob story" as proof for a claim.** For example, if someone uses the story of a tragic accident in her life as a means to convince people to agree with her opinion on war, she is appealing to emotion.

Errors in Thinking: Attacks

Poisoning the well	**Being so completely committed to a position that you explain away absolutely everything that is offered in opposition to your position.** This type of attack represents a person's unwillingness to consider anything that may contradict his/her position. For example, if a political candidate has only negative things to say about her opponent, she is poisoning the well.
Arguing against the person	**Rejecting a claim using derogatory facts (real or alleged) about the person who is making a claim.** For example, if a person argues against another person's position on taxation by making reference to his poor moral character, she is arguing against the person.
Appealing to force	**Using threats to establish the validity of a claim.** For example, if your landlord threatens to evict you because you disagree with her on an upcoming election issue, she is appealing to force.

Errors in Thinking: Misinformation

Confusing the facts	**Using information that seems to be factual but has been changed in such a way that it is no longer accurate.** For example, a person is confusing the facts if he backs up his claim by describing an event but leaves out important facts or mixes up the temporal order of the events.
Misapplying a concept or generalization	**Misunderstanding or wrongly applying a concept or generalization to support a claim.** For example, if someone argues that a talk show host should be arrested for libel after making a critical remark, that person has misapplied the concept of libel.

Taking Small Steps

When you want to achieve a goal, you do it step by step. This is especially true of goals that you expect to achieve in the future. Identify a small step or two you can take in the next few weeks—something that you can actually accomplish. This small step should be directly related to the plan you have been making. Identify your small steps by answering the questions below.

1 Today's date

2 Date by which I will accomplish my small step

3 Description of what I will accomplish by that date

4 What I must do to accomplish my small step

Inner Dialogue

Inner dialogue is a name for the talking that you do inside your head. It is the manifestation of the thoughts and beliefs you have about the situation you are in. This inner speech can be either positive or negative and can profoundly affect your ability to achieve a goal. If you are aware of your inner dialogue and realize that it is negative, you can consciously stop the negative thoughts and replace them with positive thoughts. For example, if your inner dialogue keeps telling you that the goal you have set is too hard, you might replace this negative talk with a positive statement like, "I can do this." Consider the inner dialogue you have been having about this project by answering the questions below.

What are some things I say to myself that make me feel like working harder?	What are some things I say to myself that make me want to quit?	How can I change my negative inner dialogue?

The Power of Effort

One of the most powerful skills you can learn is the ability to generate effort by controlling what is in your mind. Using the questions below, contrast your thinking when you try hard and when you don't try hard.

When I Try Hard		When I Don't Try Hard	
What I say to myself		*What I say to myself*	
My mental picture		*My mental picture*	
My physical sensations		*My physical sensations*	
My emotions		*My emotions*	

The Power Thinking Process

Step One	Before you engage in a new activity—one that is challenging to you—stop for a moment and remind yourself that effort is the key to success. Little effort will probably bring little success.
Step Two	If you don't feel strongly motivated to work hard on this new task: • Change your inner dialogue to statements that make you want to work hard. • Change your physical sensations to those that make you want to work hard. • Change your mental pictures to those that make you want to work hard. • Change your emotions to those that make you want to work hard.
Step Three	Next, set a specific goal for what you want to accomplish or have happen.
Step Four	As you are engaged in the activity: • Keep reminding yourself about your goal. • Keep monitoring your inner dialogue. • Keep monitoring your physical sensations. • Keep monitoring your mental pictures. • Keep monitoring your emotions.
Step Five	When you have completed the activity, ask yourself if you accomplished what you set out to do. If your answer is yes, acknowledge your success. If not, ask yourself what you did that worked well, what you did that did not work well, and what you would do differently. Even if you have accomplished your goal, it is useful to ask these questions. Once you have answered them, put the incident behind you and move on to your next challenge.

The Personal Project

Teacher Rubric	Student Rubric
4. The student has a clear and detailed vision of the outcome of his or her project and the steps that must be taken to realize that vision. Additionally, the student is taking concrete steps toward the vision.	4. I know what I want to accomplish in my personal project, and I know what I must do to get there. Additionally, I am doing things right now to help me accomplish my goal.
3. The student has a clear and detailed vision of the outcome of his or her project and the steps that must be taken to realize that vision.	3. I know what I want to accomplish in my personal project, and I know what I must do to get there.
2. The student has a vision of the outcome of his or her project but it is not clear and/or the student is not clear about the steps that must be taken to realize that vision.	2. I know what I want to accomplish in my personal project, but I haven't thought through what I need to do to accomplish my goal.
1. The student has no vision of the outcome of his or her project.	1. I don't really know what I want to accomplish in my personal project.

Literal and Inferential Comprehension

Teacher Rubric	Student Rubric
4. The student provides complete and accurate answers to literal and inferential comprehension questions. Additionally, the student understands the strategies he or she uses to answer these questions.	4. After reading a story, I can answer questions about information that is obvious in the text as well as information that is not obvious but can be figured out. Additionally, I can describe the strategies I use to answer these types of questions.
3. The student provides complete and accurate answers to literal and inferential comprehension questions.	3. After reading a story, I can answer questions about information that is obvious in the text as well as information that is not obvious but can be figured out.
2. The student provides answers to literal and inferential questions. However, these answers commonly have inaccuracies.	2. After reading a story, I make an attempt to answer questions about information that is obvious in the text as well as information that is not obvious but can be figured out. However, I tend to get confused and I'm not very certain about my answers.
1. The student cannot answer literal or inferential comprehension questions.	1. When questions are asked about a story, I don't really try to answer them in any systematic way.

Information-Gathering and Synthesizing

Teacher Rubric	Student Rubric
4. The student can accurately gather information from a variety of sources and can identify the key elements of the information he or she has gathered. Additionally, the student can organize the key points into conceptual categories that are useful to the completion of his or her project.	4. I know of and can use a variety of sources to gather information about a topic. As I gather information, I can identify that information that is most important to my topic. Additionally, when I have gathered the information, I can organize it into categories that make it useful to me.
3. The student can accurately gather information from a variety of sources and can identify the key elements of the information he or she has gathered.	3. I know of and can use a variety of sources to gather information about a topic. As I gather information, I can identify the information that is most important to my topic.
2. The student can gather information from a variety of sources but is not very accurate when doing so, and/or the student has difficulty identifying the key elements of the information he or she has gathered.	2. I know of and can use some sources to gather information about a topic, but I have a hard time identifying which information is important.
1. The student cannot gather information from a variety of sources.	1. I don't really know many sources from which to gather information about a topic.

Problem-Solving Skills

Teacher Rubric	Student Rubric
4. The student clearly identifies obstacles to the goal and ways of overcoming the obstacle, and carries out the most effective ways of overcoming the obstacle. Additionally, the student understands the process he or she is using to solve the problem.	4. When I face a problem, I can identify the obstacle in my way, I can identify possible solutions and try out the one that has the best chance of working. Finally, I can describe the strategies I am using to solve the problem.
3. The student clearly identifies the obstacles to the goal and ways of overcoming the obstacle, and carries out the most effective ways of overcoming the obstacle.	3. When I face a problem, I can identify the obstacle in my way. I can identify possible solutions and try out the one that has the best chance of working.
2. The student provides a rough attempt to solve the problem but does not clearly identify the obstacle to the goal or does not clearly identify ways of overcoming the obstacle.	2. When I face a problem, I have a difficult time identifying the obstacle in my way or I have a difficult time identifying ways of overcoming the obstacle.
1. The student makes no systematic attempt to solve the problem.	1. When I face a problem, I really don't have a systematic way of solving it.

Decision-Making Skills

Teacher Rubric	Student Rubric
4. The student clearly identifies the alternatives and the criteria used to select among them. The student selects the alternative that best meets the criteria. Additionally, the student understands the process he or she is using to make the decision.	4. When I face a decision, I can identify the alternatives that are available and an approach to select the best alternative. Additionally, I can describe the strategies I am using to make the decision.
3. The student clearly identifies the alternatives and the criteria used to select among them. The student selects the alternative that best meets the criteria.	3. When I face a decision, I can identify the alternatives that are available and an approach to select the best alternative.
2. The student provides a rough attempt to make the decision but does not clearly identify the alternatives or the criteria used to select among them.	2. When I face a decision, I have difficulty identifying the alternatives available to me or an approach to select the best alternative.
1. The student makes no systematic attempt to make the decision.	1. When I face a decision, I really don't have a systematic way of making it.

Imagery and Memory Skills

Teacher Rubric	Student Rubric
4. The student uses imagery and memory strategies to better understand and recall information. Additionally, the student understands why these strategies work.	4. I can use imagery and memory strategies to help me understand and remember information. Additionally, I can explain how and why these strategies work.
3. The student uses imagery and memory strategies to better understand and recall information.	3. I can use imagery and memory strategies to help me understand and remember information.
2. The student makes a rough attempt to use imagery and memory strategies but does so in a way that diminishes the effectiveness of these strategies.	2. I try to use imagery and memory strategies, but I have trouble making them work well for me.
1. The student makes no systematic attempt to use imagery and memory strategies.	1. I don't really try to use imagery and memory strategies.

Critical Thinking and Reasoning Skills

Teacher Rubric	Student Rubric
4. The student can analyze his or her thinking and that of others in terms of its logic and the extent to which it contains errors. Additionally, the student understands the process used to do so.	4. I can analyze my own thinking and other people's thinking in terms of how logical it is and whether it contains errors. Additionally, I can explain the strategies I am using to do so.
3. The student can analyze his or her thinking and that of others in terms of its logic and the extent to which it contains errors.	3. I can analyze my own thinking and that of other people in terms of how logical it is and whether it contains errors.
2. The student attempts to analyze his or her thinking and that of others in terms of its logic and the extent to which it contains errors. However, the student exhibits misconceptions or misunderstandings in doing so.	2. I try to analyze my own thinking and that of other people in terms of how logical it is and whether it contains errors. However, I get confused about how to do this.
1. The student makes no systematic attempt to analyze his or her thinking, or that of others, in terms of its logic or the extent to which it contains errors.	1. I really don't try to analyze my own thinking or that of other people in terms of how logical it is or whether it contains errors.

Self-Control and Self-Regulation Skills

Teacher Rubric	Student Rubric
4. The student has an understanding of the influence of his or her internal thoughts, as manifested by inner dialogue and mental images, on his or her ability to accomplish things and has identified strategies for controlling those thoughts. Additionally, the student actively uses those strategies to enhance his or her ability to accomplish things.	4. I am aware of the things I say to myself, the thoughts I have, and how they affect me. I can control them.
3. The student has an understanding of the influence of his or her internal thoughts, as manifested by inner dialogue and mental images, on his or her ability to accomplish things and has identified strategies for controlling those thoughts.	3. I am aware of the things I say to myself, the thoughts I have, and how they affect me. I have strategies for controlling them, but I don't always use these strategies.
2. The students has an awareness of the influence of his or her internal thoughts, as manifested by inner dialogue and mental images, on his or her ability to accomplish things but has no strategies for controlling those thoughts.	2. I am aware of the things I say to myself and the thoughts I have, but I have no way of controlling them.
1. The students is not aware of the influence of his or her internal thoughts, as manifested by inner dialogue and mental images, on his or her ability to accomplish things.	1. I am not aware of the things I say to myself and the thoughts I have.

REFERENCES

Bandura, A. (1997). *Self-efficacy: The exercise of control.* New York: W. H. Freeman.

Covington, M. V. (1992). *Making the grade: A self-worth perspective on motivation and school reform.* New York: Cambridge University Press.

Csikszentmihalyi, M. (1990). *Flow: The psychology of optimal experience.* New York: Harper & Row.

Harter, S. (1999). *The construction of self: A developmental perspective.* New York: The Guilford Press.

Lewis, D., & Greene, J. (1982). *Thinking better: A revolutionary new program to achieve real mental performance.* New York: Holt, Rinehart & Winston.

Macrorie, K. (1988). *The I-search paper.* Portsmouth, NH: Boynton Cook.

Seligman, M. E. P. (1991). *Learned optimism.* New York: Knopf.

Schlipp, P.A. (Ed.) (1951). *Albert Einstein. Philosopher-scientist.* Carbondale, IL: Southern Illinois University Press.

ABOUT THE AUTHORS

Robert J. Marzano, Ph.D.

Marzano received his B.A. in English from Iona College in New York; an M.Ed. in Reading/Language Arts from Seattle University, Seattle Washington; and a Ph.D. in Curriculum and Instruction from the University of Washington, Seattle. He is a Senior Scholar at Mid-continent Research for Education and Learning in Colorado, an Associate Professor at Cardinal Stritch University in Wisconsin, and Vice-President of Pathfinder Education, Inc. in Colorado.

An internationally known trainer and speaker, Marzano has authored 20 books and more than 150 articles and chapters in books on such topics as reading and writing instruction, thinking skills, school effectiveness, restructuring, assessment, cognition, and standards implementation.

Diane E. Paynter

Paynter is a principal consultant, Director of Early Literacy, and Director of Consortia at Mid-continent Research for Evaluation and Learning. As an international trainer and researcher, she has worked extensively at the state, district, building, and classroom levels in the areas of standards, curriculum and instruction, assessment, grading and record keeping, and literacy development. She is also a trainer for The Pathfinder Project.

Jane K. Doty, M.S., C.A.S.

Doty, a lead consultant for Mid-continent Research for Evaluation and Learning, consults and trains nationally and internationally with teachers, curriculum developers, and school administrators as they implement standards-based approaches. Jane worked as a classroom teacher for 16 years. She earned her B.S. from Keuka College, her M.S. from Plattsburgh State University, and her C.A.S. (Certificate of Advanced Study) from Oswego State University. Jane is a trainer for The Pathfinder Project.

NOTES

NOTES

NOTES

NOTES